A Time to Speak

Sir Vivian Fuchs

A Time to Speak

An autobiography

Anthony Nelson

First published 1990 by Anthony Nelson Ltd
PO Box 9, Oswestry, Shropshire SY11 1BY, England

British Library Cataloguing in Publication Data

Fuchs, Vivian *1908–*
   A time to speak: an autobiography.
   1. Exploration. Fuchs, Vivian, 1908–
   I. Title
   910.92

ISBN 0 904614 37 9

Designed by Alan Bartram
Typeset in Linotype Walbaum
by Nene Phototypesetters, Northampton
Printed in Great Britain by The Bath Press, Avon

Contents

Note
The material in chapters 10 and 11 is taken
by permission from *Of Ice and Men* published
in 1982 by Anthony Nelson. The substance of
chapters 12 and 13 is taken from *The
Crossing of Antarctica* published in 1958 by
Cassell and Company.

Foreword

Over 40 years ago Sir Vivian Fuchs and I shared a small pyramid tent whilst dogsledging in the Antarctic. Although we probably had more than our fair share of good weather during these journeys, there were many times when blizzards confined us to the tent. It was during these lie-up periods that I, as a mere youngster, listened with total fascination to Sir Vivian's reminiscences of his student days at Cambridge, Greenland days, African expeditions in the 1930s, and wartime experiences. I recall clearly having said to him not once but many times 'You should write down all these adventures for future generations'. His simple reply was 'When I have time, I shall do just that'; after all these years, his exciting life story (including in-depth details of his African and Antarctic expeditions) has been recorded for his family, former colleagues, and countless admirers to read and enjoy.

It was during those early Antarctic days that I quickly discovered Sir Vivian's decisiveness and determination. Having played the game of chess with Nature, and worked out all the appropriate 'moves', he quickly decided exactly how a programme should be pursued, and then carried it out precisely to the letter – and to success. He often said to me 'There's no such thing as good luck, it's always good planning and management' – what more can be said!

All autobiographers are inevitably faced with the same problem – *not* how to record the true facts *but* how to reveal their own personality and character for the reader; reading between the lines does not necessarily expose this important aspect of the story!

Sir Vivian is an unassuming, warm, and generous person always giving credit where credit is due, and having consideration for other peoples' feelings. His very logical and clear thinking, coupled with total impartiality in delicate matters, have brought admiration from his many former colleagues.

Most of the general public have tended to regard Sir Vivian as an 'Antarctic explorer'; in fact, this is not true, because he is a professional geologist with an extremely broad knowledge of science as a whole. His geological work in northern Kenya in the 1930s is still regarded as 'compulsory reading' for all following in his footsteps. Throughout his life he has, however, excelled in the role of advising young scientists and encouraging them to write up and publish the results of their researches, in their own interests. His Presidency of both the Royal Geographical Society and the British Association for the Advancement of Science bore the hallmark of this attribute. Even now, in his later years, he is always the first to offer encouragement where he deems it fitting.

International awards, gold medals, and honorary degrees have been bestowed on Sir Vivian, especially after his remarkably successful trans-Antarctic crossing, but in no way have these honours affected his typically unassuming and modest personality; his life has continued towards the encouragement of aspiring young scientists and explorers.

RAYMOND J ADIE

FOR MY FAMILY

To every thing there is a season, and a time to every
purpose under the heaven:
A time to be born, and a time to die;
a time to plant, and a time to pluck up that which is planted ...

A time to rend, and a time to sew;
a time to keep silence, and a time to speak ...

ECCLESIASTES 3: 1 - 2 , 7

Preface

A drowning man is said to see his life pass before his eyes, but fortunately it is few who suffer this experience. It might have a salutary effect upon intending autobiographers if such an involuntary review were to warn them of the tangled web that they are about to attempt to unravel.

Why do people write autobiographies? Is it for money, or to provide a personal memorial? Or perhaps to encourage the reader to discover what drove another wayfarer along roads that he himself has never travelled. For some, it might be to keep the record straight – better surely than to leave some stranger to interpret actions in terms of a future age, when different mores or customs prevail, making the old ways seem unreal, or even wrong.

Whatever he does, anyone who allows himself to be persuaded to write about his life is wide open to criticism from those whose beliefs, interests and way of life are different. The best he can do is to try to recount truthfully his story as he remembers it, suffering others to embellish or vary the meaning according to their whim. After all what will it matter to him? The dead cannot sue for libel!

Chapter 1

Origins

Like so many others, I now wish that in my younger days I had taken an interest in the doings of my elders and the tales they could have told. I know virtually nothing of my German ancestors except that my grandfather was Wilhelm Gottwerth Friedrich Fuchs, an artist who died in Kahla, Thuringia in 1902. By his wife Johanne Christine Caroline (née Korbel) he had five sons, of whom my father, Ernst, was the youngest, born in 1882.

However, my English mother, nurtured in the Victorian tradition of moral values, patriotism, cultured pursuits, and the habit of keeping journals, has provided a wonderful source of detailed family history. She wrote for the sheer joy of writing – poetry, stories, comments on people and events, her daily doings, book and concert reviews – everything that brought her keen mind pleasure or interest was faithfully recorded and left behind 'in case perhaps one day my son Vivian may come to be interested in the things of my day'. To my shame this day has been a long time coming, for I was well into my eighth decade before ever I looked at her many journals.

My British great-grandparents on one side were James Watson, innkeeper, and Mary Howarth, born respectively in 1791 and 1794, and married in 1814. They were Scots, and there is a tradition handed down that the Watson family was descended from John Knox, but there is nothing to prove it. James and Mary came to live in the Accrington district of Lancashire, a family of no particular standing. Eleven sons and two daughters were born to them, but four of the boys died in infancy. According to my mother's journal:

James Watson was a thorough old John Bull. A silhouette shows him with long-lashed whip in hand, low-crowned hat, top boots and all. My father always spoke of him with dislike, saying that he used to drink a bottle of port every day and always gave his seven surviving sons a thrashing every week. I always wondered whether he thrashed one each night or all seven on Saturdays . . .

Three of the brothers, John, Robert and Charles, survived to a great age, but they all fell out with each other, upholding the Watson tradition of 'opposition' and 'contradictoriness'.

The seventh son, Charles, born in 1827, was my grandfather. In his twenties he became engaged to Mary Nairn and went off to Australia to seek his fortune, later sending for his fiancée, whom he married in 1856. They had two children, a son who died in infancy and a daughter, Mary Agnes, always known as Minnie. It was not a happy union and Mary died when little Minnie was ten years old. The same year, 1867, Charles Watson entered into partnership with another Scot, John Connell.

Around 1842 John Connell, son of a Kilmarnock bank manager, had also gone out to Australia where he had established a small grocery business in Melbourne. When nine years later gold was discovered in the State of Victoria he joined the 'rush', and was lucky enough to find a valuable nugget which enabled him to start a second grocer's shop in a tent in the gold-fields. Both businesses flourished until finally he set up as a prosperous wholesale importer in Melbourne — at which point he took Charles Watson into partnership.

My other maternal great-grandfather was Thomas Blackall, coal merchant, who inherited the entailed estate of Haseley Court in Oxfordshire. He was impecunious and had ten children including two daughters — Annie and Nellie. Soon after the family had taken up residence a stranger appeared from overseas carrying papers purporting to show that he was descended from an older branch of the family, and thus the rightful heir. Thomas consulted his lawyer who recommended him not to dispute the claim, and having little money to risk, he gave up the property and took his wife and children to Australia. Later he discovered that his lawyer had been paid £1,000 by the rival claimant!

In 1855 John Connell married Annie Blackall when she was eighteen years old, and they were blessed with thirteen children. Then in 1870 Charles Watson, now a widower, married the younger sister Nellie. She was twenty years old while he was forty-three. According to the Melbourne *Advertiser* it was quite a 'do', for Miss Nellie Blackall had six bridesmaids, and

Immediately the doors of the sacred edifice were thrown open there was a general rush to secure seats ... As the happy couple entered the church Mr Horsley played 'See the Conquering Hero Comes' on the organ ... not content with sitting the crowd stood up upon the pews and behaved in a manner not quite consistent with the sacred nature of the edifice in which they were congregated ... the bells pealed out right merrily ...

The age gap proved insuperable and it was an uneasy and somewhat arid alliance which produced a son who died in infancy and my mother, Violet, half sister to Minnie. This hotch-potch of three large, interrelated Anglo-Australian families was later to produce a situation in which I, an only child, had more than seventy living cousins in varying degrees of kinship. My wife Joyce is a grand-daughter of John Connell, and thus my second cousin, Thomas Blackall being our mutual great-grandfather.

My mother, Violet Watson, was born 'in the district of St Kilda in the Colony of Victoria' in 1874. Ann Gibb, a girl of Scottish origins, was engaged to care for the new baby, and only six weeks after the birth the family sailed back to England. It was a voyage of many months and it was not then possible to have clothes laundered on board ship, so it was the custom for infants at sea to be kept in 'red flannel, blue check and such like horrors as would not show the dirt'. Unable to bear this prospect, her mother bought Violet a large number of long white nightdresses 'enough to last for the duration of the voyage'. As a result she was known for many years afterwards as 'The Clean Baby'.

The family moved into a house near the Crystal Palace called Fiésole, known to the local errand boys as the Fried Sole. At Christmas William, the footman, built for little Violet a huge snowman with a pipe in his mouth. Perhaps, too, it was to impress the pretty housemaid who had caught his fancy, for soon afterwards they both had to leave hastily and with ignominy, and never afterwards would her mother allow a man servant in the house!

Some two years later Charles Watson had to return to Melbourne on business and took his young wife with him. Violet was taken by Ann Gibb to live with her family in Ross-shire, and years later my mother still had vivid memories of her Scottish life to record:

John Gibb, Ann's brother, was a ferryman and lived on the Black Isle, across the narrow firth which lies in front of Invergordon. There was a rough stone slip or jetty ... and above it a row of little 'but-an-ben' cottages ... A 'but-an-ben' is a cottage of two rooms of which the kitchen is called 'but' meaning *to be out* or outside, and the bedroom 'ben' meaning *to be in* or within. You might be told that the wife was *'ben the hoose'*, ie in the bedroom ... The door ... is in the middle. Opposite it, between the two rooms, was the closet – a tiny room or large cupboard with a single pane of glass high up as a window.

John was a widower and had with him his other sister, Chirsty, and her little girl, Christina or Teenie. John slept in the kitchen on a big double-bed. Ann and I in another with curtained sides *ben the hoose*. Chirsty and her girl lay on a low stretcher bed in the central cupboard. There was of course no piped water, only a big water butt and a spring up the braeside. As to any sanitary convenience, no such thing existed in or near a Highland 'but-an-ben'. Humans, like dogs and cats, were sent for a run along the shore or among the bushes.

About a year later my parents came back to London and Ann brought me there to join them ... We stood in the hall and looked up a very big staircase ... Presently I saw a queen coming down! She was young and slender and tall, not a bit like Ann Gibb's family ... and she had a big crown of bright golden hair. Her dress was pink, embroidered all over with pearls, her neck and arms were bare ... I could only gaze at her with rapture. Ann pointed and said, 'Here comes your Mamma.' My Mamma!!!

I thought a Mamma was stout and old and grey ... It was glorious but far too frightening to have a Mamma like this. I did not speak a word, nor all that evening in a great sitting-room with green velvet curtains did I utter a single word to all the coaxings of Mother and Minnie, who had also somehow appeared. Only when Ann came to fetch me to bed I turned from the curtains and pointing to the ropes and tassels which held them said, 'Luik at they twa bra *tah*sels!' My Mother and Minnie were quite unprepared for a rich Scots accent and the shock launched them into peals of laughter which silenced me with fright.

Charles Watson had made his pile in Australia; coming back to England he could now qualify as 'gentry'. They took a seven-year lease on a huge house called Kingslyn in Upper Norwood which stood in a garden of three-and-a-half acres. A large square hall rose up the centre of the house to the roof, where it was lighted by a great lantern of stained glass. The floor was tessellated marble, and a gallery ran round it on the landing above. The dining-room was thirty feet long with a parquet floor on which chairs stood in pairs, between and through which Violet was soon delighting in 'swim-ming' flat on her stomach. The billiard room contained a full-sized table, a Bechstein concert grand piano, a small dinner table to seat eight, a sofa and a *chaise-longue*. There were 'marble busts, a statue, bronze figures, carved alabaster vases, gilt tables and beautiful clocks.' Always there was something going on – people calling, staying in the house, coming to lunch, to tennis or to formal dinner parties. To a wide-eyed three-year-old it was paradise – a far cry from the 'but-an-ben'.

Always there was Ann doing everything for her, constantly drilling her in the scriptures and exhorting her to eschew the world, the flesh and the devil – particularly on the Sabbath. Reading her the story of the Virgin Mary's visit to Elizabeth, Ann concluded with, 'Now remember, you are *never* to ask your Mamma what that word womb is – it is not for little girls to know.'

When Violet was six years old the accident happened which was to change her life. Her day-nursery had two doors which gave on to the gallery running round the hall, and this inspired her to invent wonderful games galloping her horse round and round them. One day a house guest joined in the romp, chasing her and then suddenly turning back to catch her as she rushed through the other door. But she was not strong enough to hold the child and they both fell with a crash. Violet rose up screaming with pain in her back which gradually got worse and worse. Eventually six doctors, unable to diagnose what was wrong, stood round her bed and under an anaesthetic she was put into a plaster-of-Paris jacket which chafed in many places, but at least she could walk. The condition deteriorated and Sir James Page came down from Harley Street. He decided that her spine was 'crumbling away' – she must be put back to bed and not allowed to move. Soon both her legs were paralysed and sometimes they contracted involuntarily, her knees rose up and Ann had to flatten them back forcibly.

For two years Violet lived in bed, on her sofa, or occasionally being pushed out in a bath-chair for some fresh air. It was a terrible ordeal but it was not time wasted. By the time she was three her mother had already taught her to read, and now spelling came naturally and without effort from the host of books she devoured lying on her back. She was never able to go to school. Her mother taught her French, including French history in the native language, and when she was nine she could speak and think in it fluently. Her lessons covered music and simple musical composition, addition and subtraction, but when Minnie was charged to teach her multiplication it was a complete failure (which lasted her lifetime!).

When at last she was allowed to walk again gently, her high spirits demanded that she 'pretend to be a wild horse, running, snorting, leaping and longing to toss my mane'. The day she escaped from Ann's constant supervision to indulge her fantasies was a further disaster. Suddenly a hot gnawing pain, later diagnosed as 'spinal neuralgia', shot down her right leg in spasms. Soon severe pain took over her life. Sleep was only induced by increasingly large doses of morphia, until her doctor refused to prescribe more, saying 'I am giving her now about enough to kill a man – and she is only nine!' Her father then proposed his 'old Watsonian elixir ... port' – which worked wonders. She was given up to half a tumblerful twice nightly, and this had no intoxicating effect but blessed relief which enabled her to go to sleep. She also wore a 'spinal ice-bag' day and night to dull the pain, and renewing this brought additional stress to her devoted Ann, who had refused to leave her side night or day throughout her illness.

Suddenly Ann cracked. Over nothing at all she turned on her employer, lost all control and began shouting and calling down the wrath of the Lord. Violet burst into howls of rage and terror. It was clear to her mother that the time of parting had come. Ann went back to her family in Scotland, and Harriet Moray, a curly-headed girl with twinkling eyes, came to take care of Violet, bringing laughter, merriment and unknown treats such as pillow fights at bedtime into what had been a somewhat austere nursery.

Eventually Violet recovered and regained her health, but her right foot remained extended making it impossible for her to walk. In the end the surgeons decided to cut her Achilles tendon, which left the foot limp and powerless, but at least she could walk again. For the rest of her life she was a cripple, moving but slowly for only short distances and dragging her right foot along at each step.

When his daughter was twelve, Charles Watson built a house called Pembury End in Tunbridge Wells, and this remained the family home until he died aged ninety. It was a large house with a square tower some eighty feet high on the Pembury-Tunbridge Wells road. There were extensive grounds with a long drive sweeping up to the front door, a tennis lawn sometimes used for croquet, and a narrow wooded area running along the Sandown road. Behind the house

Pembury End

were the stables where the Victoria and the brougham carriages were kept, for as yet there were no motor cars.

My grandfather was now a curmudgeonly old man, not in the least child-orientated, but always jealously resentful of his young wife's devotion to their daughter. Violet found great happiness with her adored mother but was always thankful when walks, picnics, excursions or parties did not include her father. She grew up full of boundless energy, enthusiastic in everything she undertook and with an enquiring and highly logical mind.

As well as her abiding cultural interests her tastes were catholic, covering astronomy and the latest scientific advances as presented by men like James Jeans and Ray Lankester. Many years later when I was going to Cambridge to read geology, I came home to find that she had already read my major text books and could discuss the subject with ease. In the mid-'twenties she assured me that in my lifetime I would see power obtained from splitting the atom, and that men would land on the moon – concepts which then seemed so way out as to be ridiculous.

As a grown-up young woman Violet and her mother enjoyed many European holidays together, delighting in German and

Italian literature and art. In 1906 she was thirty-two years old and still unmarried – in Victorian terms well and truly on the shelf. Her journal is suddenly reticent about this period, but I believe that in that year during one of their visits to the German spas she first met a handsome, adventurous and engaging young German of twenty-four. He had left home at the age of eighteen and spent the intervening years working his way round Rome, Cairo and New York to see life and learn the hotel trade, for his father, although an artist, also owned an hotel. His name was Ernst Fuchs.

During the following year they must have kept in secret touch, and in the spring Ernst came to England. The liaison was, of course, totally unsuitable, and both families were appalled. When my father's family learnt of his interest in an English woman eight years his senior, who could speak no German and was too crippled to work, they would have nothing more to do with him. Charles Watson was outraged – a young adventurer eight years her junior with no profession nor prospects, not even a job – and a man whom he regarded as a German waiter to boot! It was unthinkable. When he was told that there was a baby on the way, despite her mother's anguished pleadings, he threw Violet out of his house and out of his life, forbidding her ever to return. Altogether it was a peculiarly inauspicious beginning to a love story which was to last all their lives.

Ernst Fuchs had no means of supporting a family in England so he had returned to Genoa where he had a job. Meanwhile Violet's old nurse, Harriet Moray, had retired and was living with her sister in the Isle of Wight. In May 1907 Violet fled from Pembury End and took refuge with Harriet at Recluse Lodge, Freshwater to await developments. She was sad and very lonely, and fearful of what the future might hold, but confident that Ernst would somehow find a solution to their problems. Now her only solace was the endless books she was able to get from the library and the journals she filled with her poetry. Two months later Ernst managed to get leave of absence and returned to her for three weeks. On 6 July they were married, but it still was not possible for him to provide a home and he went back to Genoa. They were together again for a few blissful weeks over Christmas.

I was born at Recluse Lodge on 11 February 1908, and my

indefatigable mother promptly began a special journal in which she plotted my progress and chronicled my daily doings for the next two-and-a-half years. According to this a great boost to her morale was when, four weeks later,

> ... his Granny came for two nights ... and thought him the most beautiful, perfectly formed and fascinating baby she had ever seen ... His nurses and his staunch admirers, Harriet and Kate ... are inclined to agree. In fact I rather think Kate would go as far as to say that there not only never was, but never could be such a boy!
>
> His christening gifts were few but nice ... a gold tie clasp from Aunt Minnie and a gold safety-pin from Harriet and Kate ... and a silver cup and spoon from the servants at Pembury End ...

Grandfather Watson would never relent, but was now apparently the only one out of step, since even his servants seemed to be delighted at my advent. Two months later my father had fulfilled his contract in Italy and finally came back to seek work in England. He took rooms for us in Wandsworth and found himself an office job. This was their first taste of real poverty and its stresses, and my mother's first reaction to alleviate her straitened circumstances was to join the Times Book Club! Anything could be borne providing there were books. At last she was happy, and relieved too that 'Ernest* is enraptured with Vivian's society, and he with Ernest's – which is a splendid thing all round'.

Grandfather Watson apart, the family were concerned for our future in a somewhat uncongenial urban environment. In an imaginative and most generous gesture, John, Ernest, Frank and Tom Connell had a whip-round and provided my parents with sufficient funds to buy some land and build our first home. It was indeed a recognition of the esteem in which my mother was held by her Connell cousins.

We moved to the Weald of Kent, to rooms in Staplehurst where my father acquired a property of some seven acres on which he built a house called Walden. The land consisted of four open fields surrounded by thorn hedges, and included three ponds, one of which was very old and surrounded by massive oak trees. 'Old Carley' who later worked for us, said it was the best water anywhere for making tea, 'far better than any ole tap'. He walked a mile daily

*Violet always spelt his name 'Ernest' – not 'Ernst' as in German.

Walden

from his cottage to get it. The water main was a mile away but my father had a narrow-gauge pipe laid to bring it up to us, and he very happily became a market gardener. While my mother was engrossed in laying out and caring for her garden, he began breeding chickens and pigs, and producing melons, cucumbers, tomatoes and honey.

Like stars my earliest memories dot the sky of youth, disconnected yet individually sharp and bright. There was the young country nursemaid who was caught administering neat whisky to me, not as one might think to quieten my screams but, as she confessed, to find out what the demon alcohol really did to people. But I must surely give priority to my first haircut at the age of two. Seated on a stool in our verandah I learnt to my horror that my wonderful father was about to shear the hair from my head. This produced howls of terror at the thought of so much pain, and only my mother's promises allowed the operation to commence. I was amazed to feel nothing at all as the curls fell to the floor.

Collecting acorns under the oak trees to feed the pigs was a regular chore, the going rate being a penny for the large trug full – not that I had much idea, nor indeed opportunity, what I should do with it as we were one-and-a-half miles out of Staplehurst. I learnt the hard way to treat with respect the goats which provided my milk for they butted anyone coming too close.

There were no cars on the stone-surfaced lanes, nor did we even have a pony and trap. My father bought a heavy Raleigh bicycle and a curious basketwork 'trailer' in which my mother sat and was towed about to spare her damaged leg.

In 1910 one night my mother took me out to see Halley's Comet and told me, 'You will not see this again in your lifetime.' I was just over two years old but was determined to prove her wrong. Much later I worked out, quite wrongly, that its next appearance would be in the year 2000 when I would be ninety-two – and this became my target for living! When it did return I was disappointed to find that I was only seventy-seven; and also unhappy that it was so insignificant as to bear little resemblance to the remembered flare of 1910.

There must have been some family reconciliation in Germany, for when I was two-and-a-half my father took me to see his mother. As I stood by the sideboard in our dining-room ready to leave, my mother lifted my jersey to tie an addressed label to my braces in case my father was careless enough to lose me. I remember asking her, 'Are you going to post me?' Then came the exciting night voyage by steamer across a heaving sea with the sky full of stars, followed by the flares from the factory chimneys of the Zeiss works near Kahla where my grandmother lived.

This visit led to a later experience which is still vivid enough to have made me cautious about dismissing seemingly mystic events for which we cannot at present account rationally. Back at Walden, and one week after my third birthday, I woke in the night to see an arm with the elbow bent extended towards me through the lower window in my nursery, which did not open. Terrified I dived under the bedclothes, where I fell asleep. Later, plucking up courage to peer above the blankets, I found the hand had gone.

Next morning I rushed into my parents' bedroom, and as always my mother has recorded the incident.

… Vivian came to me and said 'Oh Mamma, I was so frightened in the night. I saw a hand come in at the window with fingers all stretched out. I was so frightened.' To make sure it was not a burglar's hand I said to him, 'Was it light in the room, because you know you couldn't see a hand in the dark?' 'Oh yes,' he said, 'it was all dark but I saw a hand, and I was so frightened' …

But something had also happened in my parents' room that night.

… As soon as he [my father] got into bed he appeared to be asleep … I

Broadstairs, Vivian Fuchs on left

spoke to him quietly to see if he had really gone to sleep so suddenly ... He answered me quite unintelligently and in a slow thick laboured way ... a few minutes after he sat up in a most excited way and exclaimed 'I have seen my mother and heard her speak.' I said, 'You've been dreaming, my dear, you were fast asleep!' He replied, 'No, no, no, I was not asleep. I heard you come in and heard all you said to me, and I tried to answer but I could not, neither could I speak nor move. Then I heard and saw my mother, just as I hear and see you, with her very own voice. I do assure you it was not a dream.'

At four-thirty that afternoon a telegram arrived to say that my German grandmother had died the night before. Altogether a coincident series of events, one may think – but a three-year-old child, with no conception of death, nor the imagination to make up such a story, could not have played a knowing part in the incident.

All my memories of Walden are of happy, tranquil days – it was a wonderful place for a child to grow and learn in. My parents' devotion to each other was manifest for all to witness and the atmosphere rubbed off on me. There were no strident voices nor harsh words in our home. My mother was strict but always quietly just, and never told me what I must do without providing a reasonable explanation for demanding that I conform to her wishes. She read to me endlessly until I could do so for myself, and brought me up on *Punch*, carefully explaining the jokes and the satire – this was the one thing my German father could never share, for he did not think them funny.

While my mother always took pains to expose me to all her cultural interests, she was not to know that it was going to be a losing battle, and as I grew up I must have been a great disappointment to her. My father, who was magic with his hands, taught me to make or mend mechanical things, and encouraged me to roam the hedgerows and ponds discovering natural history, and collecting everything I could carry home. We spent long summer holidays by the sea at Broadstairs, and when I was six years old I had my first bicycle. This brought me independence for I was free to ride the lanes and roam where I pleased. My mother worried lest as an only child I should be lonely. But I never wanted either company or competition in the nursery. It was my refuge, where there was always peace and quiet and the time to get on with all my activities and 'projects', without interruption or unsolicited advice from siblings.

At midnight on 4 August 1914 war was declared with Germany – and our happy little world shattered.

Chapter 2

The First World War

I was six years old when the war broke out, and remember the extraordinary widespread rumours that Russian troops had been seen travelling by train from Dover to the capital on the London, Chatham and Southcoast Railway which passed near our house. If anyone doubted this the explanation was that the troops were told to crouch in the carriages so they wouldn't be seen. Anyway they had snow on their boots, so it must be true!

Walden was in a 'prohibited area' and had to be closed. On 26 October 1914 my father, and many others like him who had been married for years to English women, were suddenly snatched away, their money and property confiscated at the same time as the breadwinners were removed. He was taken to Camp II in Newbury, where he in turn started keeping a journal:

I arrived here with many of my own countrymen, but you would never have taken them for such, some having been in England, Wales or Scotland for many years, mostly married men with English wives and children, some of them seemed hardly able to speak their own tongue ...

There are over 100 tents here, each containing ten men. There were so many unfortunate fellows here who had been already weeks at Olympia; it is sad to see them, apparently very poor and without any means; trousers through everywhere and toes sticking out of their boots ...

Had a fairly good night after wrapping myself up in blankets ... We received a very little straw as there was no more, and two blankets. Straw was just enough for your head but the rest of the body had to rest on the hard floor ... the other poor fellows who have nothing of their own suffer more and often you would find them groaning at night and complaining of the cold.

In the centre of the camp stood tanks filled with cold water, and thirty tin basins were provided for the ablutions of 1,000 men. The same water was used for personal toilet, then for washing clothes and finally for washing up the feeding utensils.

It is disgusting to wait for a tin, and getting it filthy with grease and no chance of cleaning it with hot water as one can't get any. I notice a lot of fellows with eruptions on their neck and face, and we have to wash in the same tins as them.

As winter came on the camp became a quagmire. The internees were often soaked to the skin, with no opportunity of drying out their clothes:

The mud is getting much worse and how damp the floors of our tents will become I do not like to think – they are now dirty as in a pig-sty, and no chance of washing them as we could never get them dry again.

News from home was infrequent and often dismaying:

I am very sad to read that my dear wife has been compelled to clear out of our house. Is England losing its head altogether? Is there no one to see that there is justice done to innocent persons? Why should many thousands of their own countrymen suffer where there cannot be the slightest suspicion of danger? And where there are thousands of people who could satisfy the authorities that the person is pure English and entirely English in sympathy.

The outbreak of war was a shock to the nation, but no one could have foreseen the gathering emotional storm which swept the country. It became impossible to keep a pet dachshund, their distraught owners being forced to put them down or keep them secretly in attics. Steinway and Bechstein pianos disappeared from drawing-rooms and were chopped up. People bearing German surnames from early forebears changed them from Goldschmidts to Goldsmith, Fuchs became Fooks, Fewkes, Foulkes, ffoulkes or even Fox (the literal translation). Since my father was German-born and a civilian internee there would have been little point in changing the family name. In fact I remember a feeling of disdain for those who thus sought to hide their origins. It is impossible to convey the anti-German hysteria of those days, for nothing like it occurred during the Second World War, when national hate was concentrated on Hitler and the Nazi party. It was a traumatic situation for my mother, but her courage never faltered publicly and as a child I remained unconscious of such attitudes.

After a time my mother discovered that if she could find two sureties willing to put down £100 each and guarantee where we would live, my father could be released. Coincidentally an old friend wrote from the Isle of Man inviting us to stay with them. When all was settled with the authorities, on 22 December my father returned home, and a week later we left for the Isle of Man, finally settling into furnished rooms in Strathallen Crescent on the Douglas sea front.

In February 1915, a week before my seventh birthday, I started school at a kindergarten called Ingleby run by the Misses Cowan. Each morning a farthing ticket took me a mile along the front by horse-drawn tram – open 'toast rack' cars in summer, closed ones drawn by two horses in winter, for the road could be slippery with ice and snow.

For me these were happy days when I made young friends and lived with both my parents. The war made little impact, nor did the fact that I had a German father affect my way of life. I had no idea of the stresses suffered by my parents for they never let me see their misery and always provided a stable background against which I grew up as a normal English child. It was bravely done, and only to her journal did my mother confide her true state of mind:

I began the second volume of this work when settled in my husband's house and exiled from my father's. I begin the third ... an exile from both. My father will not let me go to Pembury End, and England will not let me live in Kent ... I am an 'alien enemy'. My England calls me her enemy. I cannot keep life and youth in me unless I shut myself off a little from the pain and horror. There are hours of it every day ... if I lose my life and youth it will have served no purpose, I shall have done no one any good; and I shall have done enormous harm to Ernest and Mother and Vivian.

1915: My joy is gone from me. Dreadful things happened early in May. The Germans sank the ss *Lusitania*, drowning about 1,500 non-combatants, women and children. About the same time they took to using poison gas along their battle front. It is the foulest thing I have heard of. I will not put down the horrible descriptions of the death of those who inhaled it.

These events caused an outburst of rioting against the Germans resident in England. Shops were sacked wholesale, and people from the Stock Exchange went in procession to Parliament to demand internment of all Germans. All the people who couldn't or wouldn't join the Army set upon any German they could find, and thought they were helping England by attacking helpless shopkeepers. The result was a general internment order. 'Not so much', Mr Asquith said, 'to protect England against the Germans, as to protect German residents against the English.' ... This is a bad fall for

Violet and Ernest Fuchs

my pride in the English race ... I had always boasted to Ernest that the English liked fair play.

And so, on 14th May a detective came and took Ernest away to Knockaloe Camp on this island. I was all alone ... I had no hope of any early release, nor of an end to the war. I could only see him once a month ... I did not know how to go on and on. I lay on my bed all the afternoon. I was all strung up, I dared not break down ... I did so long for the time for Vivian to come home from school. He rushed in, and I cried out 'Oh V-V they have taken Dad away from us again. They have taken him to Knockaloe.' He looked at me, his chin twitched, two large tears formed in his eyes. Suddenly he dashed them away and said, 'I mustn't cry because Dennis and Dick are waiting outside for me to bring this boat.' He seized a boat, continuing 'I shouldn't like them to see me cry you know' and away he rushed. He had an excited conversation about the boat, dashed in for tea, talked hard about a new book at school, and spent the rest of the evening in a wild game with Dennis and Dick. So he never found time to cry at all.

He has not forgotten, however, to say a little prayer every night and this is it: 'Please let Dad come home again soon, and keep him happy while he's there, and let him have nice things, and make the people make it so that he and the others may come home again soon. Amen.'

I am trying to recover from one of those awful bronchial colds that the Isle of Man has given me. Vivian has done his best, poor little chap; carried up my breakfast and amused himself all day without 'bothering'. One day lately when going to bed he sighed and said, 'Oh Mother, I feel very sad.' I persuaded him with great difficulty to tell me why. At last he murmured 'I think it is because of Dad.' Another day I asked him, 'Vivian are you happy here in this life we are leading?' He looked at me ruminating and then said, 'Well you see Mother, I try to keep myself happy.' Poor boy, he is not quite eight, and he is separated from all his toys, his beautiful railway and trains, his big rocking-horse that even I can ride on, his stone bricks, his sand heap, the garden, the animals ... Thank heavens he has the sea – the great old playmate.

Ernest is much more comfortable than he was at Newbury Camp. They sleep in bunks in long wooden huts, a hundred men in each; and they have tables and chairs. They can work too ... I think of these things, but my own loss is as great, and more hopeless. My dear is so much to me, we are always together and happy to be together. I know the grief of the poor souls who are daily losing their men by death is much worse. But mine is so needless. He is not fighting or working for a cause, he is just taken away. If he were a danger to England I would say, 'I am bearing this for England's benefit', but it is for nothing ... I have been paralysed in mind; just sitting doing nothing most of the time. I must try.

Recently a lady wrote to *The Times* to say that too much sympathy should not be spent on the working women who have husbands at the front as one of them had exclaimed to her 'Oh! Miss, this war is just like heaven! A pound a week and *no* husband!' But I am in hell without *my* husband, a cold empty wandering hell.

I visited Ernest and had the extraordinary luck to get about an hour-and-a-half. Vivian came too, and was interested. He was even a little affected at seeing Dad ...

Ernest tells me that someone has written to a newspaper suggesting that English women married to German husbands should have their marriages annulled so that they may again be able to go into decent society. Well I will not apply to have ours annulled, and if they could annul it in spite of us then I would still live with Ernest, married or not! ... let them look to their own wives – I dare swear that their own would be very glad to see a chance of getting rid of *them*!

In tearing up old letters, I am struck with the awful things that Minnie [her half sister] has rubbed into me since the war began, when one would have thought a little cheering and comforting was indicated. All the three months of war during which we were unmolested at Walden she kept writing to us about our terrible position, and advising us to flee the country ... It was she who first scared us about confiscation, it was she who sent to Mother the advertisement asking people to join an Anti-German League which had for its object, among other things, to get people to swear never again to shake hands with a German, never knowingly to speak to a German, and to ostracize from society every British lady who had married a German. Another nice little instance of British fair play ... for this Society actually exists!

It was Minnie who said to Mother, 'How sad that Vi is forsaken by all her friends.' Whereas I often think how kind they are. When I wrote in May, very depressed, to tell her that Ernest was again interned her reply was, 'Do you think they will want to confiscate Walden too? ... We all say that all rich Germans ought to be interned: the feeling everywhere is so awfully bitter now ... I did not know people *could* hate as they do.' This was to cheer me up in my anxiety and solitude! Again she writes to me, 'You really must face things and realize that no English person will ever admit a German into their house again.'

Aug. 11: Ernest writes that he is coming to the Douglas Privileged Camp ... it is so near, just up above on the cliff, and its big electric lamps shine down and cast my shadow on the road when I go along to post my letters ... It is curious about those big electric lamps. Not a lamp is lit anywhere in Great Britain, and if the smallest shine or chink of light shines from any window, a policeman is at the door and you are suspected of signalling to the German aeroplanes or submarines. But these internment camps shine out like moons, every spot in them illuminated so that the sentries may see any attempt at escape ...

Sept. 17: Ernest is (now) in the Privileged Camp for Aliens, I have seen him twice. I may go every fortnight instead of once a month at Knockaloe, but here it is only for half-an-hour, and always in the presence of a young officer who has nothing to do but read a book and listen to our conversation ... It is good to know he is so near ...

I have never known the source of our finances at that time. My mother's journals mention £3 a week provided surreptitiously by my grandmother, and at one time a loan of £90 from Frank Connell. I knew that we were very poor, but looking back I am surprised to realize that I never felt in any way deprived. Apart from the weekly threepenny visit to the cinema, my entertainment was self-generated. I made crude model boats, climbed the cliffs, explored the caves and made my own fishing rod. How proud the moment when I brought back a fish caught with a bent pin and large enough to eat! I was fortunate too in persuading the blacksmith to give me a long iron rod of which he turned the end into a blunt hook. This was the means of dislodging reluctant but edible crabs from their rocky holes at low tide. If one came out undamaged it sold for sixpence.

My school buddies and I were fortunate in including among our number the son of a Douglas grocer who owned a small rowboat in which we paddled about the bay. Today this sort of freedom for seven-year-olds would be thought foolhardy, but the grown-ups were at war, and perhaps too busy to check on our ventures. More probably adult fears which now rule and inhibit the spirit of even much older children had not yet developed. As a result we learnt well how to take care of ourselves when boating, climbing and exploring. In later years my father was to remark that he never worried about my doings because I was far too careful of my own skin.

We lived in the Isle of Man for two-and-a-half years. In the spring of 1917 government civilian labour was so short that they introduced a scheme whereby farmers and market gardeners could apply for suitable prisoners from the internment camps to work on the land. Each man had to be sponsored by the employers who were made responsible for his good behaviour. After many enquiries, my mother found that her cousin Tom Connell, who lived in a big house with a lot of ground, was badly in need of a gardener at Walden Knowle, Elmstead Woods in Kent. Tom agreed to the sponsorship and on 26 May my father was released to take the job. Ironically we could not go with him because my mother counted as an 'enemy alien' and had to have police permission to travel. The normal bureaucratic procedures took another month.

The day after my father's impending release my mother's joy was destroyed by the news that her own mother, to whom she was very devoted, was dying of cancer. My grandfather was then ninety and somewhat senile, so when we finally left to join my father in the small lodge at the gates of the Connell property, it was at last possible for us to visit Pembury End. It was the only time I ever saw Charles Watson. I remember him with a shock of white hair which made a great impression on me, sitting in a wheelchair, everything having to be done for him by a man servant. On 5 August my grandmother died. Mercifully, in his mental confusion my grand-father seemed at last to have forgotten why he had banished his daughter. Now he welcomed her presence. He kept saying, 'Don't go away, I like to see you, you sometimes look like your mother.' Eight weeks later he too was dead – and without leaving a will.

This led to a long and appalling period of family strife. Aunt Minnie's husband, my uncle Overend Watson, was a rude, over-bearing man who drank too much, and had never heard (nor wanted to hear) of women's rights. He took it for granted that as the male son-in-law he alone was the rightful heir to Pembury End and all the family money. He and Aunt Minnie moved in and took over.

After much unpleasantness and quite a lot of skulduggery, solicitors finally had to explain to him that legally his wife Minnie and my mother Violet were the joint heirs to the property. Argumentative to the last, he then bullied my mother into agreeing to sell the house cheap to Tom Connell who wanted it for his large family. Overend and Minnie removed themselves with bad grace, and neither of them ever spoke to my parents again. It was a sad chapter.

In later years I was to pay many happy visits to my young cousins at Pembury End. When Tom Connell died the house was bought by the Gas Board as their administrative headquarters. After changing hands a number of times, it has now become the Seven Springs Cheshire Home where thirty-four disabled people live productive lives and are well cared for.

Technically on my grandfather's death my mother inherited half his fortune, but since she was still considered to be an 'enemy alien', this was promptly sequestered by the government, and she was given a small allowance on which we continued to live a hand-to-mouth existence for six long years after the war had ended.

Chapter 3

Schooldays

So many people have written such critical or scathing accounts of their unhappy days at boarding school, but this was never my experience. In 1917 when I was nine I went to Asheton Preparatory School near Tenterden. Originally in Folkstone, it had been moved to St Michael's Grange at the outbreak of war to avoid the danger of air raids. The headmaster, H F F Varley, was a splendid man with a neat pointed beard, a curled moustache and a liberal outlook, who managed to instil interest and enthusiasm into small boys.

The Grange was a fine country house with a large lake and extensive grounds. Each morning we assembled for prayers in the big oak-panelled hall with stained glass windows. On Sundays we walked the two miles to Tenterden Church, and quite frequently the older boys walked three miles to Morning Service at Biddenden or five to Benenden. Sometimes we went to a Methodist or Baptist Chapel and thus early recognized differing forms of worship.

Since it was war time and food was very scarce there had to be economies. Only lengthy essays were written on new paper; for normal classroom work in arithmetic, geometry, grammar and the like we used the insides of old envelopes which had been carefully slit open and smoothed. Our normal lessons alternated with all the practical domestic chores except cooking. We made the beds, swept dormitories, laid the fires, served at table and cleaned our shoes.

More interestingly there would be days of fetching cords of heavy logs from a forest a few miles away. These we loaded into four-wheeled horse-drawn wagons which the senior boys then drove back to school where we all unloaded and stacked them. Each term there was a special 'Wood-collecting Day' when the three Houses competed in bringing dead wood in from the grounds and stacking it neatly in the yard. The House with the largest pile earned a special supper which included delicacies such as jellies.

In the autumn a large wooden barrel was placed at the foot of a huge Spanish chestnut tree, and during the morning break we collected the well-formed nuts to fill the container. Later these provided many enjoyable teas when each boy received a plate of boiled chestnuts. A special treat, for which only seniors qualified, was to bake chestnuts on the huge recessed fire in the big hall. Three-foot logs were burnt in an iron basket, and on either side of the fireplace were seats where one could sit when only the glowing embers remained.

Another practical activity was gardening. Each of us had a plot about twenty feet square in which we grew vegetables – usually potatoes, beetroot, carrots and lettuce, with a narrow ornamental flower border. Our productivity made a considerable contribution to the school kitchen besides enhancing our education.

We were also encouraged and shown how to develop hobbies. I collected snails and water plants and set butterflies and moths, learnt fretwork, snared rabbits for the pot and salt-dried their skins. Moles, too, were a source of income, for stretched and dried skins could be sold for sixpence to ninepence according to condition. Sixpence was the standard weekly pocket money throughout the school, so this was a valuable bonus – especially as a penny-halfpenny for a stamp on our letter home and twopence for the church collection were the first priorities which had to be met.

My prized possessions were *The Handy Book for Boys* and *Let Me Explain*, which told one how to make everything from birdcages to aquaria. The new thing was 'wireless' and I was completely hooked. At home and at school I made toy sets from cardboard, map rolls, fencing wire, cotton reels and anything else around the house.

Inevitably there were some irksome facets of life too, for instance the school rule that only French could be spoken during meals. This certainly reduced the decibel level and may even have benefited our French, but it proved to be the surest way of teaching us the deaf and dumb alphabet!

During my first three years paraffin lamps were in use, the larger rooms having Aladdin lamps with their bright incandescent mantles. In the end the headmaster decided to reactivate the acetylene gas lighting which had been laid on throughout the Grange. The generator was in the stables and, as head boy, that became my particular care. The large carbide containers had to be emptied and recharged – not a pleasant job on account of the noxious fumes – but I was very proud to be given the responsibility.

We enjoyed remarkable freedoms. In my last two years I was allowed to cycle the twelve miles home to Walden on summer Sundays, returning by dusk. Once I tied a glass jar containing six goldfish caught from the thousands in the lake to my bicycle carrier. After two miles it fell and smashed on the road, leaving flapping gasping fish everywhere. My mother had said that goldfish could survive provided their gills were kept wet, so hastily soaking a handkerchief in the spilled water and scooping them up as best I could, they were rolled up in it. Six miles farther on there was a stream, but 1921 was the driest year since 1911, and I found only a very small pool in which to plunge them. In a few minutes they had recovered and I rode the last miles home in record time, finally launching them into the pond in our garden where they lived happily for many years.

At the end of the war my parents had been allowed to return to live at Walden and my father had become a chicken farmer. In 1920, when I was twelve, we first went to Scotland to spend the summer holidays with my mother's large tribe of Connell cousins. This became an annual event for the next six years. Ardentinny, on Loch Long, was then a small hamlet on the northern shore of the loch and apart from the 'big hoose', Glen Finnart, it consisted of only a handful of whitewashed cottages perched at the foot of the mountainside. After the flatness of Kent, my mother revelled in the wild scenery:

Counting children and servants, we are sixteen people in the Low Cottage. Vivian sleeps with the boys in a converted stable where they have a row of small beds in the coach house. Ernest and I sleep in a sort of large summer-house or open air shelter, wooden walls and glass in front, with dark curtains to draw along when needed ... We look out gloriously upon the loch and mountains.

Our activities included hill walking, rowing a mile across the loch to the bathing beach each day, walking three miles to Blairmore to play golf, spending the night on the top of Ben Lomond to see the sunrise, fishing or rowing across to beauty spots for picnics. A particular penance, though we did not think of it as such then, was the daily bathe. Sunshine or rain, calm or windy, everyone rowed over to Sandy Bay each morning where shivering figures were then seen to dash madly into the breakers and thankfully return to their towels in the least possible time.

In the evenings we all assembled to hear Ernest Connell read a chapter or two from the current book while the young played desultory patience on the floor. On rare occasions when the loch was smooth and still the water became phosphorescent so that every little ripple ran a line of 'fire' along the sandy shore. On one such occasion we went bathing and as we swam we were delighted to find our arms and legs outlined with a ghostly light. Sadly I am told that for some biological reason, perhaps pollution, the loch waters no longer phosphoresce.

A year later, for our second Scottish holiday, my parents took a small furnished cottage where Frank Connell, our favourite cousin, stayed with us. Along the road at Low Cottage were twelve more Connells, Ernest and Lily with six children, plus Doris and Joyce who were daughters of the eldest brother, John Connell. Joyce was then aged fourteen and it was our first encounter – but it left little impression on either of us, and it was years before we met again.

Frank Connell was sensitively aware of my father's struggle to rebuild his fortunes:

Tonight dear old Frank, with many apologies and hesitations, asked us if we would allow him to lend us £300 which he has in the bank, so that we might have a car without the necessity of waiting till the problematical day when the money will be released. We pointed out the uncertainty of our financial conditions, but he refused to consider it and refused to hear of receiving interest; but this of course we made a condition and are going to pay him the usual bank rate. There is a friend indeed! It will be so wonderful at last to drive about, and not always to be tired on my poor lame leg ... A car too! not even horses' legs to consider!

They could hardly wait to return to Walden to begin the search for what they wanted, but soon my mother was jubilant:

It has come to pass! We bought a car yesterday ... the owner gave Ernest a lesson when we tried the car and another when he brought it here. He said 'Shall I drive her up to your garage for you?' Ernest carelessly replied 'Oh no thanks, it'll be good exercise for me to take her along.' The truth was that there was no garage to take her to, nor any drive either!

According to my mother it was 'a large powerful primrose-coloured monster of unknown temper', but it changed our lives. A hot summer had baked the ground hard and my father taught himself to drive by experimenting on the front lawn. The car was a Dodge, which increasingly absorbed his energies and I was his willing apprentice. By taking it apart we learnt how cars work, and we kept it immaculate.

At long last the time arrived for my mother to begin the struggle to regain her sequestered capital:

22 Nov. 1921 – Last week Mr Norton, the lawyer, asked us to come up to see him because now is the time to put in an appeal for my capital to be 'released' to me. The Public Trustee is ordering it to be transferred from the insurance company into *his* name as owner; he can then, if so decided, use it to pay off German debts. Mr Norton himself seems to think it quite fair and natural that this should be so, and says I ought to be glad that any allowance was given to me ... But I think lawyers, even nice lawyers, get to think that what is sanctioned by law is the same as what is *right*.

It is, alas, according to law that, because Germany was at war with England, an English woman (who never wished to be a German subject but was made so against her will on her marriage with a German, by English law), who has never lived abroad and never will, whose husband has done nothing wrong and is a permanent resident in England, whose money comes solely from her English father, should yet stand in danger of having all this money taken from her and applied to paying other English people the debts which Germans in Germany have failed to pay ...

And if I am not to be treated so, how cruel to keep me in such uncertainty. Even the allowance they make me out of my own money, they particularly state is to be regarded as a 'purely charitable allowance' – a nice phrase that, and they promise nothing about continuing it ... I am so tired of it all.

It was only the beginning of a long period of weary form-filling answering inane questions like 'What are your reasons for staying in England?' and 'What are your reasons for wishing to gain possession of your capital?' It was to be another three years before any action was taken.

Meanwhile I had passed Common Entrance and was destined to go to Tonbridge. At the eleventh hour the headmaster wrote telling my father that the Governors had decided that as an 'alien' I could be admitted only after every English boy had been accepted. As there were more candidates than vacancies, arguments were futile, and my mother was understandably bitter about this last-minute refusal.

Instead I was sent to Trent College, recommended to my parents as a 'growing school'. It turned out to be a very rough place where the bullying was bad even by the harsh standards of the day. There were no wash-basins downstairs, and since we were not allowed in the dormitories by day we never washed our hands till bedtime. We ate off tin plates on bare tables. No spoons or egg cups were provided, so boiled eggs were held in the hand and scooped out on the point of a knife. I was thought to be a normally tough boy, but I found the conditions intolerable – far worse than anything I have since had to put up with on expeditions! Very soon I was pestering my parents with daily letters beseeching them to take me away. In the end they came, and were equally appalled by the situation. I was taken straight home where I promptly succumbed to such a bad attack of measles that 'Our old cook, Mrs Bryant, declared it must be smallpox.'

My parents next approached Brighton College:

There is a vacancy and the Head, Canon Dawson, writes kindly and does not mind about Ernest being a German. Such balm to find anyone who prefers one to a pick-pocket ... We found the College an attractive place and Mr Dawson an expansive and fascinating person, Irish, full of go and force. It is settled that Vivian goes there – and I hope we have done the best that is possible.

The sudden change to public school is a salutary experience, not without its initial pains. From being a big frog in a very small pond one is just a no-account new boy, the lowest form of life in what feels like a very big lake. If one was also clever, a 'swotter', and wore glasses it could be purgatory to gain popular acceptance. Fortunately I did not suffer these handicaps. I was not unduly bright, and I was reasonably adept at games. So a modest success at rugby, cross-country running and long-jump eased my way into the new community.

Later I was to represent the school at all three, but in fact it was cricket, for which I had little talent – only achieving the Third Eleven – which provided the scenario for what, out of my whole life, was undoubtedly my 'finest hour'.

It was the final of the inter-House cricket matches at the end of my first summer. Wotton (another new boy) and I were reluctantly included in the Bristol House team because we could bowl marginally better than the available talent. As batsmen we were both hopeless, and thus the two useless tail-enders in the batting order. Our opponents from School House had batted first and made a respectable total despite the inspired efforts of Kilcoin, our Captain, who was a First Eleven bowler. Against us School House fielded the school's First Eleven fast and slow bowlers who to us were pretty lethal. Perseveringly our team had battled and our total climbed slowly. When at last I went in as tenth man only another eight runs were needed to win.

This was heady stuff – and I was terrified. Four more cautious runs and the next wicket fell. Wotton advanced from the pavilion. And he had to face the last ball of the over from Adams their fast bowler. Something drastic had to be done – and my brain was racing. So was my pulse. Suddenly inspiration came, and I walked out to meet him.

'On NO account raise your bat from the crease,' I admonished him. 'Just put it there AND KEEP IT THERE.'

We took up our positions. To his credit Wotton did just that. And the ball hit his bat – *hard*. Now it was my turn, but I was facing only the slow bowler.

Keyed up to fever pitch, I missed the first ball completely. The second one, to my relief and amazement, sailed away to square leg *for four*. WE HAD WON! Not only the Cricket Cup but the Cock House Cup as well – and it was all due to Wotton's courage and determination to hold steady. We were both carried off the field shoulder high, and we went into history. It was so unexpected, and I still savour it!

In the early 'twenties all the Houses except ours had changed from gas to electric lighting. Whenever the electricity supply failed, as frequently happened, our friendly but somewhat old-fashioned house master, Mr Jackson, would gleefully point out that his retention of gas lighting had assured that we were the only ones who could present ourselves in class next day with 'prep' completed. To us this seemed grossly unfair. We devised our revenge.

In my study a capped gas pipe protruded from the wall. Without much difficulty I removed the cap and four of us took turns to blow into the pipe with all our might. First our light, then all lights in the passages slowly flickered out. We knew we had won when the large multiple mantle lamps in the 'prep' room gently died. The House was in total darkness – and next day *we* were the only ones excused 'prep'! We were never discovered but the next term electricity was installed. Only now with hindsight do I realize that it had all been a very dangerous exercise.

Maths proved to be my strongest subject and I was encouraged to pursue this when I went to university. But soon I realized that I was already reaching my limit in this, and also that I must turn towards subjects which would keep me in the open air in later life. My collecting instincts had led to an interest in natural history so I decided on geology and zoology as main disciplines, with mineralogy a weak third.

I was also still keenly interested in wireless. When I was twelve I had persuaded my father to buy a tall mast which we erected in the garden, and I made a proper twin-wire aerial. He bought me a crystal detector and sufficient parts to make my first real crystal set. After a time this was enhanced with low-frequency valve amplifiers, followed by high-frequency ones. I experimented with different circuits, many taken from Scott Taggart's book of one hundred wireless circuits. Since the valves I used were bright emitters (you could work by the light of four of them), the problem was the power supply. The nearest point for charging an accumulator was in Staplehurst, and too expensive for my purpose anyway. So I eventually solved it by permanently connecting a series of wet cell batteries to the accumulator – which provided a continuous ready source of power.

In 1920 there was one hour per week of voice transmissions from Marconi House in London, and another hour from the Hague. Later there were sound transmissions from an ever-increasing number of British and European stations; even some from the United States could be received when conditions were favourable.

My mother, always keenly interested in new inventions, shared my enthusiasm but our basic approaches were diametrically opposed. My excitement lay in the mechanics of finding programmes on the air waves – hers in enjoying them.

Last week, broadcasting direct from Covent Garden, opera began to be sent out, and we three went on the first night, Monday 8 January 1923, to the garage at the South Eastern Hotel to ask them to let us hear a little ... It was *The Magic Flute* ... so clear and good ...

Oh! if we could affort a set! Till today I feared very much that we would not be allowed to 'receive' on account of Ernest's nationality, because the forms we saw last year insisted on licencees being British. But today we bought a licence in Maidstone Post Office for ten shillings – just like anybody else ... To me it would be an indescribable miracle – something too good to be true – to be able to hear opera and good music.

It must have been a great disappointment to my mother that all her efforts to interest me in the arts were a miserable failure. I failed to understand pictures, was usually irritated by any kind of music, and would only read on practical subjects. In my defence I should perhaps put on record that later, during my African expeditions, I did work my way through all Shakespeare's plays except the tragedies – these I ignored because they depressed me!

In 1926 I reached the top of the school and sat for School Certificate, which would qualify me for Cambridge, but after the first paper I developed a most virulent attack of mumps which put paid to the examination. Some months later I had to take 'Little Go' as a substitute.

The year was also a big landmark in my parent's lives. On 1 May my mother was able to write:

At last the longed-for news in the shape of a letter from Mr Norton, 'You will be as pleased to hear as I am to tell you that the Treasury ... etc.' had decided to release *all* the capital, all the investments held so long ... I had this letter while Ernest was still asleep. After reading it twice in a dazed sort of way I gave a shriek of 'Ernest – LISTEN' which woke him up ...

No more dread and anxiety about some sudden confiscation of everything, not even a fear of reduction in means. No more doling out of one's own to one as a Charitable Allowance. And at last the feeling that one was regarded after all as not entirely an 'enemy alien' ...

My mother had paid a high price for her married happiness. Her galling situation had continued to wound her to the core of her English soul. At this time too, my father was at last able to apply for naturalization.

Ernest and I now have no nationality. We belong to no place on earth. We have both renounced German nationality and Ernest has applied for naturalization as a British subject ... According to the terms of the Peace Treaty no German was qualified for naturalization until ten years after the signing, and had first to show papers proving that they were without German nationality. I also had to renounce my acquired German nationality (which I did *most gladly*) and Ernest had to renounce any future claim of Vivian (a minor) to German rights. All this is done. Vivian is a British subject by birth ... but we two are so far nothing at all since then.

I have never known whether it was lack of judgement, sheer vindictiveness or just government bureaucracy, but it was 1927 before the final papers came through, and their long ordeal ended.

Chapter 4

University and my First Expedition

In 1926 I went to St John's College, Cambridge. My tutor was James Wordie, who had been Shackleton's Senior Scientist on his famous *Endurance* Imperial Trans-Antarctic Expedition 1914-16, and who later was to become Master of John's. He always maintained his keen interest in the polar regions, and for many years he took parties of undergraduates to East Greenland or Ellesmere Island during the Long Vac. A dour, shrewd Scot, he was a man of great reserve and few words, but with an unexpectedly pawky sense of humour. It was difficult to get close to him but his students greatly respected his wise advice and relaxed manner of dealing with their misdemeanours. In time we became good friends and throughout my African, and later polar expeditions he was always there, wise in counsel and strong in support. I owe him much.

University life was an exciting challenge, and after the rigid rules and constrictions of school, I relished the freedom to live as one chose. True we had to wear gowns, be in College by 10 p.m. and ask permission to visit London, but apart from being required to sign on for lectures there were few curbs. Suddenly we were responsible for our own learning, or lack of it, as we chose.

I must confess that I was more successful at sports than in the subjects I had chosen to read. Geology and zoology caught my attention but I soon realized that mineralogy was not for me, and after one term it was dropped. I turned to botany as a third subject in my second year.

As a consequence of the great success of the Brighton College Rugby XV I was included in the Freshmen's Trials, but my eleven stone was deemed too light for both University and College packs. Although I was often used as a replacement for a sick or injured College player, it was not until I had taken up rowing with zest (when my weight rose to over twelve stone) that I got my College colours in my second year. Even then I was the lightest of the forwards.

In summer our sporting activities were less serious. We played tennis, some desultory cricket and occasional water polo. The Sedgwick was the only geological club, in those days restricted to twelve men and six women. Since there were 120 men and only twelve girls reading geology, there was always a waiting list – and to me the female representation of fifty per cent of the male numbers was grossly unfair. A group of us decided to form a rival club which became known as The Coprolites.

Our Professor was interested in the level of the water table in the Cambridgeshire chalk, and we enthusiastically undertook a project to measure this by sounding the level in all the wells we could discover within a radius of fifteen miles. On Sundays, normally in pairs, we cycled all over the country asking farmers to allow us to investigate their water supply, and nearly always they were interested and cooperative. But one old chap, when asked if we could look at his well, scratched his white head dubiously and after a long pause he said,

'Well – what makes yer think I gotta well?'

'Because we can see your cows,' we persisted. 'Where do they get their water from?'

'From the pump, of course.'

'Yes, but where does the pump pump it from?'

After an even longer pause for thought he came up with,

'O-h-h-h – yer mean THE WELL. Well, yes.'

We gave all our readings to the Professor who then published a paper on them.

Staying out at night was not then permitted and if caught the consequences could be severe. But it was said that there were fourteen ways of getting back into St John's – apart from the front door. After one twenty-first birthday party I remember leading a posse up a sloping roof from the Master's garden and through a bedroom window in Chapel Court. I have never forgotten the surprise of the occupant when I appeared through his bedroom door asking, 'May we please come through?' On his rather dubious agreement all twenty of us trooped through his sitting-room, to disperse in the court below.

In the old colleges the ablutions were somewhat primitive and situated long distances from the sleeping quarters, so everyone was supplied with a chamber pot under the bed. The 'bedders' who arrived every morning to slop-out, clean the rooms, make beds and generally keep an eye on our domestic life, were usually motherly middle-aged women. They were also expected to report suspected misdemeanours to the Head Porter who, in turn, kept the Dean *au fait* with the general goings-on. The story is told that Peter Scott, then living next door at Trinity and already an enthusiastic ornithologist, often needed to be out all night watching the nocturnal habits of geese as far away as the marshlands of the Wash. It was easy to persuade his buddies to go in and rumple up the bed to make it look slept in, but his real friends also obligingly used his pot!

Bobby Chew, a future headmaster of Gordonstoun, shared my enthusiasm for roof-climbing. The Trinity College library immediately next to John's is a massive building with a huge chimney at one end and a gap of some four feet between the two structures. We once planned to ascend this by 'backing up', and appreciating that it might be dangerous we behaved very responsibly and roped-up. Chew ascended first and then called down for me to follow. Cautiously I began to climb and when, halfway up, I reached a daunting ridge, I called warning him to take the strain, and went on with confidence. On arrival at the top I found the rope lying loose and Chew happily exploring the other end of the library!

High above New Court, St John's, there was a large stone circle which had originally been intended for a clock face. However the idea was abandoned on the grounds that its chimes would clash with those of the Trinity clock near by. I felt compelled to rectify this situation by tying an alarm clock to one end of a strong piece of string, and the head of my geological hammer to the other. One night after dark I climbed up to the empty clock face and threaded the hammer head and string through a small square hole in the middle. This held my clock in place until next morning when it went off with a satisfactory if distant noise.

Nothing was ever proved but the Head Porter remarked that a geological hammer head was, to say the least, suspicious. It was much later that I realized Wordie himself had known quite a lot about the matter, for on returning from our summer expedition to Greenland he sent an account of its members to *The Times*. This included the statement that '... the ninth member of the team gained his [mountaineering] experience among the roofs and towers of Cambridge.'

In a local bicycle shop we found a wonderful old five-seater bicycle which could be hired by the day. Riding this monster took considerable skill for it was some ten feet long, and even mounting it required both experience and good judgement. This fearsome contraption we used for many a happy excursion, getting up tremendous bursts of speed along the flat highways of East Anglia.

Dancing and May Balls were never my scene, but I have to admit (with shame and apologies to the feminists of today) that as a group we spent happy times observing the girls who passed under the window of rooms in Bridge Street, allotting to each one points for looks on an established scale from one to ten. Some of my buddies were born philanderers, often in trouble when they got their lines crossed so that suddenly two girls were expected at the same event. Being considered 'safe', I was always the one selected to save the situation and escort the one they fancied least.

Bob Schwab, an American, had a girl in the States who once turned up unexpectedly on the morning of a May Ball to which he had invited his current English rose. I was sent to meet her and do the honours at the station, explaining that he was busy doing exams. He told her to recognize me as the chap on the platform 'who will be smoking two cigarettes'. This I refused, and he had to phone her again to change it to 'wearing a nosegay' – something else I seldom did! The upshot was that I found myself escorting an unknown but very nice American girl for the rest of that day.

During my first Long Vac my diligent mother recorded a family visit to Yorkshire:

28 June 1927: Here we are all three on the hill above Richmond. Tomorrow morning there is to be a total eclipse of the sun ... Ever since I was small I have lamented that eclipses ... were never total in England. This is my only chance.

My parents slept in the car but I refused the tent they had brought for me and spent the night walking about the parking ground watching the arrival of more and more cars bringing visitors for the event. Alas, the totality of the eclipse at 6.20 a.m. was invisible owing to thick cloud, but we saw it 'partial'.

My mother had long felt oppressed by the flat countryside around Staplehurst and longed for pines and heathery hills. Now that it was at last possible to plan for a stable future, my parents decided to buy a home in more congenial country. They began house hunting in Surrey.

... Up we went a long way through the pines. Then we saw the house in a little hollow. I said at once 'Too big' and we turned off to the left to see the grounds. Oh how lovely! I will not describe them because I fear we cannot have the place ... We all three left in a state of exaltation, and none of the places we passed after that were very much to us ...

Then called Upway, the house was near Tilford. They bought it some months later and restored the original name – Heatherdene. It was indeed too large and most inconvenient, but it stood in thirty-three acres of pine woods which my father would lovingly cultivate for the rest of his life. He began growing prize azaleas and rhododendrons, and my mother found herself able to grow rare heathers and many other plants which had not survived in the heavy clay soil of Walden.

Soon it was a model property, to which were later added another five acres of forest, and whenever I was home I too chopped and sawed, cleared away and replanted, pruned and thinned our forest land. On the hills surrounding Hindhead I spent happy and fruitful weeks teaching myself how to survey. For us it was an idyll come true.

During the Christmas vacation we went to France. The Dodge had been replaced by a Chrysler 70, an ideal open tourer, and the New Year found us in Mentone where the celebrations included a gala dinner, paper hats and streamers. I was not a party man and only with great difficulty was I persuaded to appear. But it is all down in my mother's journal!

Vivian danced for the first time in his life ... a lively Mrs McDonald asked him twice so he gave in. This morning he has asked Doris (her daughter) to go for a walk and this afternoon he has taken her and the McDonalds for a drive!

We have been here a fortnight ... the 'mauve' girl has been his constant companion ... Before they made acquaintance we laughed over the very obvious way she made eyes at him. At first he rather disliked her for this but then it began to amuse him and he would admit that he must sit where he

Heatherdene

could get the full advantage of the beam ... He has even written to Edith
(Connell) asking would they excuse him from his promised visit ...
admitting that he wished to stay on here to continue his acquaintanceship
with a girl!

But returning to Cambridge for the Lent Term I soon forgot her
in the greater pleasures of rugger. As I had no natural aptitude, and
never made the slightest effort to learn the basic rudiments of
dancing, this was perhaps a merciful dispensation of providence for
Doris.

A more immediate problem was to reconcile my now pressing
desire for a motor bike with my bank account. My parents allowed
me £400 a year, out of which I was expected to meet the university
fees and my living expenses. Despite my natural thrift, a legacy from
the war which has never left me, this did not leave a margin for
extras and I had on occasion to decide between buying a newspaper
or a bun for tea. My mother's opposition to a motor bike was
uncompromising – she considered them both noisy and dangerous.
After consideration my father made me a proposition that if I would
agree to wait until my twentieth birthday, he would anticipate my

Lepisma, my silver-grey Austin (1927)

coming-of-age and my parents would give me a small car. Thus I became the proud owner of a tiny special-bodied Gordon England two-seater Austin 7, built of pale silver grey cloth, plywood and aluminium. It cost £150 new!

Driving such a very lightly built car, and conscious of its lack of road-holding qualities, I became cautious and began to think out and practise how I might behave in an emergency. I decided that I could best protect myself by moving sideways and ducking under the steering wheel. Within three weeks I was driving through Royston at 6.45 a.m. when a motor bike and sidecar came out of a blind turning and hit the side of my car, turning it over. The entire hood and windscreen were sheered off but automatically I went through the emergency drill I had invented. The only damage I suffered was a half-inch tear in the knee of my trousers. The noise of the crash brought householders from their beds to pick the car off me and set it upright!

In our third year a group of us, under the direction of W B R (later Professor) King, went on a three-week geological mapping course to Austwick in Yorkshire. We stayed at the Game Cock Inn and during the second week decided to do the Three Peaks Walk. This entailed climbing Ingleborough, Whirnside and Pen-y-gent, a round trip of twenty-eight miles. The challenge lay in the time taken. Three days earlier I had hurt my foot badly enough to be considered medically unfit. I was indignant and mortified to be ordered to remain behind.

Next morning, fifteen minutes after the party left the inn, I set off on my own taking the peaks in reverse order – and determined at least to equal their performance. We all met halfway between Whirnside and Pen-y-gent during the lunch break. And now it became a race in earnest. My astonished rivals cut short their picnic, in turn determined to teach me a lesson. Everyone was on their mettle – and my foot was throbbing like mad! The arrival home was a dead heat for as I arrived at the back door the others burst in through the front, clocking in at seven hours and three-quarters. I claimed to have won by a quarter of an hour.

In the summer of 1929 I sat for the first part of the Science Tripos and got a Third. It wasn't a startling success but in those days it sufficed. I was relieved – and very excited because Wordie had invited me to go on his summer expedition to Greenland.

On 2 July we sailed from Aberdeen in the sixty-four-ton sealer *Heimland*. Besides Wordie, four of us were geologists together with two surveyors, a doctor and a physicist who came as our wireless operator. With all sails set and a two-cylinder coal-burning steam engine, *Heimland* could manage seven knots in good conditions. She carried a Norwegian crew of nine but we also took turns at the wheel and in the engine room. For the first three days we rode out a series of gales, when all of us except August Courtauld lay miserably wedged into our bunks overcome with seasickness. On the second night out the cabin I shared with Vernon Forbes was flooded by a heavy sea to a depth of several inches, and this quickly cured our normal untidiness, for everything on the floor was soaked. The ship was plunging her nose badly and in an effort to steady her all the deck cargo of extra coal was moved aft. When the storm had passed there was a deep and uncomfortable swell.

Six days later, in latitude 71°N we entered the pack ice and it soon became apparent that it was a bad ice year – progress through the free-floating pack was painfully slow. The Captain was often anxious but we newcomers were enthralled. I began my first journal:

A beautiful sight. Great masses of ice of every conceivable form and size, assuming fantastic shapes. Great piles and pillars, huge toadstools and arches, some consisting of many years' accumulation formed of blocks of ice built up into a sort of large cairn which glowed in the crevices with a blue fire like some gigantic electric radiator ... The ice has an eternal fascination for me. Floes of different shapes and sizes piled upon one another in an indescribable confusion, or beautifully smooth level fellows which seem to invite one to walk upon them.

Frequently the ship was completely halted by pressure, and then we set out across the ice to hunt seals or bears, or to play our own somewhat unorthodox brand of rugger. This entailed getting very wet, for tackles usually landed both parties in small melt pools of icy water, much to the delight of the crew watching this mad English pastime from the ship's rails.

Slowly *Heimland* pursued her sinuous course through the ice, crashing her way between the floes, shuddering thuds shaking her from stem to stern, the brash — accumulations of floating ice fragments less than six feet across — bumping and slithering along her sides. On 10 July we hardly moved at all and if the estimated southward drift of twenty miles a day was correct, we went backwards. We were then in a pool of open water about three miles by a mile, which we circumnavigated three times trying to find a way out.

The floes surrounding us ... are of immense size and thickness ... in the neighbourhood of fifty to one hundred square miles, sometimes reaching fifty feet or more in thickness. We made an attempt to force a passage through a small crack ... but got firmly wedged, unable to move either way. Failing to pull ourselves out with a wire rope from the windlass donkey-engine to an ice hummock, we were reduced to blasting with dynamite.

In all the Captain spent four weeks trying to fight a way through the ice in the direction we wanted to go, but none of us really appreciated the dangers he faced on many occasions. For us life was always busy for there was much to be done. The ship normally carried four tons of water but by 12 July only a ton remained.

It is a laborious business watering ship ... One moors alongside a convenient ice floe with a puddle of water ... making sure ... that it is free from salt, a procession of buckets starts ... these are filled at the water hole by three men and handed to me ... I lift them over the side and carry them to the Mate and Parkinson, who are pouring the water down a small funnel set in the deck ... which meant that (today) I handled three tons of water — which is just what it felt like!

The sealer *Heimland*

I keep on feeling how impossible it is to realize my luck in being here to revel in and marvel at all these things ... I wish I had thought of wintering ... it would have been great fun and very cheap, especially as I could hunt, and if at all successful this would at least make it pay my way.

During tea in latitude 73°30'N the Mate suddenly called out 'Seals!' and in a flash we were all out on the ice. Fresh meat was badly needed, and the crew had a special interest in our success for the skins were their special perks and fetched good money back home in Norway. Once we walked far afield, hopping over intervening water channels – known as leads – and often jumping from point to point on pieces of ice which turned over and over. Sometimes we could only progress by pushing off across a broad lead, standing on perhaps a square yard of ice. This was slow, and far from secure but there was a thrill as one paddled slowly with great caution across water 3,000 feet deep on a wobbly bit of ice.

As I returned to the ship people were yelling from the rails 'Look

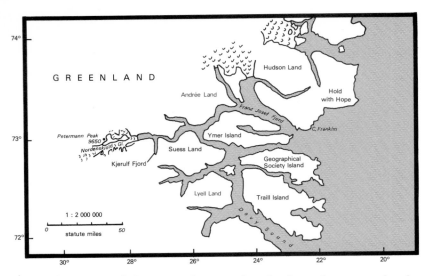

behind you!' and I saw a bear a hundred yards away clearly following my trail – and able to swim and run faster than a man. As he gained on me Whittard and Dykes came to my rescue with rifles and dropped him at eighty-five yards. Next day we ate bear for lunch, which is rather like veal, tender and delicious, greatly preferable to seal, which is always black.

On another walk I found shells and seaweed on the surface. This set everyone hunting for them and by evening we had fourteen different species. Various theories for their presence were argued – transport by melt water, flooding coastal ice, or perhaps in the shallows the sea froze the bottom, entrapping them. Later if the ice floated away accretion to the bottom of the floes would encase shells, mud and seaweed. During these days the animals and birds we collected were all skinned and labelled, for we were trying to procure properly identified specimens for the Cambridge Museum.

Day after day the ice remained impregnable, but on one glorious occasion when the sun shone brilliantly and there was no wind, the water temperature was 33°F (0.5°C). Wakefield, Varley and I bathed, and that evening our 'winter sports' took the form of sliding down an ice slope using tea trays and shovels as well as proper skis. The largest shovel made a beautiful sledge when towed by three men, but it was an accomplished rider who could stay the course of bumps and puddles through which his steeds dragged him.

July 28 was a heartbreaking day for we could see sea water only three miles away which promised a passage if we could reach it. The expedition divided into three watches to assist the crew, and we chopped and cut and poled and hacked away to breaking point, but the ship only moved a quarter of a mile.

Again fast in the pack ... This morning the ice began to move towards the east and the ship got squeezed at the stern and amidships. We tilted about five to ten degrees to starboard, but before I could get my camera she slipped back ... For several hours there was tremendous pressure on the rudder and sternpost. After it became free ... the rudder had been bent through thirty-five degrees ... We are completely unable to straighten it and even if we could it would probably break off. This means that we can go hard aport but only very little to starboard. This will make it difficult to steer through the pack.

At last at the beginning of August we saw the Greenland coast fifteen miles away, but once more the pressure increased. Floes on the starboard side moving quickly drove ice under the stern. This bent the rudder and sternpost in opposite directions until it seemed impossible that they did not snap. Huge pieces of ice rose under the stern raising the ship three feet. Cabins creaked and groaned, beams bending and seams opening until we feared she must pop and let the water in. By the 4th the Captain had fought through to 'land water', and that evening we thankfully anchored a mile offshore in Mackenzie Bay. There we found an isolated hut occupied by two Norwegian hunters who had two polar bear cubs tethered near by. We never discovered what they were going to do with them but they seemed very vicious captives. Four of us went ashore, astounded at the wealth of vegetation, and came back laden with specimens. By midnight we were on our way again, sailing up the 150-mile long Franz Josef Fjord, finally to anchor in Eleonoren Bay in Kjerulf Fjord.

We were badly behind schedule and field work began at once – Parkinson and Whittard geologizing, Wakefield, Courtauld and Dr Varley surveying Eskimo hut sites. (For some unknown reason the Eskimos had all departed or died out in the late eighteenth century.) Vernon Forbes and I went off to find musk ox, and five miles up the valley we saw three adults and two calves. But the distance from the ship was too great to get them back so they were not touched. They were wonderful great black scraggy animals which looked almost square owing to the hanging masses of long hair.

Next day six of us started on the trek to Petermann Peak, then thought to be the highest mountain in the Arctic. Since this was not an elaborate enterprise employing porters, it had to be done on the absolute minimum of food and fuel which we could carry ourselves. This together with tents, cooking equipment and survey require-ments amounted to fifty-two pounds per man, but on the first day everyone, together with three crew members, carried loads of thirty-six pounds to establish the first camp. Forbes, Courtauld and I comprised the vanguard, choosing the site and pitching three tents at 3,800 feet. From here the support party returned, and next morning we were on a glacier and had climbed another 2,500 feet. Lunch consisted of one biscuit, two bars of chocolate and six lumps of sugar, with no water. Now each of us carried fifty pounds which felt very heavy, and I was thankful when we roped up to cross a crevassed area where agility seemed likely to be at a premium.

Having negotiated this the two ropes parted company, Wordie himself with Forbes and Varley going on to make camp, while Wakefield, Courtauld and I veered east towards a peak from which we could survey the area. The day ended with all of us in camp at 11.45 p.m. at 7,300 feet with fourteen degrees of frost, and my journal records, 'Dead beat and damn cold.' It snowed all night.

In the morning everything was obscured by fog. Four of us returned to base camp to fetch up more food, and we were thankful to get down into warm sunshine where we stripped off and dried clothes. We also drank until we swelled! Then Forbes and Varley set off to climb a neighbouring peak of 7,000 feet, and Courtauld and I started our return journey – now carrying thirty-four pounds each. We chose a shorter route but it proved to be dangerously crevassed and we had several near misses. Indeed as darkness fell we had to pitch our tiny two-man tent, and continue the next day.

Meanwhile Wordie and Wakefield carried supplies up to 8,600 feet to 'Outlook Col' and returned to their rendezvous with Forbes and Varley without having found water. Next morning all four carried rations up to this Col, returning so thirsty that they collected together all the available mugs and their two saucepans and climbed 200 feet up to a small pool which they had seen in the distance. They ate their frugal lunch there, breaking six inches of ice to get at the water, and having drunk all they could hold, they returned to camp with all their utensils full.

On 9 August we awoke to twenty degrees of frost and it was snowing hard, but by midday we could move back to Outlook Col and there, at last, before us was Petermann Peak, the centre of a wide vista of rocky peaks and snowy slopes stretching to either side. The following days were full of alarms.

I think I have never been more continuously frightened than I have today ... we made a traverse along the flank of Outlook Col and came across ... pretty bad crevasses ... lower we came to rock which was difficult to get off. But worse was to come for as we climbed the next snow slope we found avalanche snow in abundance, while below ... were the yawning bergschrunds [a bergschrund is a crevasse which separates the moving glacier from the rock wall and the ice apron attached to it] ... we reached the summit, which showed we had to descend 1,000 feet and immediately climb another 800 feet on to the Knoll ... We soon found that [the descent] hid both crevasses and bergschrunds in abundance which, with much glassy ice, made the descent a pretty terrifying experience ... then began the steep ascent of the Knoll ... Once up we could find no camping ground, so descended 800 feet of extremely steep scree ... by a somewhat difficult little rock climb.

It was here that Wordie dropped his pack – I think in preference to himself – and it went bounding down 800 feet. One had a very good idea of what one's own body would look like flying through the air! At the bottom we camped in an extremely dangerous position at the foot of the scree on a mass of ice and stones. (From there Wordie's pack was recovered.)

Next day we ascended to a high col with peaks on either side. From the summit of one we established that the way to Petermann now lay across the great Nordenskjöld Glacier ahead. We camped at 6,500 feet, and next day returned to Outlook Col to fetch more supplies. This was a two-day assignment in bitter weather with surfaces like glass. Icicles formed in our beards and faces lost all feeling. So it went on for several days until finally Varley's boots just gave out, the soles parting from the uppers, and he was forced to stay put.

Curious thing is he doesn't think he knows the way back in case we do not return. We have tried to describe it to him and have left him a tent and enough food. I am sleeping with Courtauld and Cuthbert (Wakefield) three in a tent. It is pretty cold with a strong wind.

Next day we climbed what we named the Disa Glacier, reaching a snow field which led up to a col whence we had another wonderful view of our objective. By now lunch consisted of tea and oatmeal in ice water, and we camped in a screaming wind coming over the cliffs to the glacier below – marvelling that the tent-guys did not snap. On 16 August Wordie, Wakefield and Forbes made the final assault. The doctor's absence spelt disaster for my high hopes, for Courtauld had no crampons and anyway Wordie decided that the final climb was too dangerous to be attempted with less than three men on a rope. It was a big disappointment to us both. We settled down for a long wait, our boots frozen solid on our feet and with faces that had lost all feeling. In the tearing gale we took a boiling point reading with a view to establishing our height.

Wordie's party roped up and set off across a seventy-degree slope of green ice. It was a dicy effort with 3,000 feet of nothingness yawning below and nothing on top. Presently we heard their cheers and knew they had reached the summit. They were about 100 feet above us.

Getting back to the ship was now a matter of urgency for there was very little food left. We found Dr Varley safely. He had spent his time profitably by mending his boots with copper wire and attaching crampons to them. On the other side of the Nordenskjöld Glacier we had left a small depot of food and some instruments, but these were now cut off from us by a deep pool. Varley volunteered to swim over and fetch them but dared not remove his crampons which were all that held his boots together. He got across safely but while swimming back his right crampon caught in his left trouser leg. Since he had two pounds of pemmican in each hand and the strap of an instrument between his teeth, he was forced to let go of something as he went under. We lost the instrument but the food was more than welcome, and we travelled till 1 a.m. Towards the end of this day Forbes had declared himself too done in to go any farther.

I stayed behind with him and kept him moving. Had I not ... I am sure he would have laid himself quietly down and frozen. Fortunately I insisted on us being roped as he fell down more than one crevasse. If we had lost him it would have been serious, for the rest of us would have had to look for him without food, and without being able to cook as he had the utensils.

By the 18th we had nothing left to eat so decided that we MUST reach the ship in one spurt. To save time we crossed the side slopes of a snow dome instead of going over the top. This was nasty for it could have started an avalanche, but we got away with it. Farther on

Wordie fell up to his shoulders into a crevasse. When we held him up, he made no attempt to get out, frantically emptying his left-hand pocket of everything imaginable. In the end a burning box of flamer matches came out – the cause of the trouble!

In the evening we were on our way down the last slopes some 3,000 feet to the fjord ... we saw the ship and gave a great shout, In return they ran up a flag and put out a boat for us. They had been about to leave for work elsewhere an hour after the time we arrived, so we were lucky. The cook had a grand meal ready for us, and how I over-ate, even if it was 0200 hours. As we climbed on board the crew shook hands with each of us – a nice gesture!

We were all pretty done. The ship sailed immediately and four hours later it was breakfast time. After that I remember not being able to find any comfortable position in which to write up my journal because I had over-eaten so much! But youth is resilient and next day we were out geologizing and excavating some Eskimo huts we found in Kjerulf Fjord. Two nights later nature took her toll.

Last night Forbes and I had an extraordinary experience. I awoke to hear him saying something about ice, and then I realized that half the tent floor had sunk and the whole was overhung by ice. I cried out that we were down a crevasse and everywhere I looked was hung with green icicles. Forbes got out of bed and went on deck to find out how badly the iceberg had crushed the ship, saying that we had better not tell the others yet for fear of alarming them. I looked out of the port hole and could still see nothing but ice outside. Between us we made quite a commotion – and that is how confused ... a nightmare can be. Never will I forget how vivid was the crevasse down which we had fallen.

I recovered but Forbes' nightmares persisted and on six consecutive nights he wandered dazedly about the ship suffering hallucinations about crevasses. Somewhat heartlessly my journal records, 'I can't imagine how he manages to walk in his sleeping bag'!

For a few days we cruised up neighbouring fjords still collecting interesting museum specimens such as hares (which were very difficult to find) and Arctic owls, but on 24 August it was time to make for home – with fingers firmly crossed and a fervent prayer, the Captain steered once more into the pack ice.

Four days later *Heimland* swung heavily on to an ice foot (the underwater projection of an iceberg's base) and was damaged. Part of the rudder post broke away, the propeller was bent in several places, and the shaft itself was bent two inches out of true. The broken rudder made it difficult to turn to starboard, the bent shaft meant we could only sail at half-speed, and if we went astern it was possible that the propeller would come off because the lock-nut appeared to be loose. We spent a day in thick fog repairing what we could. The ice was in fairly rapid movement and the ship was subjected to several 'squeezings', the beams groaning and the rudder chain rattling. Again we all kept round-the-clock watches with the crew as our indomitable little vessel finally fought her way to open water. Eight days later we were in Jan Mayen. For me it had been a memorable baptism of ice.

In October I went back to Cambridge for a fourth year to take Part II in Geology. As a result of our work in Greenland Wordie encouraged Whittard and myself to write a joint paper on the occurrence of marine shells and other material on floating ice. This, my first publication, appeared in the *Geographical Journal* under the title 'The East Greenland Pack-ice and the Significance of its Derived Shells'.

Our weekend geological excursions were resumed and occasionally we unearthed the remains of old Roman pots and vases. Louis Clarke, then Director of the Museum of Archaeology and Ethnology, took an interest in our findings, many of which found their way into the Museum. He was a wealthy man of great charm and impeccable taste, an epicure who delighted in the arts and knew everyone. His personal collections included paintings, porcelain, jade, old books, ivories and parchments, and he took care to hide his greatest treasures whenever Queen Mary visited his house for she was famous at parting collectors from pieces which she herself admired! To my less cultured mind his portrait by Augustus John and his bust by Epstein were awe-inspiring, but after I got married and bought a house with a large garden adjoining his, we became good neighbours and shared a common interest in breeding huskies.

Dr L S B Leakey was then a Research Fellow at St John's and through my association with him I became interested in East African archaeology. His parents were African missionaries who had brought him up with the Kikuyu tribe. From infancy he had learnt their native lore, their customs and could speak their language fluently.

Vivian Fuchs 1928

When he came up to Cambridge Louis Leakey had proposed to read Modern Languages, offering Kikuyu and French, in which he was also fluent since his mother was French. It was an easy option, which would enable him to spend nearly all his time studying archaeology. The university authorities were taken aback, and decreed that Kikuyu was not acceptable as the Statutes said that only languages spoken by at least five million people could be recognized. Louis quickly proved that there were more than five million Kikuyu, which left the university in a quandary for there was no one who could teach the language – much less examine a student. An urgent appeal to the School of Oriental Languages revealed that only two people in the country were competent in Kikuyu – one was in Oxford, the other was a certain Louis S B Leakey who had recently arrived in Cambridge!

Not surprisingly Louis completed his examinations with First Class Honours, but archaeology was his real interest and he soon made his mark in pursuing the prehistory of East Africa. His was a fascinating personality from whom I learnt not only about the past climate of Africa and the stages of palaeolithic and neolithic man, but also such useful things as the art of making fire by rapidly spinning a carefully chosen stick on a block of wood (my record was nineteen seconds), and the construction of the most complicated and elaborate string figures which put to shame my earlier school-boy skills at cat's cradle. It was Leakey's influence which first turned my thoughts towards Africa.

In June 1930, as my university days were finishing, Dr E B Worthington, then working in the Department of Zoology, was organizing The Cambridge Expedition to the East African Lakes. Its object was to study the biology of Lakes Baringo and Rudolf in the Eastern Rift and Lakes Edward and George in the Western Rift. He wanted to include a geologist to study the geological history of these lakes with special reference to previous climatic fluctuations and the fossil freshwater faunas. To my amazed delight Wordie suggested my name. This was better than anything I could have hoped for – when Worthington offered me the job I jumped at it. So began my journeyings in Africa, which were to continue intermittently for the next nine years, until the outbreak of World War Two.

Chapter 5

The Cambridge Expedition to the East African Lakes 1930-31

It was a four-man expedition planned to last one year – Dr Barton Worthington, Leader/Zoologist (accompanied by his wife); Leonard Beadle, Chemist; Richard Dent, Fish Warden of Kenya; and me as Geologist. Beadle and I left Tilbury in ss *Llandaff Castle* on 9 September 1930, to be joined by Dr and Mrs Worthington at Genoa eleven days later. It was a relief to find that I was no longer upset by the motion of the ship no matter how rough the sea, and I took energetically to deck tennis. At Port Said we were surrounded by the inevitable mob of excited yelling Arabs trying simultaneously to sell us necklaces, sweets, fez, walking sticks and pornographic post-cards. On 3 November we reached Mombasa and boarded a train to Nairobi.

The railway engines were then wood-burning, which produced clouds of sooty particles that settled everywhere when running into the wind. But when the windows could be opened exotic scents of the tropical night permeated the carriage, and when we stopped at Voi the trilling of a thousand cicadas made an impression I have never forgotten. In Nairobi we found Louis Leakey, already en-gaged on the archaeological work which was to make him famous throughout the world. He was generous with advice and material assistance, allowing us the use of one of his lorries. In addition Worthington bought a box-body Ford. Instruments and equipment from one of his previous ventures were routed out from the Game Department Store, and we bought fishing lines, hooks and swivels, together wtih spare parts for the wireless set which I had built in England and carefully nursed all the way out. In four days of working round the clock we were ready to set out for Lake Naivasha.

Both vehicles were packed solid. Beadle and Dent drove the Ford, Worthington and I following in the lorry with an African 'boy' somehow clinging precariously to the top of the load. As we climbed the slopes towards the great Rift Valley the gradients necessitated driving almost continuously in second gear. Every ten miles we stopped to refill the radiators, and then suddenly we were plunging down 1,200 feet to Dick Dent's house on the lakeside some miles from the little township of Naivasha. This was our first head-quarters, and my first task was to set up the wireless.

These early African years were to prove a revelation. This great black brooding continent caught my imagination and interest as completely as the Arctic pack ice had done. Sometimes the heat was intense but I acclimatized quickly and revelled in the strenuous outdoor life. Never in all my years there did I subscribe to the afternoon siesta during the heat of the day. The hot starlit nights too were a wonderful experience, when we listened to the cries and calls of strange animals. I soon learnt to imitate some of them to the point where they would answer me back. Usually the only geologist, I was to spend many torrid days under a baking sun in isolation as I worked around the lakes. In the evenings I learnt to speak Swahili from the African 'boys' and the porters who, from time to time, accompanied our safaris.

Roads were either non-existent or indescribably bad, and all our work was done against a background of incessant punctures and a constant struggle to get our vehicles to the points we wished to investigate. In order to examine lakes boats were essential, and to transport these from site to site we required lorries. But in places of geological interest where it became impossible to get vehicles over the ground, we organized safaris on foot supported by camels, donkeys or native porters. It was a supremely satisfying way of life, and I was happy and very content.

For work on Lake Naivasha we had a flat-bottomed boat with a twelve-horsepower outboard engine, and we planned to take this to Lake Baringo some fifty miles to the north. For this exercise it was overhauled and the engine fitted, but the first test run was a disaster. When the boat turned too sharply, the diagonal thrust of the propeller, coupled with the vibration, jerked the clamp off the stern. Barton Worthington valiantly held on to the steering handle of the violently racing semi-submerged machine but finally the rubber grip came off in his hand. The engine then sank to the bottom in ten feet of water.

We marked the spot immediately but although we dived repeatedly and then used long poles to probe the bottom, the engine had apparently sunk without trace. Next morning oil was floating on the surface. Taking this as a promising sign we resumed the search. Owing to six feet of clinging weed in the water, diving in this new patch was impossible, but Worthington and I repeatedly pushed a long pole vertically to the lake bed, climbed down it and trod a circle in the bottom feeling for the engine with our feet. Two hours later we realized that a more systematic method must be devised, and it was Beadle who thought of fitting a piece of corrugated iron to a wooden handle, thus making it possible to 'sweep' a much greater area at each thrust. By this means we found the engine, brought it to the surface, took it apart and laid it out in the sun to dry.

All this had delayed our departure for two days. On the morning we planned to start again it was discovered that the engine of the lorry was only loosely held in place by two bolts, the front not being attached in any way whatever. By midday this was rectified and the boat somewhat precariously fixed on top. When we left, the convoy consisted of our Bedford lorry, Dent's box-body Dodge and the expedition's Ford. Four nights and a few mishaps later we were camped near the shores of Lake Baringo. *En route* the Dodge had broken a back axle, the Ford suffered four punctures in rapid succession, and the lorry had stuck fast in the mud. While Dent was searching for a suitable camp site on arrival, a rock broke a large hole in the bottom of his petrol tank — but all these were then normal events when motoring over African tracks!

Our main camp was pitched a hundred feet above and four hundred yards from the lakeside. A small tent was erected at the water's edge to house the specimens we had come to collect. Here our surroundings consisted of dry dusty bush, acacia thorn trees including the curved thorn wait-a-bit bushes, and the average midday temperature was 94°F (34.5°C). Providing food for the party was simple, since hares and guinea-fowl were abundant. We fished and washed in the lake, albeit with some caution for it was also full of crocodiles.

By boat we visited a small unexplored island where I was particularly excited to find trees which none of us could recognize. These were covered with lianas growing in fantastic drooping bundles. Beneath, giant veranus lizards four feet long crashed through the bushes like express trains when disturbed, while huge spiders with legs that spanned a man's hand came out and looked at us. The yellow strands supporting their webs were as thick as carpet thread. In some almost inaccessible caves I found traces of past habitation and a curious tailless rat.

Back in camp that evening we found that fresh meat was required for the larder, so arming myself with a .22 rifle I went out after guinea-fowl. It was still just light enough to see when suddenly just ahead of me there was a slight scuffle and a cloud of dust arose behind a bush. I rushed forward and saw with some shock a rhino making his way through the bushes. Discretion being the better part of valour at ten paces from a rhino, I made off silently in a different direction.

Going for walks along the lake shore I would sometimes surprise basking crocodiles, and always I was escorted by hundreds of dragon-flies ready to pounce on anything edible which my feet might disturb. Indignant storks would march majestically ahead; if I quickened my pace they took wing with tremendous flapping noises. Once I met a family of Grant's gazelle – a buck, a female and two little ones – all almost fearless, for they allowed me within thirty yards of them. It was a relief that the camp was not then short of meat for it would have been impossible to reward such friendliness with a bullet.

It was at this time that I became aware that the 'boys' now called me Bwana Songura (Swahili for rabbit or hare). This was not because of my English nickname Bunny (which originated at my prep school) but it was curiously in keeping. It apparently originated from the fact that I was constantly shooting hares rather than birds or other animals for the pot.

On 10 December, our work at Baringo finished, we broke camp and set off for Kitale on our way to Lake Rudolf. This time the sun's heat was melting the patches of our previous tyre repairs. We fitted two new inner tubes to the Ford but in less than ten miles both had burst. Beadle and I reached Kitale in two days, but Worthington and Dent in the Ford made a digression to Kisumu on Lake Victoria to fetch a boat which was to have been specially built for the work at Rudolf. In fact this had not been done, so they had to search for a substitute, finally settling for a Kenya Uganda Railways and Harbours twenty-foot lifeboat made of steel. This, of course, was too large and heavy to carry on the lorry, but the King's African Rifles were willing to take it up to the lake on one of their much larger vehicles.

They were ready to leave on the 19th but when the boat and their lorry were brought together, alas the former was the larger! By dismantling the body, including the cab, and building in strong supports, they finally secured the boat on top with only a seven-foot overhang. It was decided to ignore the fact that the whole contraption was now dangerously top-heavy, and they arrived without incident in Kitale.

The following morning we all set off on a hair-raising three-day journey to Lake Rudolf, the convoy consisting of two King's African Rifles lorries and the expedition lorry and car. Two escarpments had to be crossed, the road down the first one being precipitous with a surface of loose stones and large boulders. On the second the surface was better, but in an uncomfortably large number of places the bends swung out over more than 1,000 feet. The whole safari crept down with extreme caution, and I am still astonished when I think about it.

We left the lorries at Lodwar and the four of us set off in the Ford on a reconnaissance of the road to make sure that the last fifty-five miles of track to the lake itself would carry the heavy army vehicles. On arrival we took the opportunity of a quick bathe but found the water unpleasantly soda-rich. Starting back to report, we had travelled some twenty miles when there was a strong smell of burning and the ammeter began to glow red. The wires were encased in a metal tube which precluded cutting them. They had to be disconnected from the battery and for this we had no tool, but half-an-hour of improvisation put the trouble right, and by this time it was dark. Setting off again we had only covered a short distance when the headlights fused. Driving with only a spot light we got back just as another conflagration was starting.

Next day it was my turn to drive the car. Leading one of the army lorries, we set off ahead of the main party. At intervals one or both vehicles stuck in the soft ground; then we had to cut down palm leaves and bushes to lay under the wheels until they could grip on the sand. The main party caught up and eventually a patch of abominably soft sand barred the way, and all the vehicles dug themselves in.

Turkana fisherman

We turned out a hundred or so of the men from round about and with their help got all the cars out and down to the shore. This sounds simple enough but it was far from that. Every man had to be shown where to push, how to push, and when to push, or else he stood and watched the others standing and watching. Once we got the cars moving ... a horde of natives shouting and yelling ran beside and behind brandishing palm leaves. Whenever we came to a soft point I would shout and sound the horn, at which they all heaved and shouted in unison ... they enjoyed it enormously! When we had got everything to the shore, the boat in the water, and were settling down for the night, they came and did a *ngoma* (native dance) and sang ... and then asked for tobacco. Each man got one quid which seemed to delight them.

The local Turkana people were greatly intrigued by all the unintelligible scientific work we were doing and groups of them constantly hung around the camp. On Christmas Day we all went on a fishing expedition and on Boxing Day I set off to do some local geologizing, taking with me, on his first-ever car ride, a very excited local chief. Our progress was triumphant, the chief shouting loudly at any of his subjects we passed, until shortly the gearbox gave out. With the willing but somewhat disastrous help of my passenger, who promptly managed to lose some vital bolts, I had it to bits and mended after an hour or so, and we were off again. But on arrival at my target area I was disappointed to find no sign of fossils in the old lake beaches.

A few days later I set out early on foot to examine Losodok, a flat-topped hill some ten miles to the west which seemed to show indications of old lake beaches. Having walked for several hours in the burning heat I was still short of my objective at lunch time, when I discovered that my canvas chargel had been leaking and was now as dry as a bone. In these circumstances the sensible thing would have been to turn back, but one is not always wise.

Now that I had gone so far I was jolly well going to get up to the supposed head so I started off again ... Near the top I came upon the grass line which showed from a distance and which is definitely a beach. The top, nearly a hundred feet above, is a level surface of rounded pebbles showing that this, though not a beach, was at one time within wave action. Having gone a short way down the other side and taken several photographs ... I started back for camp.

I never want another march like that. A burning sun reflected from bare sand and rock, no water, and about ten miles to go. I went about a mile out of my way to a *manyatte* (or temporary village of huts) on the edge of some palms to try to get water but could not. After another four miles, about the worst I've ever had to walk, I reached the palm belt. The only way to keep going was to pick on a point, walk to it, then choose another and walk to that.

Half-a-mile farther I came to another *manyatte* and rested. There I found an old man who managed to make me understand that there was a water hole a mile farther upstream, if I could only make the effort to reach it. I started again.

On reaching the water hole I drank cautiously but a great deal, with the result that after a short rest in the shade I was able to continue towards camp. Having been misdirected, however, I went three miles out of the way ... I got in just as it was getting dark and drank tea, and tea, and more tea. Thus ended a successful but very tiring day.

With hindsight I realized that it could have turned into a serious misadventure. In fact I had in two hours drunk one-and-a-quarter gallons of water and thirteen mugs of tea, without any effect on my bladder.

A major event was a visit to Central Island, locally known as Choro, which entailed a boat trip of nearly three hours until we landed on a small beach on the western shore. We thought ourselves to be the first people to reach this island, and our landing scattered an enormous number of surprised crocodiles, some more than fifteen feet long. A steep climb brought us on to the rim of a dry crater, which proved to be the first of twelve of different sizes. Three of

Turkana woman watering camels

these held lakes which teemed with crocodiles, the females apparently burying their eggs in the soft volcanic ash, for I saw a veranus lizard digging some up for a meal.

The highest point was 550 feet, where a strong sulphurous smell emanated from a complex of fissures and two small fumaroles below. The latter were emitting spumes of sulphur as I watched. Walking round the shore, we found the surface to be covered with boulders and lava, and the birds were so tame that they allowed one to within ten yards before flying off. Small cliffs and beaches, together with driftwood, were evidence that the lake level had been falling. Soundings made on the return journey gave a maximum of 150 feet near the island.

Living in stuffy tents in temperatures of 100°F or 38°C was trying, so the local Turkana built us a *banda* of wood and Dom palm leaves. All our scientific work was out in the sun, and it was a great relief to return each evening to this splendid shelter. In order to simplify our return to Lodwar we also built a hard-surfaced road across the sand patch which had bogged down our convoy so badly.

After three weeks it was time to leave and it was a somewhat sorry cavalcade that set out, for by now our lorry was without a front engine bolt, Dick Dent's car had only two leaves of one spring left, while Leonard Beadle and I brought up the rear in the Ford with scarcely any petrol and very little oil. By milking some petrol from the lorry we just reached Kitale. The climb back up the escarpment had proved even more frightening than the descent had been. On the bad corners overhanging the precipices we had to keep engines going hard or we would not have made the gradient, consequently the vehicles slithered about alarmingly on the loose stones. After only four more punctures to the Ford we were very thankful to reach the comforts of the hotel. From there it was another hundred miles, including a climb up to 10,000 feet to Ravine, but by 16 January 1931 we were back in Naivasha.

A week later the next phase took us back to our old camp on the shores of Lake Baringo by 23 January. Accompanied by two African 'boys' I began a personal safari round the lake geologizing and taking pictures. The repeated punctures were normal, but once a tyre flew off a wheel and bowled along beside and just ahead of the car, much to the terror of my passengers and posing me a problem of how to stop without decanting us all!

The first evening I camped between three villages.

The inhabitants turned up in force (thank heavens I am getting used to the smell) and it seemed one long cry of 'dower, dower' (medicine). One fellow had been fighting and had a cut on his forehead about three inches by half-an-inch completely bare to the skull. It had to be stitched ...

After this ... the whole village was more or less in a state of fester. They came for sores and cuts, ears rotting off the children, fingers off the men. The women, many with ghastly skin diseases. It is awful to have nothing to give the poor people. I've been reduced to engine oil for the skin and permanganate for eyes that they could not see out of owing to some sort of pink-eye. Their faith is incredible and as patients they are marvellous. The man I treated for his skull wound was laughing and talking while I was washing his bare bone – I think I disliked it more than he did. They apparently appreciated my efforts, for milk and eggs turned up from somewhere, for which I was very grateful.

Next day while climbing among some caves in a gorge I was three times chased out by swarms of bees sitting like a cloud on my head – fortunately my hair had grown too long and thick for their stings to penetrate it. I worked surrounded by impala, grant, hundreds of zebra, and always the tracks and traces of elephant, though I seldom saw them.

One night one of the Njemps ran into camp just before sundown imploring me to go quickly and shoot the crocodile which had just eaten his son. The place he described was a mile distant, and it would certainly have been dark by the time I got there. I asked if he was quite sure that his son was dead, to which he replied *'anakwisha kabisa'* (it has finished him completely). So I explained that I would complete my work round the lake, and would then come back and shoot the crocodile.

Four days later I was back in camp, and within half-an-hour the father arrived to ask if I would go at once and treat his son who had been eaten by the crocodile. I was appalled. 'But you told me that he was *dead*,' I said. 'No,' he replied, 'when I went back I found that others had chased the crocodile back into the water and frightened it so that it let go of my son.'

Hastening to the primitive shelter he called home, where goats wandered in and out, I found a very sick boy. The crocodile had taken him across the middle of the body with one arm pinned to his side. The wounds were a series of circular punctures in two rows across his arm and shoulder on one side and his ribs on the other. After four days they were in a terrible state. I cleaned them, bound him up till he looked like a mummy, gave him some aspirin and hoped. When the others returned to camp with our full medical gear I treated him again. In three days he was running about playing with his fellows and full of beans – a remarkable demonstration of the wonderful resilience of the African.

By 2 February the science was finished and we returned to Maragat. Two days later I became seriously ill with a soaring temperature, and Worthington was sending worried telegrams to my father. In Nakuru hospital my condition was first diagnosed as a form of

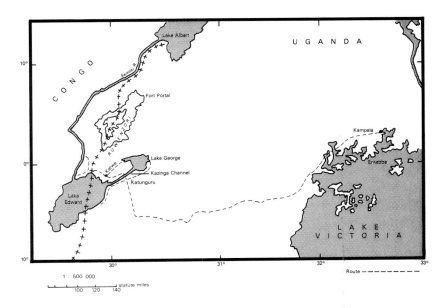

typhus, but some weeks later, after I had had to be moved to
Nairobi, it was found to be malaria combined with relapsing fever. It
was two months before I recovered sufficiently to rejoin the expedition, which by then was on its way to Uganda to investigate Lake
Edward, Lake George and the Kazinga Channel which joins them.
One oft-discussed puzzle was the absence of crocodiles in these
lakes while they flourished so prolifically in all the others. Was there
a physical or chemical factor against them in these waters, or were
they distributed throughout the East African lakes before ever Lake
Edward came into existence? Later I was to find their fossils in the
old lake beds, so they had once been there but had been killed off
when the lake had dried up about two million years ago.

At Katunguru, midway along the Kazinga Channel, there was a rest
camp built of grass huts with cane or mud walls. With tents pitched
alongside, these provided comfortable headquarters and the bathing
was magnificent. In the distance Mount Ruwenzori towered up in
the clouds, and through binoculars we could pick out snow fields
and great ice precipices. Here the climate was congenial after the
sizzling heat of Baringo, but it was wise to consider one's health for
sleeping sickness, malaria and spirillum fever were rampant.

The natives used enormous heavy 'dug-outs' to cross the channel,

73

and cars could be ferried over on a raft made from two of these tied together with boards across the top.

The amazement of the population was extraordinary to see when I took our canvas boat down to the water and it swam so easily on the surface. The speed of it when rowed seemed to take their breath away. This, however, was nothing to the excitement when we fitted our 12-hp outboard to the back of a forty-foot dug-out. It drove the old thing along at about seven knots, causing great waves to rise at the bow.

The other crews, the ferrymen and everyone within sight or sound left what they were doing to watch the miracle of a boat going along without men paddling. Many of them clapped their hands in astonishment. The 'boys' we had in the dug-out with us were momentarily nervous but soon they could not contain themselves for laughter ...

Beadle and I began a ten-day safari along the south side of the channel, taking porters to carry our equipment and accompanied by the local chief who insisted on being invited. On many evenings extra 'banana men' brought out food for the porters from the village, and then we had as many as thirty mouths to feed, for whom sufficient meat had to be provided from surrounding game.

At Kateta steep cliffs overhung the lake which I wanted to investigate. It was here that I found myself being chased by a hippo whose preserves I had inadvertently invaded. I retired with speed if not with dignity. Later crossing the flats, another one was sitting basking in the mud, and I succeeded in creeping to within twenty-five yards of him from where I got splendid close-up pictures. The water was full of them. When we wished to bathe we first threw stones to scare them away, but to our surprise they were very quick in the uptake and soon they quietly submerged as one raised an arm to throw.

Two islands in the north gulf of Lake Edward were thickly covered with wood and bush through which it was only possible to travel along hippo paths. We found abundant evidence that they had once been inhabited by humans too, but the population had long since been driven away by the prevalence of tsetse fly and sleeping sickness.

Later on the north side of the Kazinga Channel we approached Lake Katwe. There we met heavily laden porters all carrying loads of salt, the great local native industry.

The lake lies in the bottom of a crater, and though perhaps one-and-a-half miles in extent, it is never more than one or two feet deep. The bottom is formed of salt which the natives heave up in great blocks like solidified sand complete with perfect ripple marking ... They are prised up from the lake floor and stacked where they are, out in the lake. A man then comes out to these stacks towing a series of small rafts on which the salt slabs are floated so that they can be towed to the shore where they are again stacked till they can be carried by porter to the village above, on the rim of the crater.

Two more days' marching brought us across the border into the Belgian Congo. We camped at Rubangu where we were obliged to discharge our porters and take on local men.

This evening after supper we put the light low and listened to the noises of the night. Sitting in the mouth of the tent the stars shine above us, the Southern Cross catching the eye ... Close to us the guard camp fire shines through the reed-like grasses, while in the distance is the irregular beat and thrum of drums above which one catches the sound of a native chorus. Somehow this is a thing detached from the night noises of nature, the shrilling of cicadas or the no-less-common chirp of a cricket. Above all is the incessant high trilling of the frogs, no more like a croak than a flute is to a bassoon ... Before the light died ... we saw great stretches of snow on Ruwenzori and the Marguerita Peak, the highest of them all towering to nearly 17,000 feet. How we longed to go up there. We must now be camped very near the actual centre of Africa from north to south and from east to west.

Under Belgian administration it was forbidden to hunt; in consequence there was a considerable problem in feeding the safari. The native greeting also changed abruptly. In Kenya and Uganda everyone said 'Jambo' or 'Jumbo', but here these half-civilized people greeted us ceremoniously with 'Bonjour Monsieur' in impeccable French accents!

We changed our money into Congo francs and centimes, finding the rate was ten francs for one East African shilling. This was certainly in our favour for a thousand bananas now cost us one shilling (5p in today's British money), a chicken twopence at most (0.8p), forty pounds of sweet potatoes ninepence (3.5p), a bottle of milk twopence again, two pounds of beans or six eggs one penny (0.4p). I calculated that we had fed ourselves and twenty porters for nearly three weeks for little more than six shillings (30p).

Resuming our journey we found ourselves marching under enormous trees that towered up and up, with great bare poles, to spread out in a beautiful green canopy overhead. It was much pleasanter travelling in shade.

Once I dropped a little behind the safari, then I could hear the echoing of the porters' marching songs as if in some great cathedral, this effect being increased by the pillar-like form of the tree trunks all around. As the singing died away in the distance the voices of a multitude of birds living far above in the foliage began to make themselves heard. The rather fantastic effect of the whole scene was enhanced by the curious buttressed base of all the trees. At about four feet from the ground woody wings grew out, perhaps seven or eight feet long and gradually diminishing in width away from the trunk, thus forming wide natural boards, often no thicker than three-quarters of an inch, and almost never more than two inches. When one was struck with a hammer, the sound was of a multitude of planks being dropped in a huge empty hall, the whole forest resounding with reverberations. Walking along the brown leaf-strewn native path, with mossy roots and ferns, the surprising lack of undergrowth for an equatorial forest, together with the cool freshness of the morning, gave the impression of walking in some English wood that had outgrown itself.

In places there were marshy pools, their inky blackness and the rotten branches protruding from the water gave an air of dank putrescence to the surroundings. But this effect was banished as we suddenly and surprisingly emerged into one of the open clearings lit by brilliant sunshine. In some of these we found a group of huts in a banana or maize plantation, but often the whole clearing was deserted, the forest encroaching as if it was healing its open wounds.

The reason for this journey was to discover why there were crocodiles in Lake Albert but none in Lake Edward, since the two are connected by the Semliki River. On reaching Malahunde we learnt that there were two falls on the river, and that crocodiles lived below the second one. As we searched for them, the way led through thick forest to a cliff about a hundred feet above the water.

On climbing down we found the entrance to a gorge where the river narrowed and deepened, the water swirling along with increasing speed. Forcing our way through dense undergrowth the noise of rushing water increased until at last we could see below us the frothing, tumbling river surging over gigantic boulders. Here indeed was a barrier to crocodiles, for no such sun-loving creatures would trek through the dense undergrowth that mantled the margins of the gorge.

As night fell the natives began to congregate for a *ngoma* or dance. Proceedings were led by two drummers followed by a chorus of wood pipes in four different sizes each giving a different note and remarkably well tuned. They stood in a close circle, each group blowing successively while the players were bowed forward, jigging in time to the music. Any change of rhythm was signalled by the drums. Then they all straightened up and blew all together but soon reverted to the original monotonous series of blasts.

A women's group jogged slowly round the edge of the players. Sometimes the pipes stopped, the pipers dancing off in a long snaking line to the beat of the drums, then suddenly the circle reformed and started off at full blast once more. The noise was deafening, and finally drove us back to our tents.

After our return to Katunguru from the Congo, on 6 July we set off to visit the point where the Semliki flowed out of Lake Edward. There surroundings showed a shallow delta fan which indicated that the river had once flowed into the lake. It was there that I had a personal encounter with a hippo. With one of our 'boys', known as Lucy, I was returning to camp in the outboard-driven boat which also towed our canvas dinghy. Lucy was steering, I writing my notes, when he suddenly clapped me on the back and pointed astern where I was just in time to see a pair of enormous wide open jaws snap shut, just missing the dinghy by inches. But this hippo was persistent. Travelling fast under water he kicked off the bottom, reared out of the water and again snapped wildly at the dinghy. At his fourth attempt he was finally successful, and got a mouthful of canvas and steel ribs. We were slowed down as the dinghy began to sink, but fortunately our attacker seemed ready to call it a day for he remained where he was, snorting and blowing clouds of spray into the air. We saved the dinghy, but it was never quite the same again!

When work on Lake Edward finished we spent a month studying Lake George and its surroundings, visiting many small crater lakes including Bunyampaka where there was a flourishing salt industry. Though not as rich a source as Katwe, here there was a marked difference in the way salt was collected. Instead of prising up slabs from the bottom, the lake was divided into separate small and muddy ponds by long dikes. As evaporation took place the salt

Alan Cobham's Short Valetta seaplane on the Kazinga Channel

appeared as a crust on the surface of the pools like ice on water.
When it was thick enough a man waded out towing small wooden
bowls into which he skimmed off the salt crust. The sodden mess
was later spread in the village street to dry out.

Our scientific work completed, we returned to Katunguru on our
way back to Kampala. Some weeks previously we had heard that Sir
Alan Cobham was to attempt the first flight from Cairo to the Cape.
He was expected to land on the Kazinga Channel to refuel.
Four-gallon debbies (petrol tins) had already arrived, and a mooring
buoy had been anchored in the channel. On the day of our
departure we suddenly saw his Short Valetta seaplane skimming
low over the water to alight. With him were three mechanics and
two photographers who all came ashore to have tea with us.

Cobham was a short man, slightly bald, inclined to stoutness, and
seemed to be in a constant state of fluster. He gave the impression of
being a valetudinarian, for he kept imagining mosquitoes where
there were none and saying how awful it was to come to such places
where one might catch *anything*! Perhaps it was the cultural shock

of being transported in only a few days from the soothing English countryside to a native shack in hot unknown central Africa. After tea we ferried his petrol out to the seaplane in a forty-foot dug-out — truly a contrast between the old and the new, which can never have happened before and might never happen again.

Cobham was very worried about the next leg of his flight to Lake Kivu for he had to cross the Mfumbiro Mountains which he believed to rise to 13,000 feet. On the day of his departure we also left Katunguru, and it was some years later that we learned that he had crossed the mountains but decided not to alight, and returned to Katunguru on his way home.

This was the last episode in the story of the Cambridge Expedition to the East African Lakes, and all that remained was for us to return to Naivasha and prepare for the voyage home. But for me it was not to be the end, for it was my good fortune to continue working in Africa.

Chapter 6

Olduvai and Njorowa Gorge
1931-33

In 1913 the German explorer Professor Hans Reck had led an archaeological expedition to Olduvai in Tanganyika Territory (now Tanzania). His party had discovered important fossil beds which yielded an extensive fauna of extinct species, and also the skeleton of a man. The latter had created world-wide interest, for Dr Reck maintained that it belonged to one of the earliest phases of human existence, but as he had been unable to find any evidence on the site to date the deposit his claim was not upheld.

At this time Dr Louis Leakey had already spent several seasons doing archaeological work in East Africa. Now he was to visit Olduvai, accompanied by the Professor who had come from Germany specially for this purpose. Knowing of my recent work with Dr Worthington's expedition, to my great delight Leakey invited me to join his team, and I grabbed this further opportunity to remain and work in Africa.

The main objects of this expedition were:
(a) To re-examine with Dr Reck the exact spot from which his human skeleton was obtained, and to check over the evidence upon which he had claimed that it was contemporary with the extinct fauna from Olduvai.
(b) If possible to find stone-age tools *in situ* in the deposits.
(c) To discover some means of establishing a correlation between the Olduvai fossil series and the Pleistocene sequence worked out for Kenya by Leakey during the past two seasons.
(d) To collect a series of fossils from the Olduvai beds for the national collection in the British Museum (Natural History) and, hopefully, to find new species not discovered by the 1913 expedition.

Leakey and Dr Reck arrived at the site at the beginning of October 1931. Donald MacInnes, a palaeontologist, and I joined them two weeks later. Olduvai was a great open undulating area of grassland into which sheer-sided valleys had been cut, giving a good imitation of the Grand Canyon in Colorado on a very small scale. The Professor was a tall elderly man with a round cheerful face and very bright blue eyes. Never excited or flurried, he was exceptionally earnest about his work. The last two members of our party were Dr U T Hopwood, a mammalian palaeontologist from the British Museum and J R H Hewlett, Honorary Game Warden of Kenya, who was with us as a white hunter and engineer.

At first sight it was clear that the material in the beds was fragmentary and there seemed little hope of finding complete skeletons, But one of the first most startling discoveries was a partially articulated skeleton of a dinotherium – an extinct mammal allied to the elephant, remarkable in that the front part of the lower jaw was bent downwards and bore two tusk-like incisors also directed downwards and backwards.

In the first four days we found tools and a rich collection of fossils of extinct animals, which seemed to establish that Dr Reck's Olduvai man belonged to the Acheulian Period – and was in fact the earliest human being found in East Africa up to that time. However, careful examination of the site, still marked by the four sticks which the Professor had left behind, finally showed that it was a fairly recent burial, perhaps a few thousand years old.

Our work was not easy, and sometimes it was far from pleasant. The nearest water hole was fifteen miles away by lorry and then another half-mile on foot. Sometimes the supply was a mere drip when it took up to forty minutes to fill each debbi. To supply the camp for two-and-a-half days meant the absence of one European and seven African 'boys', with a lorry, for twenty-four hours.

The first of the pools stinks, the second is drinkable when boiled, the third we wash ourselves and our clothes in, the fourth is almost inaccessible … though the green scum is not present as with the first three, we have not yet made use of it.

There had been no rain for months so the whole countryside was parched and dust or sand got into everything. Big game were a constant nuisance, for leopards raided the larder while lions and hyenas prowled around the camp practically all night.

One had come to my tent and stood with its head and shoulders through the

81

door, as was shown by its foot marks – I'm glad I was asleep for an apparition like that not more than two foot from one's face would have been startling ... Hopwood tells me that one walked under the fly of his tent and then 'laughed'; this was too much so he ... fired two pistol shots into the air which drove them off for a while.

One night Leakey fired at a leopard by torchlight but missed. The animal then charged him, but not being able to see it he rushed into the ring of the kitchen firelight to escape, and it disappeared into the night.

We also had our medical and domestic problems. Somewhat nonchalantly my journal records that

Hopwood has intestinal bleeding, which is rather worrying, especially as I have something wrong with my oesophagus, and in view of the fact that some little time ago I found broken glass in the sugar ... I'm going to have a good look at it at the next meal!

Fortunately this alarm led to nothing. No more glass was found, and both Hopwood and I had no recurrence of our troubles.

Besides my geological work there was always a great deal to do in connection with the game specimens being collected for the Museum. Everything had to be numbered, catalogued and packed for shipment to England. In one day we managed to take two wildebeest, a female klipspringer, two male impala, one young one for comparison, and the head of a zebra. That kept the skinners busy all night. In those days, nearly sixty years ago, the concept of 'endangered species' was not a public concern. Even so, we never shot animals except for food or museum collections.

We also entertained a more domestic menagerie in our tent.

A young fox which consumes small birds at an alarming rate and keeps up an incessant but intermittent yowling that can only be compared to the skirl of a spurwing plover ... two tortoises, Terence and Clarence, who make no sound, eat no food and cause no trouble – a delightful contrast to the other little devil.

One day Leakey and the 'boys' who had gone with him on a water safari arrived back carrying a large rhino which he had been forced to shoot in self-defence. They had suddenly met it unexpectedly and the animal had charged, successfully 'treeing' them all and then prowling hopefully up and down under them. I was on the next trip for water, and found a troop of baboons running along our path.

Vivian Fuchs in Naivasha, Kenya 1931

Needing a mask as a specimen I shot and decapitated one of them, returning to camp feeling rather like Perseus carrying the Gorgon's head.

When work at Olduvai finished our cavalcade of lorries left for Limuru, contending as always with incessant engine troubles and burst tyres. As the Professor was anxious to look at some other parts of the Rift I was deputed to accompany him. Apart from his years he also had a weak heart, so it was a responsibility which turned into something of a nightmare.

On the first night we camped near the foot of the escarpment, four miles from the slopes of Suswa. Next morning we clambered up to the rim of the outer cauldron, to a marvellous view of a great sunken basin eight to nine miles in diameter, its sides almost vertical. To the south there arose a huge cone built by some later phase of activity and then cut through by a fault, forming a second inner cauldron in which stood a great flat-topped mass that was the sunken half of the cone. The Professor insisted on visiting this so we trekked across great cliffs and ridges of lava, overgrown by bush so thick that it was difficult to force a way through. He took an inordinate time, both with his notes and the photographs, and it was half-past three before he was ready to turn back.

By five o'clock we were back at the foot of the outer cauldron wall when the Professor's heart told on him. He was in distress and could not climb more than fifty feet at a time. When we rather painfully reached the top it was nearly dark and he had to have a short rest. He then set off to the right of a landmark I had taken for the return journey, and when I expostulated he would have none of it – no amount of guile would persuade him. When we finally reached the point from which we should have been able to see the car, below us we saw nothing.

Fortunately I had realized that something of this sort might occur and had sent Ngoma, my African 'boy', on ahead with orders to switch on the car lights. This ruse worked as planned and in the darkness we picked out two tiny points of light 1,000 feet below us and nearly two miles to the left. For the Professor this now meant walking over some very bad ground – down into and out of gullies and all in darkness. Very soon he was saying that he could not see and could go no farther. He was obviously completely done in, but by moving only a few yards at a time while clinging fast to me, and because of the fact that Ngoma came up to us with a lantern, to my enormous relief we managed to get him, quite exhausted, back to the car.

That ended the excursion. We all returned to Nairobi where we each gave lectures at the Coryndon Museum on the work accomplished. So the Olduvai venture drew to a close on 19 December 1932.

I had already paid several visits to Njorowa Gorge, and had

determined to map it and study the geology before returning to England. At one time the gorge must have been an outlet for Lake Naivasha when it was much deeper. Now the northern entrance to it is dry grassland between high lava cliffs. On the west side a relatively recent lava flow, Hobley's lava, filled one-time side valleys in the lower part of Njorowa. This was a deep cutting in the level floor which could only be reached on foot, or by donkeys from the northern end. The whole area was wild and attractive, especially to me, for the geology was quite unknown, so I now turned my attention to Njorowa.

In early January 1933 I set up a camp with three 'boys', Ngoma, Dedan and Mbogwa, in the upper gorge. My first task was to make a plane-table survey of the area at a scale large enough for the geology. In all I was to spend some two months on the project. I was fortunate in finding a pool in the lower gorge with a few inches of warm water which ran down the walls of volcanic tuff. I finally made it into an excellent 'bath' by banking up the outlets. However I soon found that I could not linger in the water for it was inhabited by large *Dytiscus* beetles which insisted on biting my white skin painfully. At numerous points in this lower gorge were steam jets, which proved to be very useful for it was possible to condense the steam with a contraption of sloping boards. In this way we obtained about four gallons each night, for it was only then that the air was cool enough to allow condensation.

There was plenty of big game about, chiefly buffalo, rhinoceros, leopard and lion. One morning I woke to find that a rhino had been churning up the path only a few yards from our camp, and that a leopard had paid a visit and stolen our meat out of a tree. That night I set a gun trap baited with more meat. In the morning we found that the trap had not fired – but tracks showed that not one but two leopards had paid a visit. On the third night they came again and actually ate the meat off the string without pulling it sufficiently to fire the gun!

This had now become a challenge. On the fourth night I sat up till two in the morning but saw nothing. However, daylight revealed that they had paid another visit. Finding me there they had waited until I went to bed and then walked up and chewed the bait off the string again. Once more I set the trap, and this time the gun fired. But the last laugh was with the leopards, for it was a small jackal which had tugged the bait. The sound of the gunshot caused forty or fifty buffalo to stampede past the tent only six yards away.

One morning I worked round the Hobley lava flow in pouring rain. Soaked to the skin, I was wandering along a narrow almost vertical-sided watercourse when I was aroused from my dreams by a crash – there was a buffalo charging me full tilt some five yards away. Mbogwa was carrying the rifle, and in any case it was at too close quarters and too sudden for it to have been of use. I leapt for the side but the buffalo got there at precisely the same moment, so that he helped me up with what would otherwise have been a nasty toss. I lost my hold and slid down a little way, facing the buffalo so I was still within his reach when he had a second go at me. By some rapid wriggling I avoided his horn, but he tore my shirt to shreds.

By the time he had turned round for his third attempt I had a firm hold, but was unable to climb any higher. Fortunately I handed him off with the heel of my left shoe in his eye. This gave me enough lift to reach the top. The buffalo, disconcerted by the blow (and perhaps uncertain of the nasty growlings I found myself emitting) made off rather uncertainly. I should think that few people have had so close an encounter and blacked the eye of a buffalo, getting away with no more than a scratch and a bruise. A moment later Mbogwa came up with the rifle – but I refrained from revenge.

My working day got longer and longer as the programme extended farther and farther from the camp.

This morning we set off at a good pace as I now have five miles to walk before reaching the scene of operations. Tomorrow it will be six-and-a-half. Another two miles will be the limit as we have to do a lot of trekking and climbing ... and these continual long distances are not doing the 'boys' feet any good ... Although it can be hot enough to make it impossible to touch the instruments, yet the nights are exceedingly cold ... Today we drank a lot of the condensed steam water from the vent beside the dyke ... as it has to fall such a long way after it had been condensed, it reached us stone cold, although we were standing on hot steaming clay that sizzled like a shut-down steam engine.

By the end of February my map was complete, and all the geology I could do in this area was finished.

I was also completely broke. On 14 March I sailed home from Kilindini, Mombasa in ss *Tanganyika*, travelling Second Class only because it was impossible to get into the Third. And relieved that she would land me in England after the end of the financial year! A month later it was very good to be back at Heatherdene in time for the daffodils.

Chapter 7

Marriage and the Lake Rudolf
Rift Valley Expedition
1934

In 1933 I was twenty-five years old and my parents were concerned that I should be settling down in some permanent employment. I realized the sense of this but now Africa held my interest, and in particular I wanted to make further contributions to Rift Valley geology, then in hot dispute as to whether it had been formed by tensional or compressive movement. I had also acquired a particular interest in the Pleistocene climatic variations and their effect upon land and lacustrine fauna. These things, and the call of the African wilderness, made me determined somehow to return to Lake Rudolf for I was sure that some of the answers lay there. This time I intended to lead my own expedition.

I began to formulate plans which I submitted to the Royal Society, the Royal Geographical Society, the British Association, the Percy Sladen Trust and other organizations who might make grants. Fortunately all of them were reasonably generous. Even so I quickly learnt that it is much easier to carry through an expedition in the field than it is to find the money to mount it. Today it seems unbelievable that the final cost of the expedition for six men for a year was just over £2,000!

During this period my cousin Joyce Connell, whom I had not met since a shared family holiday at Ardentinny when I was fourteen, came on a visit to my parents. She was a good companion, sharing my interest in hill walking, mountain climbing, and indeed all fresh air activities. Within a few months our friendship had blossomed into an engagement. On 6 September 1933 we were married very quietly in a church in Hampstead, and in 1983 we celebrated our Golden Wedding surrounded by our children and grandchildren.

My wife was herself a traveller in her own right. Before the days of easy air travel she had already spent a year going round the world. This led her to Malaysia, Australia, New Zealand and Canada. At

Joyce Fuchs (Connell)

first she was accompanied by a girl friend who went as far as New
Zealand before turning back – perhaps because she found it too
strenuous to accompany Joyce to the top of every nearby mountain!
Undeterred, Joyce sailed from New Zealand to Canada, where she
landed at Victoria on Vancouver Island. After some time she found
herself at Prince Rupert, 500 miles to the north. There she arranged
a canoe trip down the Parsnip River to the point where it joins the

Finlay to form the Peace River. This was long before the Peace was dammed to form the present straggling fjord-like lake which now lies in the Parsnip, Finlay and Peace valleys. Coming to the end of navigable water, she walked through the eastern Rockies to Pouce Coupe – thence by truck and train found her way across Canada and home.

My expedition plans were almost finalized when we got engaged. Joyce was happy to begin our life together with an adventure and enthusiastically she agreed to come along and share it. When my geological work took me into areas inappropriate for her, she would see as much of the country as possible on her own. We would travel back together overland before making a home in England.

The main objects of the Lake Rudolf Rift Valley Expedition were geological and survey work in the northern part of the Rift Valley in Kenya Colony, but since this area was then so little known, I also wanted to attempt as many other lines of investigation as possible.

Our party consisted of myself as Leader/Geologist; Cuthbert Wakefield who had been at Cambridge with me, Surveyor; W R H Martin, Surveyor; Dr W S Dyson, Medical Officer; John Millard, Archaeologist; and Donald MacInnes, Palaeontologist. Wakefield came from the Sudan Survey Department, Martin was a qualified forester and undertook to collect botanical material, Dyson was to be in charge of zoological specimens and would also do as much anthropological work as possible. In addition David Buxton of the Agricultural Laboratories, Kampala, who was then particularly concerned with the locust problem, planned to join us during the months we were to stay in Turkana.

On 4 January 1934 the expedition left England to embark in the ss *Llandaff Castle* at Marseilles where we travelled 'steerage' in some discomfort for the sum of £35 per person for the seventeen-day voyage to Mombasa. It was memorable because of the unusual weather conditions. At Port Said we wore mackintoshes, in the Red Sea overcoats, and it rained at Aden! We disembarked on a Sunday when no banks were open, but managed to get sufficient credit from the Kenya and Uganda Railways to get us to Nairobi. There we spent twelve days buying equipment, a lorry and three cars – one being for Joyce, who was not allowed to enter the Turkana Province which was then restricted to men. I also recruited a number of 'boys'

Expedition members with Kings African Rifles escort;
Vivian Fuchs sitting third from left

for the expedition, and one called Mbuthia to accompany Joyce as
her personal servant.

During her travels Joyce visited the Ituri Forest in the Belgian
Congo, where I had walked with porters in 1931 – only three years
later she found a newly constructed road. Even so when travelling to
the volcano Nyamligira in the Mfumbiro Range she used porters
provided by the Belgian District Commissioner. Likewise in climbing up to the snows of Mount Baker in the Ruwenzori Range she
hired porters from Fort Portal in Uganda. She climbed Mount Meru
(15,000 feet) in Tanganyika and Mount Elgon (14,000 feet) in
northern Kenya. These ventures, which included big game photography, kept her busy while we were about our business at Lake
Rudolf.

The lake is approximately 1,230 feet above sea level and 180
miles long, with a maximum width of thirty-five miles. The greater
part of the surrounding country is desert, the only permanent river
flowing into it being the Omo which rises in the Abyssinian
highlands and flows into the northern end of the lake. There is no
outlet and the whole of the western shore lies in Turkana Province.
Many years later, after Kenya became independent, the lake was
renamed Turkana.

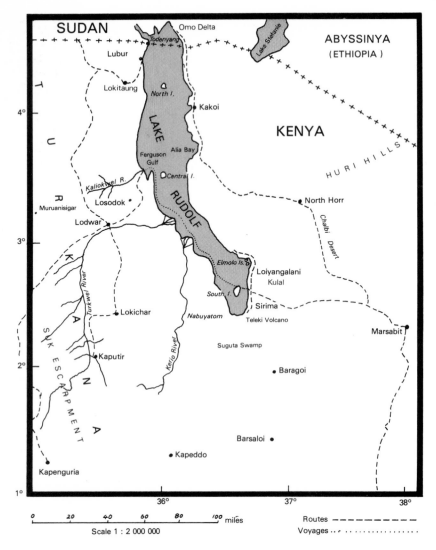

SUDAN

Omo Delta

Todenyang

ABYSSINIA
(ETHIOPIA)

Lubur

Lokitaung

North I.

Kakoi

LAKE

4°

Ferguson
Gulf

Alia Bay

KENYA

Kaliokwel R.

Central I.

RUDOLF

HURI HILLS

Muruanisigar

Losodok

North Horr

Lodwar

3°

Chalbi Desert

Elmolo Is.

Loiyangalani
Kulal

South I.

Sirima

Lokichar

Nabuyatom

Teleki Volcano

Marsabit

Suguta Swamp

Kaputir

2°

Baragoi

Barsaloi

Kapeddo

Kapenguria

1°

36°   37°   38°

0   20   40   60   80   100 miles

Scale 1 : 2 000 000

Routes — — — — — — — —

Voyages ..· ....

Originally we had hoped to make a continuous journey around the lake starting from Lodwar, the administrative post forty miles from the western shore. But the Abyssinian government refused us permission to enter their territory, which meant omitting the extreme northern end. Instead we organized the work in two sections – first on the west and then up the eastern side.

We reached Lodwar in February, still hopeful that we might be able to get into Abyssinia (now Ethiopia) if personal contact could be established with the local Ras or governor of the Maji Province. Whilst awaiting his expected arrival at the frontier we began work among the Losodok Hills which lie between the lake and Lodwar Post. Here Millard discovered numerous *coups de poing*, the crude chipped implements of early man, here of late Acheulean age – the first pre-neolithic implements to be found in the Lake Rudolf Basin.

I made a trip to Ferguson Gulf where we had camped four years earlier and was enthusiastically welcomed by our old friends the two Turkana Chiefs who promptly ordered a dance in my honour. This lasted for three hours in the heat of the midday sun. I was astonished at the change in the shore line. Since January 1931 the water level had fallen approximately six feet, which meant that on this gently shelving beach the shore had retreated over a quarter of a mile. On the mud flats thus exposed the Turkana were now growing millet.

I had brought with me from England a considerable quantity of small mirrors, bead necklaces and wooden-handled shoemakers' knives, all useful for bartering – also many pounds of coarse local tobacco bought in Kenya. In Nairobi I learnt that the government had levied an annual hut tax of six East African shillings in the Turkana district. Apparently this was in an effort to introduce the conception of the central government having a responsibility to the people. As things were they had no idea of money, except for an occasional Maria Theresa dollar which from time to time appeared as a curiosity from across the Abyssinian border. The taxes were therefore being paid with live animals – goats equalling two shillings, sheep three. I was now asked officially to attempt the introduction of money to the Turkana.

This request called to mind a previous occasion in Masai country where the government had tried to start a beef export trade. Their intention was to use Masai cattle, but the people refused to part with them since cattle represented a man's wealth. In an effort to overcome this problem special coins were minted bearing the image of a cow instead of the King's head, but the Masai remained obdurate on the grounds that 'coins do not breed, do they?' Faced with having to explain the intricacies of a money market the authorities abandoned the whole project.

I could see myself facing a similar reaction in Turkana, but hoped

I had one trick up my sleeve. As things stood, when the tax became due a number of men had to spend weeks driving animals more than a hundred miles over sub-desert country to the main police post at Kapenguria. Using my to them ingenious method, one man could carry the whole tax for a village in one bag and only be away a few days. After some pretty hard talking my ideas were accepted, I put away my pretty beads and they agreed to sell me the animals we needed for food at the price representing the tax. One serious problem remained. As soon as a man had sold us three goats or two sheep, and thus had the tax money for one year, he refused to part with any more. They also could see that 'coins do not breed'!

However, it was a beginning. I had perhaps successfully introduced coinage in primary numbers, but how to get across the idea of smaller denominations? I decided that in future we would buy sheep for two shillings and fifty cents (half the standard shilling). Thus each man had to sell us three animals to acquire his tax money. We benefited by being able to buy more animals and the natives began to think in terms of half-shillings. I never got as far as the unattractive copper coins of lower value.

As soon as news came through that the Ras had arrived at the frontier we packed our lorries and left with all speed for Lokitaung, the chief military post in northern Turkana. Thence we travelled down to the lake through an impressive gorge which opened out on to the plain left by the retreating waters many thousands of years ago. Twenty miles farther north we reached Todenyang, the British fort on the shore only three miles from the Abyssinian post of Namoraputh. The recent retreat of the lake was a threat to the surrounding country, for the prevailing south-east wind dried the bare sand and blew it inland in the form of dunes which swept forward at the rate of fifty yards each year.

The Abyssinian and Kenyan authorities had arranged a 'peace meeting' between two tribes, the Merille and the Turkana, who lived on either side of the boundary. We arrived just in time to witness the ceremonies. The ratification of peace necessitated the killing of a white sheep and a white bull, both supplied by the Elders of the aggressor tribe. The Chief of the Turkana was present but took no part, for he was still a *moran* (warrior), and therefore he led them only in battle.

Termite nest near Lodwar

The Elders squatted in two rows opposite each other while the animals were ritually slaughtered in front of them. Strings of fat taken from the entrails were draped round the necks of the Turkana by the Elders of the Merille. When the bull was killed a bone from a front leg was broken with a stone and the marrow sucked from half of it by the Chief Elder of each tribe. Everyone then sat down to feast on the carcasses of the two animals.

Feeling that the occasion might be auspicious, I cautiously took the opportunity to seek the Ras' permission to enter his territory. He readily assented, promising to send the necessary safe-conduct to our camp the following day. But alas he forgot, or perhaps he never intended to remember, for he left to return to Maji in the early hours of the morning – and the letter never arrived.

On one occasion a local *sultani* (chief elder) called Akal sold us two goats. A week later my personal 'boy' announced that another *sultani* had come to call with a sheep he wished to present to us.

Hastily putting on some clothes and a cartridge belt (for impressive purposes, for I had been lying without a stitch on) ... I went out to meet the Chief expecting to have to give him an appropriately large present in exchange ... He said that he had heard from a *mtoto* (child) that Akal had sold us the goats. He did not consider this at all the thing. We were Big Men together, and as such did not buy and sell to one another. He had therefore brought me a present of a sheep.

After suitable remarks I said 'Thanks very much' and that I would like to give him some tobacco ... in return. He refused (an unheard of thing for a Turkana), and even when pressed would take nothing ... At last he said that if we were coming by that way another year he would like us to bring him a shirt. I told him that if he returned in the morning we would see what could be done about the matter, but he must come early as we were breaking camp.

He turned up after breakfast and I called him to the tent to receive the present we had prepared ... one rather smart looking bluish-red bush shirt with belt and bright buckle, together with a mirror and a shoemaker's knife ... this brought forth a sigh of ecstasy as he saw it ... he swore to give us many sheep when we came again.

In this northern fringe of British territory all parties were compelled to have escorts, so at our next camp we numbered thirty. This included a section of the King's African Rifles, native police, camel and donkey 'boys' and their own cooks, and our servants. The water supply had to be reduced to forty gallons per day for the whole party – this to include cooking, washing and drinking. It allowed for one and a third of a gallon per man, which we found just sufficient, but it entailed constant supervision of our men. For the remainder of the expedition we aimed to maintain the supply at two gallons per man per day, for we found that this was the minimum which prevented quarrelling among the 'boys'.

The water shortage in the district was becoming serious for the local population. There had been no rain for two years and large numbers of cattle had died. The poorer people were in a bad way. Akal, the Chief Elder, had implicit faith in the white man's powers if he chose to exert them, and asked repeatedly that we produce rain, or at least that we should mention the matter to God – or preferably the government. If no rain fell his people would have to go raiding in the Merille or Karamoja country. Nothing would convince him of my impotence in the matter.

In desperation, and on the strength of some gathering clouds over the Abyssinian highlands, I told him that rain would fall within two weeks. Two days later, our work finished we left Komogin. Fortunately for our reputation we later learnt that on the fourteenth day six inches of rain fell in four hours!

Watering camels

There were discrepancies between the surveys of Kenya, Uganda and the Sudan, so our next objective was to climb Mount Labur (the north peak) to fix its position by astronomical observations using wireless time-signals for the first time in this area. To attempt this from the west we returned to Lokitaung, whence the donkeys were sent on with the instruments and supplies, while the surveyors followed the next night to spend a successful period of seventy-two hours on the top of the mountain. This enabled many errors in the map to be corrected.

With the work on Mount Labur finished, we left Lokitaung for Naramum, some seventy miles to the north. This was in a part of the Sudan then controlled by the Kenya military authorities. The place was no more than a waterhole in a level-floored valley between the Kaitherin-Lokwanamur Range and the mountain mass of Lorientom. The position of Kaitherin was badly out, for we found that to reach the top we had to walk for two hours beyond the point at which it was shown on the existing map.

A few days later we visited Lokitoi, the northermost military post guarding Turkana from Merille raiding parties. The fort was built at the crest of Lokitoi Pass, whence I could see some interesting geological features a few miles to the north. Since these were beyond the military line it was strictly forbidden for anyone to enter the area. I had therefore to be extremely circumspect, and taking with me Beyu, my personal *kanga* (authorized Turkana policeman with rifle) I surreptitiously descended a gully to the plain. There we undertook the difficult task of marching some miles while remaining hidden from the fort and from any possible Merille ahead. The trip was a success for I found incontrovertible evidence of pressure deforming the rocks in this part of the Rift Valley.

On returning to Lokitoi I found the Commanding Officer nervous about some soldiers he had sent down the hill to collect firewood, for they had not returned. He had others out looking for them in all directions. I could have eased his mind by telling him that there were no marauding Merille within miles, but then he would have wanted to know how I knew this!

After another week's work in the area we returned to Lodwar, and saw the dramatic effect of the rains. The dry river beds had been washed out, making it necessary to stop and rebuild tracks across them. Large areas of previously barren countryside had assumed a green flush as all the waiting seeds took their opportunity. The apparently dead thorn scrub had begun to clothe itself anew. Large numbers of Grant gazelle had come from more barren areas to feed on this fresh growth and the sandy bouldery track was now relieved by red and yellow lilies that had burst into flower.

Our next move was to return to the lake shore at Ferguson Gulf. There Wakefield and Martin began remapping the gulf for comparison with earlier efforts, including one version drawn by Dr Worthington in 1931. During the expedition we had endeavoured to ameliorate the very soda-rich water by the addition of citric acid. This had produced a fizzy drink like Enos fruit salts, which was indeed palatable, but unfortunately we soon found that it also had a medicinal effect and we had to reduce our consumption. Remembering this, I had had constructed in England a wood-burning 'still' weighing about 100 pounds. Its output in the sun, even when the shade temperature rose to 110°F, (43.5°C) was one gallon per hour. This gave us twelve gallons or three debbies during the day. At first it tasted of sawdust, metal filings and oil that had accumulated in the bottom during manufacture and shipment. But in time it produced clear drinking water which was very acceptable. Any reluctance on the part of the 'boys' to keep it going was overcome by

Suk warriors

telling them that they could daily use any amount they distilled over six gallons.

From this camp two journeys were made to Central Island, which lay nine miles across the water, and for this we used a small Hudson collapsible wooden boat fitted with an outboard motor. Just before our first visit Arthur Champion, the Provincial Commissioner, came to see how we were faring, and to my surprise he brought Joyce with him. Apparently his niece had persuaded him that she, Joyce Mortimer, and my Joyce should be allowed a brief visit. So it was that I was able to take her over to Central Island, the first and only woman to visit it. On a second trip Dyson and Millard spent eight days there, making complete botanical and zoological collections to find out to what extent the lake acts as a natural barrier to the migration of fauna and flora from adjacent areas.

It was then planned that while the surveyors worked in the north-west of the province, Donald MacInnes and I should visit the Dome Rock area south of Muruanisigar which forms the northern edge of the Moroto embayment in the Uganda scarp. We had only travelled thirty miles to the Lorogumu River when a storm, heralded by an ominous yellow cloud of dust, swept up from the south. Within fifteen minutes the surrounding country changed from a flat expanse of sand into the semblance of a lake, from which a few drowned bushes stood out.

We decided on retreat but now found ourselves cut off by a second river which had come down in flood behind us. It was not until the following morning that the water subsided sufficiently for us to get back to our previous camp, where we were greeted with the news that the rains had washed away part of the motor track down the Suk escarpment. This meant that both we and the Provincial Commissioner's party were now prisoners in Turkana until the road could be rebuilt.

Our camp was pitched under some acacia trees beside the River Turkwel. A few nights later it suddenly overflowed its banks, seriously threatening our living quarters. The vehicles and equipment were hastily moved to the top of a nearby hillock which itself was only twelve feet above the water level. It was very cramped quarters for five tents, a lorry, two cars, the kitchen and ten native 'boys'. Lodwar Boma had also become an island, and the District Commissioner rowed over the intervening quarter of a mile of water to have tea with us.

When the flood subsided we were able to visit Kaputir, the southern Turkana administrative station. By then the rains had brought out large numbers of new species, and we asked the natives to bring in specimens of the local fauna, promising payment to be agreed according to the condition of the material collected.

This has brought in great and small lizards varying from an inch-and-a-half to nearly four feet, jerboas that look like mice, civet cats, squirrels, mongooses, dik-dik, foxes and numerous birds with and without eggs. These, together with a large number of snakes and incidental insects such as tarantulas, centipedes and scorpions, makes a large list ... which we should never have otherwise obtained.

A large number of the animals are brought in alive in snares and it is a problem how to kill them. The reptiles are easy for the smallest bit of nicotine from a pipe put in the mouth causes them to die immediately. The birds have to be killed by squeezing the heart so as not to spoil the feathers ... the mammals have presented rather a problem ... Most we have tried to keep as pets ... at one time we had a young dik-dik with a broken leg (mended by the doctor), two ground squirrels and two bat-eared young foxes.

After going back to Lodwar we were at last able to begin the return

Above the Lake, near Sirima

journey to Kitale. From the top of the Nepau Pass a great change
could be seen as far as the foot of the Suk escarpment. In the eleven
days since the last rain had fallen everything had had time to grow.
Instead of a dusty red track stretching into the distance through a
sea of lifeless thorn scrub, the road was now a grassy path shut in on
either side by an impenetrable wall of tall green grass beneath the
acacia trees, the air heavy with the scent of flowers.

At Naivasha in the Kenya highlands the expedition refitted, and
arrangements were made with the military and administrative
authorities for the second leg of our programme to be carried out in
the Northern Frontier District. Our party was now reduced to four,
for Wakefield had to return to duty with the Sudan Survey and
MacInnes felt that the disappointing palaeontological results he had
obtained on the west side of the lake did not justify his remaining
with us longer – particularly as the rocks were almost certain to be of
the same series.

The last 'settled' area was left behind at Meru on the lower slopes
of Mount Kenya. From there we travelled 180 miles to Marsabit,
crossing the Guasso Nyiro River and then a great plain covered with
thorn scrub which was the home of a large variety of game,
including the spectacular reticulated giraffe and the long-necked
gerenuk.

From there Martin and Dyson crossed the southern part of the Chalbi Desert to the foot of Kulal, where we had arranged for camels to meet them. Kulal is approximately 7,500 feet high, and was to be the first of a series of astronomical points which they intended to 'fix' on this side of the lake.

Meanwhile John Millard and I travelled 100 miles to a water-hole at Sirima, about eight miles from Lake Rudolf, where we established our main stores base for the next month. Two days later we left with baggage camels in an attempt to reach the lake itself. Although ultimately we were successful, the rocky broken nature of the country, and two very steep scarps down which it was only just possible to take camels one at a time, provided its own difficulties and risks. Relays of four porters carried our boat, each team taking a turn for a few hundred yards at a time. When we finally reached the waters Millard undertook to sail it to Loiyangallani where we had arranged to meet Dyson and Martin coming from Kulal. I continued the march along the bouldery coast with the camels.

When we were all reunited we pitched camp beside some hot springs which formed a stream running down to the lake. Soon some of the native Elmolo tribe shyly appeared, offering us a sight of their morning's catch of fish. A bargain was struck, the price being one gaudy glass necklace for as many fish as we and our 'boys' could eat.

When they were first discovered von Höhnel recorded that 'Elmolo' means the 'poor ones'. In 1888 they had numbered about 500. By 1934 this had dwindled to only eighty-four. They lived entirely on fish, crocodiles and water tortoises caught in the lake which was also their water source. It lacked calcium, and it seemed that this, combined with their diet (also deficient in available calcium) had resulted in nearly all of them suffering from a forward – and sometimes outward – bowing of the shin bone. In some of them this had reached a degree that made walking difficult – one man even appeared to have a second 'knee' somewhere above the ankle.

Dyson was greatly interested in anthropology and measured every adult member of the tribe, making notes on their general health and finding a tendency to scurvy, pyorrhoea, decayed teeth and arthritis. These people knew only two cures for ailments – either blood-letting or burning the painful spot by applying a glowing ember

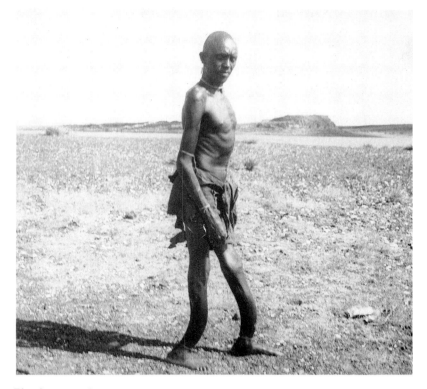

Elmolo native, showing exaggerated form of typical leg deformity

through a piece of goat skin. As a result most of them bore innumerable scars.

Soon after this Millard was suddenly and unexpectedly recalled to Marsabit and ordered to a government post in Basutoland. Thus we were reduced to three as we made ready for a long-anticipated visit to South Island, where we looked forward to fruitful work. This island is about thirty square miles and lies some four miles from the eastern shore and fifteen miles from the southern end of the lake. We had observed that over the water weather conditions were constant in a regular daily cycle. Every morning there was a very strong wind with accompanying rough water until 11 am after which it gradually died away. By early afternoon a flat calm prevailed which lasted until 4 pm. Then the wind gradually rose again until it blew so strongly that we used to dismantle the tents and cover them with heavy stones.

Before attempting the crossing we moved camp to a point some five miles south of Loiyangallani because this allowed a certain northward drift which we hoped to make use of – the prevailing wind came from the south-east.

On 25 July Martin and I made the first visit to the island, taking an hour-and-three-quarters in rather rough conditions. We ran into a sheltered cove to make camp under some sloping rocks. The next day we explored and began the arduous climb up treacherous slopes. At about 800 feet we found the tracks of a four-footed animal – a big surprise as we had expected to find only birds. From the highest point at 1,500 feet we looked down and saw a herd of thirteen domestic goats grazing on some scanty tufts of grass. They were as wild as the wildest antelope and it seemed that they had never seen a man before. Later we came across another thirteen goat skeletons in various parts of the island, also a fragment of a broken pot and some human bone – proving that at least one man had reached and lived there before us. There was a central ridge running north-south composed of a series of ash cones, on some of which we erected cairns for the survey which Martin intended to begin the next day when I returned to the mainland.

From the Turkana I learnt that they had a legend about the island which could account for these finds. They believed that long, long ago some of their people were herding goats when the water suddenly rose over the land, cutting them off from the shore. There they had perforce lived and died until none were left. I asked how it was known that men lived there for years after this event, and was told that a number of fires could be seen on the island, these becoming fewer and fewer until finally there were none, and it was assumed that everyone had died.

Our discoveries seemed to support this story. Indeed, other factors also contributed to its veracity. At the south end of the lake there are numerous faults running out into the water towards South Island some fifteen miles away. Astride them is an extinct but perfect volcanic cone, Nabuyatom. Not far distant is the small Teleki Volcano which von Höhnel found to be active in 1888. Perhaps the faulting and its associated vulcanicity has caused the ground to sink beneath the lake. If so, it is probable that the event took place a very long time ago – the story may have survived for thousands of years. The piece of fossil human skull and half a primitively ornamented pot both lay on the west side of the island on a ledge of precipitous rock face some fifty feet above the 1934 level of the lake when we found them. Perhaps the lake was that much higher when the people were cut off to live and die there. I have been inclined to believe the story for we were the first known visitors to South (Höhnel) Island, since the Turkana and the Elmolo had no boats.

Twenty-one years later George and Joy Adamson visited the island, where they too found live goats and pottery, but the story of how people came to be on the island was different. In Mrs Adamson's account in the December 1956 *Geographical Journal* it is said that 'The Elmolo and Samburu people have a legend that a long time ago the southern portion of the lake was dry land and that people used to live there. One day a young pregnant woman was herding her goats and came upon a spring bubbling out of the ground. Having nothing better to do she idly picked up a stone and started to hammer away at the orifice of the spring. Suddenly it burst open, and a great deal of water shot out flooding the land. The young woman fled with her goats to the hills, which soon became an island. There in due course she gave birth to twins, and thus the island was peopled.' The weakness of this story is that there is no account of how the birth of the twins came to be known!

My journey back to the mainland was made in a flat calm, and the following morning Dyson took a boat-load of supplies over to join Martin for the survey work. I travelled to the southern end of the lake to geologize in the Teleki Volcano area. Before we parted it was arranged that should Martin and Dyson be in need of assistance on the island they would light three fires as a distress signal. We decided to make it *three* to avoid misunderstanding in case they wanted to work at separate sites and to camp at different points. If ever the African 'boys' saw three fires a message was to be brought to me immediately. The plan was that the survey work would be completed by 5 August, and it was agreed that the party must *return* to our stores camp at the latest by 15 August.

My geological work completed, I returned to Sirima on the evening of 4 August.

On the 7th I began to be concerned about the rations of the 'boys' at the lake-side camp, and annoyed that the others [Martin and Dyson] were delaying so long ... [On] the 8th I packed off a syce and a camel with some potatoes, sugar and maize cobs ... Luckily I shot an oryx that morning, and we were able to send a good mass of meat as well. The syce crossed with Katunge coming up from the lake camp to say that their food was finished, and that they had not seen a fire on the island for some days ... the only sign they had seen of those on the island was on the 5th, when they saw a fire in the north bay ... These times are probably fairly accurate as Mdele was winding the chronometer every day. I gather that they lit fires every night after that on one or other of the headlands.

I was perturbed by this news. Although I was expecting them to be working on the far side of the island for some time, I felt they should really have returned on the 5th. On the 9th I went down to the lakeside camp to try and establish contact, but neither then nor on the two following days could I get any response from the island. A sixth sense was beginning to warn me of trouble and I began to consider what measures to take if they became overdue on the 15th.

In order to have everything readied in case of need I travelled to Marsabit, whence I sent telegrams enquiring about the possibility of obtaining an aeroplane. Replies were received from Nairobi on 14 August. On the 15th I returned from Marsabit accompanied by a police patrol ready to search the shore of the lake.

Martin and Dyson had not come back so I immediately went back to Marsabit in order to send a telegram asking for a Wilson Airways machine to pick me up and proceed to the island.

Unfortunately the plane was delayed and it was not until the 18th that Mr Pearson (pilot), the Superintendent of Police and I left to search the island and the lake shore. We flew low over their known first camp and then all the other suggested camping sites, but saw nothing. Examination of the five small adjacent islands and the shores of the lake from Bor on the east and the Kerio River on the west, to the south end of the lake gave us no clues. Returning to Marsabit we found that a wireless message had been received stating that Dyson's topi had been found on the west shore in the Ferguson Gulf region seventy miles to the north. I immediately telegraphed asking that a plane be sent to that area too.

From 18 to 22 August Donald MacInnes and John Millard, both of whom had flown to Marsabit in the search plane, helped me to break up the camps at Sirima and the lakeside. We then intended to search the western shores of the lake, where it would be possible to launch a boat and so make another complete search of the island on foot. But half-an-hour before our departure a message was received from Lokitaung reporting that two fires had been seen across the lake on the *east* side. We immediately left with a police patrol for the point indicated, which was 250 miles north. Arriving on 27 August we found the remains of fires, but it was plain that they had been lit by natives. We turned back — now certain that the last chance of finding our companions alive had gone.

I had been hoping against hope that we should be greeted [on arrival] at Sirima by the lost ones but I was doomed to disappointment ... The poor 'boys', who have not had proper rations since 19 July, had the water boiling ready to put the rice in directly I arrived. We also brought them sugar, salt, maize cobs, tobacco and ghee – after all, they deserve something for the way they have stuck it out without complaining.

Before finally accepting our loss, and feeling that possibly traces of the disaster might yet be found on South Island, we arranged to transport a metal lifeboat, lent by the Kenya and Uganda Railways and Harbours, from Lake Victoria to Lake Rudolf. Donald MacInnes and I spent the next eight days sailing southwards towards the island searching for clues. Owing to government instructions issued from Nairobi, we were compelled to follow the weather shore instead of sailing south under the lee of the east coast. The result was that one night the boat dragged her anchor and sank on the boulders. Precious time was lost effecting recovery and repairs, and as soon as this was finished the weather became too rough for boat work and MacInnes went sick with a high fever.

After all these frustrations we had finally to decide on a one-day dash across to the island itself. All went well until we had covered fifteen of the twenty-miles' distance when a strong wind began to blow directly off South Island. Half-an-hour before darkness fell the outboard engine was swamped for the third time, and when only two miles from our objective we were finally forced to turn and set sail before the wind.

Our troubles were not over. As we unfurled the sail a scorpion fell out and stung MacInnes, causing him to let go of the ten-foot sweep with which he was steering. Fortunately we had another one. It was now pitch black and the rising storm made me decide to sail north along the length of the lake until dawn. By then my personal 'boy' had tied himself to the mast and MacInnes was in great pain. Then suddenly away to the north-west I saw a flashing light – one of our 'boys' from the camp had been intelligent enough to light a powerful lantern. Five hours later we were safely back in camp.

Lack of both petrol and food precluded another attempt, and we never found out what caused the accident to our companions. During other searches which were also being made, two tins and two oars were found on the west shore of the lake, as well as Dyson's hat, which had been picked up seventy miles north of what must have been the scene of the tragedy. Not the least mysterious aspect of the whole sad affair was the disappearance of their boat and the two four-gallon buoyancy drums that were carried in it.

So the first expedition I led ended two months prematurely in a terrible human tragedy, although not in scientific failure. Millard and Wakefield returned to their African posts, MacInnes to England. I collected Joyce from her travels and we prepared to drive home overland. Twenty-one years later George and Joy Adamson visited South Island, and she reported this in her *Geographical Journal* paper.

On a high-water mark about twelve feet above the present level we found, among other debris, a four-gallon steel petrol drum corroded with rust, and beside it a length of red motor car inner tube. Both the objects were obviously very old, the former being a type well known before the war. Since the expedition boat carried both petrol drums and an inner tube, there can be no doubt that these remains came from the wreck of the boat.

I brought home Dr Dyson's notes on the Elmolo, and a full report was published under our two names.* My own work was published two years later by the Royal Society.† Martin's biological collections went to the British Museum (Natural History). Thus we ensured that the last work of our two companions, who had endeared themselves to us all in the few happy months we had spent together, was not all in vain.

When at last all the expedition's affairs had been settled, Joyce and I prepared to return home from Naivasha by road. I retained one of the expedition cars, an aged 1929 box-bodied Chevrolet. Much had to be done to her – stronger springs, an extra fourteen-

*W S Dyson MB *and* V E Fuchs MA PhD, 1937. 'The Elmolo'. *Jour. Roy. Anthropological Inst*, Vol. LXVII.
†V E Fuchs, 1939. 'The Geological History of the Lake Rudolf Basin, Kenya Colony'. *Phil. Trans. Roy. Soc*, Series B, No 560, Vol 229.

gallon petrol tank and a general overhaul. At the last minute it was found that one of the longitudinal chassis members was cracked and this had to be cut out and replaced. It was but the beginning of a long series of troubles which led us to name the car 'Laura' after a certain truculent camel we had read about.

Our route led through northern Kenya, Uganda and the Sudan to cross the Nile at Juba. Thence through the Congo (Zaire) and the French West African territories, via Cameroun and Nigeria, before heading north over the Tanezrouft plateau of the Sahara to Morocco. From Tangier we sailed for Gibraltar, and so home across Spain and France, to take a boat from Boulogne to Folkestone. The trip took forty-six days during which we travelled 7,687 miles, with only three hours spent at sea on the Mediterranean and Channel crossings. Throughout this time Joyce drove each alternate fifty miles, and took a full part in all but the engineering. It is her journal which is the record of this journey.

Today it is remarkable to think that we set out to pass through so many territories with British passports alone – the thought of getting visas never even crossed our minds. The only frontier problem was the occasional need to make a Customs declaration. Usually any interest in our cameras was dispelled by diverting attention to the cage of five chameleons we carried. Invariably, even at Folkestone, we soon had the Customs officers catching grasshoppers or flies so that they could watch the chameleons eating with their long five-inch tongues! With luck they could also see them change colour – green, black, yellow, blue or blotchy to match some new background.

Besides having no visas we had no maps. Before starting we had compiled a list of place names so that by enquiry we could move from one to the next. But many of these 'places' consisted only of an assembly of grass huts, and it was often difficult to know where we had got to. 'Is this a place?' we would cry, then seek local information and, hopefully, directions to the next one. Everywhere we found the Africans friendly and helpful. We were fascinated by the different people and the cultures we encountered, and some of them seemed equally curious about us. Many had never seen a white woman and I often found women stroking Joyce's arms, persumably to see if the white came off, or to discover whether she felt the same as they did.

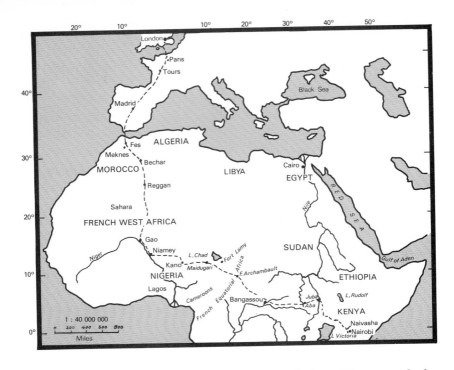

As we crossed frontiers the nature of the villages and the cultivation changed, and we became aware of different modes of dress. We were well acquainted with the unclothed males of northern Kenya where anklets, wristlets, earrings, lablets and coiffeur were more important than dress. But as we entered southern Sudan we found the women also wearing less and less. However, they were nearly all overdressed in necklaces, earrings and bracelets.

In the Congo we had to cross numerous rivers, the larger ones by pontoons composed of several dug-outs decked with boards. These were driven either by men hauling on a taut wire stretched across the water or by paddling and poling. On the downstream side of the pontoon were numerous vigorous paddlers, encouraged by a musician playing a native gourd-piano and singing in unison with the paddling. On the upstream side stood a number of men punting with long irregular poles. By some miracle we would arrive at the appropriate landing place on the far bank in spite of the rapid current. There, as when embarking, considerable skill was required to leave the unstable platform.

In the region of Buta we were surprised to encounter at intervals a number of albinos, some of whom were heavily tattooed. There were other surprises, as when we stopped beside a tall grass hedge to visit a local District Commissioner. When we returned to the car the 'hedge' had gone, leaving no sign of it having been there. A mile farther on the mystery was solved, for we found that the hedge was in fact a number of huge bundles of tall grass being carried by a line of women. Where we had stopped they must have been resting facing away from the road, each neatly tied bundle standing close together and upright.

Farther on came the extraordinary sight of growing telegraph poles. Apparently freshly cut trees, stripped of their branches, had been used to carry the wires – and these, with astonishing vigour, had sprouted a head of new green growth at the top of each. We were never to know if this was only temporary or if they succeeded in rooting.

At Bangassou we entered French West Africa (now Central African Republic), where the chameleons worked their usual magic and we only had to pay five francs. Pressing on, we passed through cotton country where the crop was spread out to dry in innumerable trays. Then through coffee plantations and forest, to open country where a gaunt clump of trees stood alone. Thinking that this would provide splendid firewood, we set up camp. Soon came disappointment for none of the dry dead wood I collected would burn. Even with the aid of paraffin the most we could achieve was a temporary glow. We never discovered the reason for this but realized that had it been burnable all the wood would long since have been removed by the local people.

Passing on through Fort Sibut and Fort Crampel to Fort Achambault we learnt that Lake Chad was in flood, and the road to Fort Lamy was under three feet of water. This meant that the lake must have extended some fifty miles beyond its normal margins. The region is indeed precarious for its people – for the long-term repetitive rise and fall of the lake means that they alternately suffer either flooding or drought. In recent years it is aridity which has tended to depopulate the area.

At the time our only concern was to find a passable route to Maidugari in northern Nigeria. We discovered that by turning west then south into the Camerouns we should be successful. There we met two Germans, von Wichmann and von Hertzberg, who had been in India selling motor car spares. Apparently they had been attempting to do the same in Africa. At Fort Achambault they were awaiting a spare armature for their dynamo which had burnt out. As they had a deadline for reaching Germany they were only too glad of my offer to charge one of their batteries in our car while they ran with the other. So it was that they left for Kano with us. Our route led through Maroua, which was very picturesque, and the native horses were gay with scarlet harnesses. After visiting the Administrateur, where we paid twenty francs each for passing through the Camerouns, we left for Maidugari.

Eighty miles on we came to a wide unbridged river with a soft sandy approach in which Laura stuck. In no time a horde of willing men arrived with loud cries of 'Poose, poose' which they did with a will all round the car. When I had organized them all to push in the same direction Laura was successfully extricated to solid ground. Another dash at the sand and the unpleasantly deep river, and aided by our 'poosing' friends, she emerged on the far bank rather full of water.

A mile or two later fumes of over-hot oil came from the engine. Only then did I realize that the radiator had been pushed back on to the fan, which had cut a large hole in the honeycomb. Providentially we had bought a supply of plasticine in Kenya for just such an event and now it came into its own. That evening we arrived in Maidugari and called on the British District Commissioner, for we were now in Nigeria.

At the post office next morning we heard that a message had arrived for the District Commissioner saying that yellow fever had broken out in Kano and local leave should cease. Fearing a long enforced stay we discourteously left at once, without saying goodbye and chancing an order to remain where we were. After driving 350 miles we arrived in Kano.

I was relieved to get some assistance from a garage for the maintenance of Laura. During the 3,284 miles we had covered so far I had already replaced one back axle, mended innumerable punctures, freed a seized-up distributer shaft, cured an overheating dynamo armature and temporarily mended the radiator. Laura was living up to her name. Now the front wheels needed alignment and the steering column needed replacement.

Three days later, when all was done, we left for Niamey on the River Niger in French territory, a distance of some 450 miles. Thence the way led northward via Gao (then known as Gao-Gao, and now in Mali) to the tiny village of Tabankort and the beginning of the Sahara crossing.

Although the hole in the middle of the radiator had been filled with cement (not the best thing for the Sahara), at Gao I had found it leaking again, this time from the very base where the metal frame had fractured and the edges had worn through the radiator. This I had soldered up, but throughout the Sahara crossing it was necessary to remove the radiator every morning and resolder it before starting. Towards the end of each day, and indeed whenever we stopped, there were cries of 'Basin' and with this we saved every drop of water we could.

We found the first hundred miles after Tabankort difficult driving, for the last vestiges of vegetation in the form of long grass tufts had collected sand, which formed a maze of anthill-like bumps that tortured Laura and her passengers. Once on to the bare sand we made better progress, except for the occasions when the back wheels sank into it. To extricate ourselves we had brought two twenty-foot lengths of coconut matting, each eighteen inches wide. These helped, but tall rolls of chicken wire squashed flat were simpler and more effective – as we later learnt from our German friends. It was now Christmas Day 1934. In mid-Sahara we celebrated 25 December by eating a small tinned cold Christmas pudding brought for the occasion.

By this time we were well on our way across the 700 miles of the Tanezrouft sand plateau. Fortunately at that time there was a French encampment known as Bidon Cinque for resupplying aircraft. As we approached it was not the few low tents that we noticed, but the surprising presence of a glistening white petrol pump standing all by itself in the Sahara sand. There we were able to fill up – petrol for 12/6 (62p) and water for 6/- (30p) a gallon. Although petrol was five times its price in Kenya and over six times what it was in England, it was perhaps justified, since everything had to be either flown or trucked in.

After a further sixty miles that day, we camped in a smooth area of sand. Standing on the roof of Laura was like being at the centre of a gramophone record – a perfectly circular horizon without an undulation in sight. The western sky was blue-green, in the east it was a soft pink, both shading into slate-blue.

Two days later, owing to problems of soft sand, our petrol ran out when we were still thirty miles from Reggan, on the north side of the desert. In the cool of the evening I set out to walk, leaving Joyce in the car. But I had hardly covered 100 yards when von Wichmann and von Hertzberg arrived, bringing with them eight gallons of petrol – which we gratefully accepted. We spent that night in the Reggan Hotel, where a very friendly cheetah was chained to a pillar in the middle of the entrance hall. He purred as one stroked him.

From Reggan our route led to Adrar and on to Beni Abbes, but we turned north through the beautiful oasis of Igli nestling among huge terracotta-coloured dunes, magnificent against the clear blue sky. That night, 30 December, we reached Columb Bechar, a centre for the French Foreign Legion. It was pleasant to find an hotel, for the nights were now cold: indeed, I had been sleeping in a sleeping-bag that I had used in Greenland. This was a double bag, one inside the other, so we had one each. This surprising change of temperature was due to the cold air from the snows of the Atlas Mountains pouring down over the northern Sahara. Beyond Columb Bechar, at a place called Bou Denib nearer to the mountains, we were surprised to find ice in the courtyard in the morning.

Our arrival at Bou Denib was eventful. Before reaching it we came to a small post at dusk, and found an Arab placing a barrier across the track. 'No,' he said, 'No one may travel after dark.' However on my insistence he took us into a hut and cranked an ancient telephone which he said was connected to the Foreign Legion fort at Bou Denib. When I was asked to speak on it I mispronounced a French word when I said that I was an English geologist. It later transpired that those at the other end thought I was an English *general*. We were given permission to continue our journey. Presently we saw a number of flashing lights in the distance advancing towards us. When we met they turned out to be a posse of Foreign Legion trucks coming out to meet the 'English general'!

Now somewhat shamefaced, we were deposited at the Café du Légion where the Patron's wife showed us to a room. When congratulated on her command of English she retorted with a strong northern accent, 'And so I should, I was born in Manchester.' But our humiliation was not yet over, for the next morning the Commandant asked to see the passes for our cameras. These it seemed should have been procured in Columb Bechar – now 114 miles back.

Two days later we returned to Bou Denib (those bothersome English again) with the necessary permits. It was New Year's Day and we sat down to lunch in the café. At the bar in the dining-room there were a number of Legionary officers drinking to the sound of a gramophone. Suddenly we recognized the strains of the Marseillaise and sprang to our feet at the table. This was a great success, and with cries of *'Vive la France!'* and *'Vive l'Angleterre!'* we were pressed to join in the drinking. Thereafter our troubles were over.

It transpired that the road over the Atlas Mountains could only be travelled from south to north and north to south on alternate days. It happened that the day of our desired departure was a north-to-south day, but 'No, it does not matter,' decreed our new-found friends, and off we went. The way led over the Atlas, where we found snow at 8,000 feet, to Meknes. At the barriers we encountered we said we were English and had agreement for our travel from Bou Denib, and they always let us pass.

After driving through the huge walled city of Meknes we reached Tangier on 5 January 1935, and two days later crossed the Straits to Gibraltar. Another six days and we were in Folkstone, on our way to Heatherdene. Then it was that Laura made her final protest by breaking the main leaf of a rear spring – the only spring she broke throughout our journey.

At Heatherdene there was a champagne welcome and many telephone calls. The chameleons finally came to rest in the freedom of my father's large conservatory, where spiders, flies and other insects were theirs for the taking.

Chapter 8

The Suguta Valley
and Lake Rukwa Expedition
1937-38

The time had come to take stock and decide where we were going to live, and to think about where I was going professionally. I had brought back sufficient material for publication and, I hoped, with a view to obtaining a higher degree. So Cambridge seemed a good place to establish ourselves. We rented a small house while we searched for a more permanent home. For months we found nothing suitable and felt so hopeless that one day we decided to tour the outskirts of the city just for the fun of choosing a house where we would like to live whether it was for sale or not. That afternoon we saw three, but none were for sale.

Only a few days later the estate agent phoned to ask us to go and look at 72 Barton Road, which had just been offered on the market. To our amazement it was one of our chosen three, and when we rang the bell the door was opened by a man in the Zoology Department whom I knew quite well. 'How nice of you to call,' he began. To which I could only reply that I had not known he lived there and this was not a social call – we had come to look over his property with a view to purchase. It was his turn to look startled. 'But my new appointment was only confirmed yesterday. How could a house agent know we would be leaving?' That point was never resolved, but before long we were the happy owners of our first home, and a few months later, on 17 February 1936, our daughter Hilary was born.

I had been accepted as a research student at the Sedgwick Museum to work for a PhD, and spent nearly every day there for the next two years writing a thesis on the geology of the Lake Rudolf Basin. In 1936 I got my doctorate, and in 1938 the material was published by the Royal Society under the title of 'The Geological History of the Lake Rudolf Basin, Kenya Colony'.

During these years Donald MacInnes was working for his PhD in the Zoology Department, while a geologist, Ian Cox, recently returned from Akpatok Island in the Canadian Arctic, was also researching at the Sedgwick. The three of us shared pub lunches most days, and this led to the idea of making a survey of all the public houses in Cambridge. We decided that at least two of us must visit each site to discover the type of draught beer sold and the games of skill that were available. Bottled beer and games of chance were ignored, but the College Butteries were included. The final total was 199.

When all the 'field work' was accomplished, Ian Cox, the artist among us, drew a very splendid eighteenth-century-style map decorated with ladies in crinolines, chaps fishing on the river, little red buildings representing colleges, and numerals indicating the position of the pubs. A list of names showed what make of ale was available at each, and symbols denoted the games of skill on offer. It was a work of art, and five hundred copies were printed for us by the Cambridge University Press. We sold them very quickly, chiefly to the breweries or tourists, at eight shillings and sixpence for a hand-coloured copy, half-a-crown (12½p) in black-and-white.

I was thinking seriously of finding a job with one of the East African Geological Surveys, especially as I had African experience. But first I thought I needed a little more field experience; and I had not forgotten that Gertrude Ellis, one of my early mentors at the Museum, had strongly urged me to 'go out and be active – don't bury yourself in a stuffy museum'. So began the planning for another expedition, this time to Lake Rukwa in Tanganyika (now Tanzania). The intention was to extend knowledge of the great Rift Valley and, in particular, its Pleistocene history. In those days it seemed that in Africa lay the best opportunities of future employment.

In 1937 we began negotiations for the purchase of No. 78 Barton Road and an adjacent plot of land, making some three acres in all. After considerable alterations to the house – which were only completed after my departure for Africa – Joyce was able to move into what was to be our home for the next fifty years.

I organized the Lake Rukwa Expedition mainly for geological work in what was then a little known part of the great African Rift Valley. I was interested in the basin rather than the lake itself, and Donald

MacInnes was anxious to extend his palaeontological work in the same area. His wife Dora was a botanist and I asked them both to come with me. We also planned to travel north from Lake Baringo, through the arid Suguta Valley, before going south to Rukwa. There our objective was to seek evidence of what we believed to be the one-time southern extension of Lake Rudolf.

Financial support came from the Royal Society, the Goodman Fund of the British Museum, and the Royal Geographical Society which also lent us survey instruments. By the end of December 1937 the three of us were in Nairobi buying a car, a stout lorry, and negotiating for camels which would enable us to travel through the Suguta Valley. There were also stores to be purchased and personal 'boys' to be hired. Finally we spent Christmas with my old friends the Pickfords.

We went into the field on New Year's Day 1938. It felt good to get back to work, and my thoughts turned nostalgically to my very first camp in Africa at Naivasha in 1930.

We are sitting in the open with a brilliant starry sky but no moon. Innumerable cicadas are shrilling all around and a light air is blowing from the north. A little while ago I heard a curious sort of vibrant hissing which we searched for and finally found to be a sort of 'safari' of white ants, many of whom were sitting on dry sticks – and particularly on dry acacia pods lying on the ground. At irregular intervals all those so situated would quiver so quickly that their heads became a haze. This quivering affected the whole body, but in particular it caused the head to strike rapidly on the stick or pod, so making the curious vibrant hiss I had heard. They could be induced to do it by touching or stroking the pod on which they were standing. A curious point is that those walking on the ground do not ... take part in the 'dance'.

We travelled down the River Kapthurin geologizing and collecting specimens, spending the evenings skinning or preserving the material, writing up notes or shooting for the pot. At each camp I held the now inevitable 'sick parade'. It was the rainy season and what passed for roads were frequently flooded, the rickety bridges swaying perilously. Only too often these gave way under the weight of the lorry, which then had to be unloaded and dug out. It was backbreaking work as well as very time-consuming, but by 20 January we were at Kinyang and making for Loruk.

All was going well until we came to a hairpin bend near the bottom of an escarpment where the turn was too short for the lorry to round it in one, and the outside was a steep drop on to a lower flat. Having unloaded my passengers, I tried to get round as far as possible with full lock, intending to back up a steep gully to complete the turn. But the 4,000-pound load and the steep gradient merely caused the wheels to spin on the stones, and I found myself pointing straight over the edge, unable to move either forwards or backwards. There was only one thing to do – cut away the steep edge of the slope and build up a road on to the flat below. This we did and I drove down what felt like the wall of a house with all the loose items in the lorry falling about my ears.

To add to our troubles the rain had brought out myriads of insects. At night there was a perfect plague of ants and insects of almost every size, colour and shape around the lamps. As one had to sit near a lamp to see at all, I wrote in a haze of flying and walking creatures. Added to this the eyes could be damaged by large crickets, huge solitary locusts and innumerable hard beetles as they winged their energetic ways. I sat in my pyjamas and they persisted in crawling up the sleeves and down the neck until I felt as though my back and chest were a hive of activity – which in fact was true!

All day the 'boys' searched for good water. All we could get was like strong cocoa, and the matter in it was so fine that we could not strain it out. However, we were able to precipitate a certain amount by putting wood ashes into it. For the rest we used some of the lake water that we got with much trouble on the donkeys. The difficulty with that was that – apart from being slightly brackish – it tasted strongly of boiled algae and other vegetation, as well as of (I suspected) crocodile and hippo dung which fringed the shores everywhere in large quantities. Altogether horrid.

Getting away from Kinyang entailed crossing the river, and before the vehicles could negotiate this it was necessary to make up the river bed into some semblance of a road. First filling the hollows in the bare lava with boulders, we laid down a carpet of branches bedded in with sand dug from a cutting in the river bank.

It is the local custom to feed herds of goats by cutting down whole trees or the more succulent (and of course thorny) branches. Consequently we were bothered by a number of goats who would come and eat our 'roadway'. So enthusiastic were they that they disappeared into the depths of the branches before they could be cut and beaten down into a compact mass. I therefore walked over the stouter wood whacking the backsides of goats wherever visible. Incredible though it seems, they merely dived deeper and refused to budge. But we got them out at last, and covering all our basal preparations with sand, mud and gravel, we have hopes of going over it at the first attempt tomorrow ...

This experience with goats was not surprising since we had previously seen them gather round a man high up in the top of a tree with his goats standing round gazing up at him – some even on hind legs in their anxiety. As the branches fell they pounced upon them and stripped every vestige of greenery in a few minutes. No wonder the Kenya slogan we had seen on posters said 'If you want a desert keep goats'! On the other hand, they are one of the few domestic animals which can survive in semi-desert conditions.

The next day we attempted the river crossing which we had so arduously prepared.

What a day – what a day! We started off at 9.30 am from the camp at Kinyang and three or four minutes later arrived at the crossing ... I got everyone off the lorry and made the first attempt fully loaded. Hardly had we crossed the rocky river bed and started the climb when we stuck with wheels spinning. The lorry was then pointing up at about thirty degrees so we unloaded her ... and then cautiously backed on to the river bed. So steep was the incline that the engine oil poured out through the main bearing into the clutch housing and thence in a black stream on to the sand ...

Having taken all the load off we tried again and again, each time putting down more and more branches in the hope that they would bind with the sand. Even chains did not help, so we bribed a number of Suk men and women to help us dig away the road to a lower level. Two-and-a-half hours later we reached the top amid general rejoicing ...

Once more on our way, we found the country became less and less bushy and continued its gradual decline northwards. Soon the track led us to the bottom of a gorge where the vertical walls of yellow pumice were so close and the course so twisting that it was almost impossible to steer the lorry without touching the sides. Certainly it was impracticable to avoid any of the enormous boulders which strewed the floor. Never had I put a lorry to such a test in so short a time. Hummocking and bucketing over huge stones, avoiding the walls at all costs lest I tore off the body or precipitated tons of the slabby rock on top of it, I felt it was scarcely possible that tyres and axles could stand the shuddering jars as the wheels clambered and

The hazards of motoring

slipped over the unseen (from the driver's seat) obstacles. Finally we arrived at a more open patch where a splash of very green grass indicated water.

This was the saline springs we had heard of. As it was very hot even in the late afternoon we looked for a better camping place, but up above there were only two or three bushes and a wide expanse of grass ... Going down again to the brackish water it was very clear – the most beautiful water we have seen for weeks and full of fish. We finally decided to try and get out again and back to where we had seen some camels grazing ... Back through that awful gorge, where Donald told me afterwards it seemed as though he could see light between the load and the body as we bounced over the boulders. At the point where I had nearly slid into an abyss on the way down, she stuck on the way up. However, after three attempts she was away and out on to the flats, with only a little hesitancy as the engine boomed its thousands of revolutions to maintain a speed of three to four miles per hour.

Now we are in camp at a good place with plenty of muddy river water and nice shade. Karpeddo is perhaps a mile-and-a-half away. Hardly had we arrived when Gitileet's grandfather came for medicine to ease various aches and pains which I diagnose as rheumatism. This stretches to head and eyes as well, but our *dower* (medicine) is good for everything! For his headache and to make him sweat he got Empirin and aspirin, for his colic three veg. lax. besides a quinine tablet for luck. Quite a sight it was seeing him swallow them one at a time, each with a dose of water. I also gave him vaseline to rub on his joints, and this was a great pleasure ... considered more 'powerful' than all the others put together ... He is also troubled with 'impotence', but as our medicine chest contained no cure for this I suggested the combined action of all that I had given him should perhaps effect a cure. Doubtless his graphic descriptions will be continued tomorrow as he is a very talkative old man.

We spent the next few days in camp at Karpeddo, from where I established a number of survey stations in order to correct inaccuracies in the local maps. The whole region was very hot and the water very contaminated – the tea tasted very strongly of goat, which was a bit ominous!

When we arrived a camel had produced a calf more or less on our doorstep. It was unable to stand and lay a limp mass of incredible boniness. This morning it was gone, but I think the owner must have carried it away. He had built a thorn *boma* round mother and toto, and also kept fires burning all night – both precautions to keep off leopards.

The following extract from my journal describes a typical working day.

Woken at 6.10 am by Katunge with tea; we are already feeling the daylight as the sun is rising and our beds are outside in the open to get as much air as possible. Keeping the mosquito net down because of the myriads of early-morning flies (this is a cattle watering hole) we read for a quarter of an hour while drinking the tea ... while our washing water, shaving can and gear are laid out by our beds. Directly they are ready we rise, and sitting on the edge of the bed swot flies and shave with much dexterity while balancing the mirror on one knee ... This done, breakfast is ready, consisting of doves or hare or mutton, followed by toast and marmalade together with one or two pints more tea. If we have the excuse that there is no meat in camp we may get sardines or tinned sausages.

Directly breakfast is cleared, Donald sorts the previous night's collection of beetles while I set the barograph, take aneroid readings and bottle or tank any spirit specimens left over from the previous day. By 8.30 am I am ready to leave camp. Accompanied by one or two 'boys' carrying such survey gear and cameras etc as they can be trusted with, I set out for the day's trip. This will last any time from five to seven hours – the latter being exceptional. On returning to camp a wash of the mouth followed by two pints of water and/or lemonade leads on to a meal accompanied by drinks amounting to another two pints, and followed by a pint or two of tea. By this time somewhat inflated, especially if the cook happens to have decided it is spotted dog day (made without baking powder as there is none), one is glad to recline and read for half an hour.

The next move is to sally forth for a short walk of a few miles, usually with a gun or rifle and accompanied by one of our 'boys'. During this trip I make general observations and collect reptiles and food for the pot, very often in this dry country finishing up with some sand-grouse shooting after the sun has gone down. On return to camp the first thing is a couple of glasses of water, then clean the guns. By that time the canvas bath is ready and I wash as well as possible in water that would be a thick clay colour if one could see it in the gloom of the tent. After the wash I get into my pyjamas and mosquito boots and read for a quarter of an hour while taking the evening tot of whisky. Directly the second of us (we take it in turns to be first) has finished washing the soup arrives.

After the meal, which is accompanied by about a pint and a half of drink, we have a pint of tea and settle down to read and write up such notes as these, and clear up the day's efforts. With great regularity we go to bed between 9.20 and 9.40 pm and sleep like logs.

On our return to Baringo we headed for the east side of the lake and southwards to Lake Hannington, which was very saline. A rocky path wound along the steep screes on its eastern side, and as I walked the reflection from the water in the heat of the day made me long for a bathe. I asked my escort of locals how deep it was. 'How should we know?' was the reply – they laughed at the idea of anyone going in. When I suggested to my 'boy' Gitileet, that he should test the depth with a stick, he hastily refused. But a little jeering, and the desire to be thought a brave fellow by the Kamasia (he being a Suk), finally nerved him to venture in. Realizing that it was fairly deep I began to undress, confident that the bevy of women who had by now appeared along the path would either be driven away by modesty or would not see it as peculiar. I soon found that the matter of greatest interest to them was the whiteness of my skin where the sun had not got at it. Then as I dived in and started off at a rapid crawl they were truly astonished – but still thought me mad! The rich soda solution was not the best thing for nasal passages, so after some fifty yards I turned back; drying out in the sun I found myself completely encrusted with a white powder of soda crystals.

By the middle of February we had worked our way back to Sterndale, the Pickfords' house at Naivasha. There the long and eagerly awaited news arrived that Joyce had had a second little daughter and both were well. We were both delighted at her arrival. We had decided to call her Rosalind, and I was thankful that all had

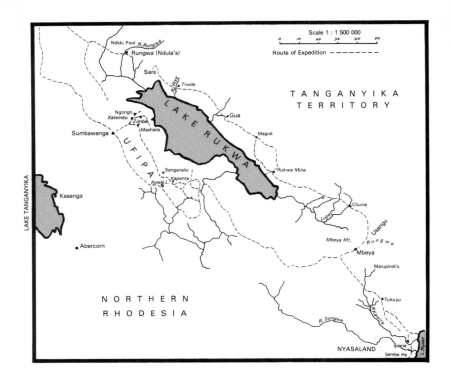

gone smoothly. My very perspicacious father felt uneasy and thought there might be something wrong with this beautiful child, but since Joyce was so happy, and the doctors seemed satisfied, he kept his own counsel. None of us could foresee the heartache which was to come.

Early in March we left Tanganyika, a territory which had been removed from German administration after the First World War. It was then under a League of Nations mandate. We were not impressed with the country. Roads were as bad as anything I had experienced in Africa, and consequently the hard-working lorry was usually in low gear, and frequently in trouble. It was a laborious journey to Mbeya which lay under the southern end of the range from which it takes its name, and which was the administrative centre of south-western Tanganyika. To the north lay the great rocky hog's back of Mbeya, the highest point rising to well over 9,000 feet. When we climbed it we found that above 8,000 feet the grassy slopes were brilliant with red-hot pokers, irises, white delphiniums and innumerable orchids. During an excursion which lasted less than two hours Dora collected seventy-five different species.

We made camp under the west flank of Mount Mbeya in the Wasafui country, where we found that the natives were superstitious and timid. Frequently our approach was the signal for flight, and we were amused to learn that our visit to the top of the mountain – combined with my peculiar habit of chipping the rocks as I climbed – had made them regard us as friends of the devil himself.

On one occasion when I was sitting with one of the 'boys' off the track we heard voices approaching. Presently two women bearing enormous bundles of firewood on their heads came along the path. As they passed my 'boy' made a noise. Turning their eyes, but not their heads, towards us they caught sight of me. They continued for a few paces until they were out of sight, then crash went the bundles into the grass as they tore away screaming at the tops of their exceedingly high-pitched voices. Never had I heard anything like it. The proverbial stuck pig could not have competed in either volume or shrillness. This acute sense of fear seemed all the more remarkable because there had been many mission stations all over the country for thirty-five years.

We spent two weeks working in the country west and then north of Mbeya. As it was the rainy season we found large areas covered with the most surprising plants, many with superb flowers. There was also a predominance of weevils and bugs, multi-coloured varieties which Donald collected assiduously, while Dora concentrated on the plants, I on the spiders, molluscs, amphibians and reptiles.

At one point when driving along a track difficult to follow on account of the tall grass, five to eight feet high, we did some involuntary collecting.

As the car brushed through it seeds flew in all directions. Soon we were irritated all over by innumerable kinds of pricking, creeping and piercing seeds that covered our clothing. One advantage of this tall grass was the enormous number and variety of beetles and other insects that were left on the radiator gauze and in the piles of grass heads that decked the mudguard valleys and running boards.

On 15 March we drove back to Mbeya and learnt there that Hitler had invaded Austria.

It sounds bad because of all the talk, but the general opinion seems to be that they are German people in a sense, and it is not peculiar for the German boundary to include them. The trouble is that everyone will now begin to wonder whether the Czech-German minority, Switzerland and/or Belgium will be next.

Leaving Mbeya, we passed through Chunia and by 25 March reached Bayldon's Rukwa 'A' Mine at Marambangombe, the most northerly of the Lupa goldfield. We had arranged for forty-five Wawungu porters to meet us for the march up the east side of the lake. Ten days were spent dividing our belongings into suitable loads of forty-five to fifty pounds, visiting the mine and other places of geological interest, and of course, collecting insects and reptiles. When ready to leave our party numbered fifty-three.

We carried food for ourselves and the personal servants, but part of that for the porters would have to be found along the route. This could limit our range because the country was only sparsely populated owing to a recent outbreak of tsetse fly, and the year's crops were not yet ready to be harvested. Before leaving I made a last excursion into Chunia for mail, and was delighted to get the news that the Royal Society had accepted my paper, 'Geological History of the Lake Rudolf Basin', for publication. I felt this was something of a triumph and set off in good spirits.

We made our way down to the lake shore over the very precipitous 250-foot escarpment which formed the eastern wall of the Rukwa Rift. The cook was suffering from relapsing fever and on the second night out his temperature rose to 105°F (40.5°C). Dora was also finding it tough going.

Yesterday's rather long and hot march (twenty-four miles) was not helped by the fact that we had no opportunity of eating on the way. Fortunately I do not mind missing my meals, but it makes Donald extremely irritable and is tiring for Dora. They were both very tired ... Dora was quite knocked up.

The cook fortunately recovered, but several of the porters suffered temperatures ranging from 99° to 103°F (37.2°–39.4°C) and required constant medical attention. In six days we reached the Gua River and then struck off through forest to camp under the northern slopes of Mount Iloma. From then onwards with rare exceptions of a small swamp or river bed, we found ourselves marching continuously beneath a pall of branches that shut out any view of the

Porters in the marshes NE of Rukwa through which we walked for six days

surrounding country. The forest itself was neither dense nor tall, the trees averaging only a foot in diameter, but at thirty feet their interlacing branches effectively blocked any view, which was a source of irritation hard to bear.

At the River Gua we found a concentration of over 3,000 natives, with widespread cultivation and a White Fathers' mission station. We learnt that farther north there were no occupied villages and it would be impossible to obtain food for at least a week. But as our chief object was to reach the north-west corner of the lake where we expected to find deposits, it was imperative to push on. It was impossible to carry sufficient food for the whole party, so Donald and Dora offered to turn back, travelling to Marambangombe by a different route, while I went on with thirty porters.

In this way it was possible to reach my objective, Sara Hill, and we also saved money. Dora had been over-stressed for some days although she marched bravely and without complaint.

We had been troubled by buffalo flies, but on this last day together they became a serious pest. Donald killed one hundred in ten minutes in my tent, but it seemed to make no difference to the numbers. They were about the size of a small bumble bee and buzzed furiously as they flew, with a sharp proboscis which extended about a quarter of an inch in front of them. Fortunately their instinct was to attack their victims from below, so they spent most of their time prodding the underside of the tent. Only occasionally did they make one leap from one's chair as they experimented with some part of one's anatomy. We found that they could even penetrate the uppers of our leather shoes – we pitied the poor buffalo.

Parting from the others at Gua, my way led over undulating ground covered with dense forest. At numerous points we were delayed by the volume of water in the streams which made it difficult for the porters carrying heavy loads. That day I climbed up a hill standing some 1,200 feet above the camp. This too was mainly covered with the all-pervading forest, but it was sometimes possible to look over the surrounding country. In the distance lay a large expanse of Lake Rukwa surrounded by a marshy shore.

On my way down to this I found myself in dense grass standing well above my head, when suddenly I came upon a rough trellis-work fence made from branches. This I knew must be quite old, for we were now in deserted country. The people had been moved because the tsetse fly was infecting them with sleeping sickness. Why had the fence been built? I thought perhaps it was to guide game towards a trap. Sure enough, moving carefully along it I came to a pit covered by branches, some of which had fallen away. It was the first of three elephant traps. As they had been dug shaped like an hourglass, I would hardly have been able to get out had I fallen into one. By now it was dark and I had to strike a match to read my compass, for I knew the track to our camp lay to the east. I had told my men to come calling for me if I did not return by nightfall. Soon I heard them and saw the light from a lantern flickering through the trees.

On the third night I was camped just east of Tiwile when really heavy rain began to pour down. As I was using only the outer fly of my tent, I could not close either end, and the rain swept through in a fine spray. Soon numerous black glistening faces of my porters appeared out of the darkness hoping to be allowed to shelter. I let them in, having first showed my disapproval of their improvidence in not building a shelter when the weather was so threatening . As a result I slept with fifteen men crushed into every corner not occupied by my bed and the sacks of food.

Porters crossing Lukwati River east of Lake Rukwa

The rain continued till dawn – and what a dawn! Grey and cold, with the whole world sodden. I had shot an eland for the pot, and the meat should have been drying all night on a wooden frame. Instead it was just horrible lumps of wet and sooty flesh hanging limp and forlorn – a most unpleasant sight. We waited for it and the tent to dry out, but the meat remained soaking. In desperation we packed up and started off through the long wet grass. As we left I noticed a tree from which a panel of bark had been chipped. On the bare wood was an inscription in Swahili which said:

We came here with a Bwana named Fokoze who went out into the forest and shot an animal called an eland and now we have meat this day. 18/4/38.

Such is fame! Soon it began to rain again. Hastily I had the sacks of maize flour (the 'boys' rations) piled in a heap on which I could sit with the skirt of my huge cape spread out round me to protect them. I remarked to them that I felt like a broody hen, which brought forth shouts of delighted laughter despite the depressingly sodden state the 'boys' were in.

North of the River Yeye we marched over a flat shelf bounded on the west by the Rukwa trough. The ground was swampy, and in these marshes there was little game except roan antelope and elephant. There must have been hundreds of elephants for we walked for two days through country laid waste by them: trees torn up and thrown about, and great areas of grass and bush stamped flat among the shambles of the surrounding vegetation. Apart from the danger of running into a herd, we were most troubled by their deep tracks in sodden ground. As always they had followed the easiest route, leaving the surface pitted with holes. In places it was impossible for the laden porters to avoid deep water-filled tracks. It was a strain trying to make their way carefully along the crumbling ridges between the giant footprints.

Mosquitoes were another curse. Even at midday everyone's back was a clustered mass. One or two men had badly swollen faces, while others suffered poisoned limbs through incessant scratching. I ate my evening meal wearing pyjamas, thick khaki trousers and mosquito boots. My upper clothing consisted of a parka with the hood tied tightly round my face. On top of all this my waterproof cape provided further protection. Even so my face was left bare, and I had to blow mosquitoes off each mouthful of food!

On 22 April we reached the Sara district where I had hoped to find the lake beds cut into by the River Rungwa, but the German sketch map proved to be wrong and instead of running due north the scarp continued its north-west direction. Thus to find the beds it would have been necessary to continue the journey to Tungwas, and the unexpected rise in the lake level owing to the recent rains would mean walking for two or three days through water up to the waist – as well as risking a shortage of food. I decided to turn back, following the same route as far as Gua and then keeping farther east, thus crossing the Lukwati-Kikamba much higher up than before, and rejoining the old route for the second time near Magua.

By this time I had discovered that in Isador I had the local (Malezi) schoolmaster as headman. I asked after his pupils whom he had left behind, to be told that they were nearly all with him as porters – the others had been given 'homework' to do!

Two days later I rejoined Donald and Dora.

Since my return I find that Dora has been looking after the stores and catering for their party. As she now has a good idea of the system we run on and the amounts required, I suggested she might like to relieve me of that

Expedition porters entering village

burden? This she has agreed to do, so henceforth I hope I shall only have to help when bargaining with Indians. I have told the 'boys' that the memsahib is O.C. stores and all requests must go through her.

As the chickens which we have kept from those we bought to eat have now grown up and are being fed – an experience they do not have when kept by the natives – they have started to lay. We therefore get three or four fresh eggs a day which are very welcome. They go obediently to a packing case placed on its side and lay there in turn, the inducement being an egg blown by Donald and filled with plaster of Paris. An interesting event with these hens was witnessed by Donald and Dora. A hen rousting round for a place to lay came into the messroom and found her way down behind some tents and sacks where she laid one egg. A little while later she came with another hen and led the way to the same place. They both stood looking at it for a moment, then the new one went in and was seen comfortably established by her guide, who then left her to it. A few minutes later there was a second egg.

No mention of the hens would be complete without saying something of our cock, now named Jasper on account of his sinister appearance. He is really rather a fine bird and has a most peculiar and aggressive crow ending on a sort of gargle. We have seen him grow his comb and try his first crow, so he is now one of the party – we shall never eat him.

At Marambangombe the porters were paid off and sent home. On 6 May we began the return journey to Mbeya, spending two days *en*

The precarious bridge over the Mtembwe River, Ufipa

route at 8,000 feet near the top of the Usango escarpment. Here the cold seemed intense and we ate our breakfast wrapped in blankets. From the higher points the distant views were magnificent, and here Donald added thirty new specimens to his beetle collection. But we were glad enough to get down to the warmth of the Rest Camp at Mbeya once more.

The next part of our programme was a short visit to the northern part of the Nyasa valley to see something of the Quaternary deposits of that lake and also the volcanic range which fills the Rukwa-Nyasa rift where it is intersected by the fractures of the Ruaha valley. We camped at Marupindi near the head waters of the River Kawira, under the northern slopes of the Rungwe volcano which rises to over 10,000 feet. The country was heavily vegetated and we all became involved in adding to Dora's botanical collections.

Today I started turning the *Weekly Times* into blotting paper for Dora's plant collection. By soaking the pages in a saturated solution of citric acid they became porous when dried and can be used as good drying agents. The shortage of blotting paper was becoming acute when I suddenly had a vague memory of making it as a child with citric acid.

We had planned for us all to go down to the north-west of Lake

Dugouts at NW end of Lake Nyasa

Nyasa but now Donald developed a poisoned leg and had to be left within reach of a doctor. Dora stayed with him and I prepared to make the journey alone.

We hear that the mosquitoes there are really bad, and so large that they bite through the chair seats! However, things are never so bad as one is told, so I expect I shall still be able to sit when I come back.

Accompanied by my 'boys' I took the lorry to Tukuyu and thence to Ipiana in the Konue country. With the rains still falling the road was very treacherous. With relief we arrived on the banks of the now broad River Kawira over which I intended to cross in a dug-out. Next morning a team of Wanyamkusa porters arrived and the loads were distributed.

There was one extremely leaky dug-out to take us across, and as there was a long split in one side only a few inches above the water-line, it could not take more than five men and their loads at most. It was nearly 2 pm before we all got over and were on our way again.·
After a little way the fun really began, for – the whole countryside being under water – we walked shin- or knee-deep for three hours. At first through rice fields and later open grass and marsh, sometimes up to our chins in water – often waist-deep. Where the water was really deep the tall

men carried the short ones on their shoulders. In one place I was lucky enough to turn round and see our very dwarf-like cook apparently sitting on the water – but in a moment or so the faithful Alphonse's head slowly emerged from beneath the swirling current.

It was at the point where this occurred that I was swimming with considerable difficulty on my back (for my sodden shoes weighed me down), when I was swept away and ended up minus my hat in a very prickly submarine thornbush. However, I managed to preserve my bundle of clothes in a semi-dry condition at the expense of a lacerated tum.

At the end of this rather trying day we climbed up on to the bouldery foothills of the Ijembe Hills and there, just below the forest, was a well-swept clearing before a whitewashed school. It turned out that it was a mission school established by the Seventh-day Adventists. In charge were two native teachers who went out of their way to be helpful. Fortunately they spoke English, for now I found that Kiswahili was of no use in Nyasaland – even so short a distance from the boundary.

In the grass at the edge of the forest we pitched our camp. Here the irritating temperament of the Wanyamkusa porters made itself felt, for one and all refused to do anything the Kapitan told them and I was compelled to enter into the fray. Momentarily they were inclined to argue but the secret was to pick on any man who started to grumble and tell him to go for a debbi of water (four gallons weighing forty pounds). This produced laughs from the rest – until it became their turn – and so the sit-down strike was broken!

From the Ijembe camp I crossed the hills to an area of Karroo rocks in which there was a seam of coal about twenty feet thick. This extensive exposure flanked the whole side of the valley. Sparsely overgrown with grass and bushes, it had at some time been swept by a bush fire which had ignited the coal at a number of points. Once begun, these had continued to burn and smoulder for some months, thereby forming conical pits five or six feet deep. This had greatly astonished the locals who thought that the fires heralded the arrival of Satan. Fortunately they went out before he actually reached the surface!

By 31 May I was back at the Kawira River Fish Camp where I began to reorganize for our trip to the west and north of Lake Rukwa. On the eve of our departure a number of local people arrived and began to dance in the middle of the camp. The sound of the pipes, single notes blown at irregular intervals, soon brought together every man, woman and child from both sides of the river. The women and children formed one long line, many of the former dancing with babies on their backs – some old enough to be enjoying it, others completely hidden in the skin pouches. The men danced freely about the band which also kept up a lively movement but remained as a group. From time to time one man would make a dash towards the women, then three or four others would seemingly chase him back again. The whole time everyone pounded madly to the music with their feet and periodically the groups merged in a mêlée of whirling bodies.

All this was entertaining, but why had they come uncalled to dance for me? A little gentle questioning of the Chief and Elders merely elicited the fact that they had come to show me what their dance was like, but previous experience warned me that such an expenditure of energy would not be expected to go unrewarded. Unfortunately these natives did not chew tobacco as did so many of the other tribes, and I was momentarily stumped for something to offer them in return. As I cogitated about this the Chief suddenly announced that they were feeling tired and 'what about stopping?' I suggested that they should then go for I was delighted to see how well they could dance. Neither this, nor my 'boy' Katunge's smiling assurances that we had seen enough had any effect.

I then asked what I could do to help them? To this he suggested that each one of them, and there were certainly 100, should be given something – but he would make no suggestion as to what would be acceptable. Fortunately I had over fifty pounds of sugar in camp so I asked Katunge to put ten pounds in a basin and told the Chief that it was up to him to share it out. He was really delighted, and it was surprising how quickly the dance came to an end!

For the share out all the men and male children down to the tiny two-year-olds came first, the women and girls remaining clustered in a group apart. Nevertheless I noticed that not only did the little children get as much as the men, but plenty was reserved for the women when their turn came.

When all was accomplished the Chief came with profuse thanks but with a slightly wistful look in his eyes; I therefore asked if there had been enough for him? At this he cheered up a bit and admitted that there had not been. So I sent Katunge off to fetch another mugful which sent the Chief away very happy.

While the doling out was going on I had lurked in the shadows studying the expressions of the recipients. All were delighted, first sugaring a finger, then licking it with surprised enjoyment before wrapping up the whole in a corner of whatever cloth they were wearing. If nothing, then a piece of leaf did nearly as well. The children were the most delighted and it was probable they had never tasted sugar before, except perhaps by chewing sugar cane. The ten pounds of sugar had cost me three shillings in Mbeya – and that was expensive. I wondered if so small a sum had ever brought so much pleasure to so many people.

Our next essay was to visit the western and northern shores of the lake. For this we were joined by Arthur Champion, ex-Provincial Commissioner of Turkana, who accompanied us for a time. He was a good traveller and was keen to add to the survey, which he did at every opportunity.

We soon found that even where the tracks were passable, we had constant trouble with the old rickety bridges built from local tree trunks and branches. Often these had to be rebuilt or strengthened and on several occasions we were lucky not to fall through to the river below. So it was that we took to using porters again.

Even marching with porters had its problems for larger areas through which we passed were infected with *pupu*, a kind of scrambling bean which grew amongst the tall grass. Its seed pods appeared to be furry, for they were covered with fine translucent spines like spun glass. The beans could be avoided, but when we were there in July they were shedding these spicules in countless thousands. Thus the grass became dusted with them, and brushing against it we were soon covered with the stuff which felt like being continually stung by nettles. Being so fine, the spicules penetrated our clothing, and once inside irritated the skin making things worse than ever. On the way to camp we hardly knew whether to run, walk or just stop and scratch. A bath relieved the irritation, but that night my temperature rose to 102°F (38.8°C). This *pupu* appeared to be confined to the lower part of the Ufipa escarpment west of Lake Rukwa, and we were relieved to find that it disappeared about 1,000 feet from the bottom. When we had climbed some 2,000 feet with the sun on our backs, and not a breath of wind, we rested beneath a leafy and apparently deciduous tree. Within a minute or two we were again itching and scratching, for it was shedding its dry leaves, which in turn scattered millions of irritating hairs. These seemed invisible, but the maddening skin irritation drove us away.

Vivian Fuchs and Donald MacInnes with crocodile at Ndidu Pool

Even then Ufipa had not finished with us, for we were suddenly pursued by the tiny stingless bees so often encountered in the drier parts of East Africa. These moved in clouds, and being attracted by sweat, they settled on exposed skin. They could not be waved away but had to be rubbed off by hand. Even then there were so many, and they were so persistent that they finally wore us down and in no time were exploring our eyes, ears and noses.

After working our way slowly up the west side of Rukwa we came to the River Rungwa at the northern end. A few miles from the lake the river plunges 100 feet over a scarp to form a large pool of clear water about 100 yards long and sixty yards wide. Here there seemed to be an inexhaustible supply of fish, for every day there were large numbers of men spearing or gaffing them along the shore. One hazard was a large crocodile which inhabited the pool, and was said occasionally to take goats or even children. After ascertaining that it bore no fetish, I shot it in the interests of local safety. It turned out to be old but only thirteen feet long, and apart from the usual stones there was nothing in its stomach.

Next day Donald and I walked for nine hours over a circuitous route which led us home along the course of the river. This had a wide rocky bed which would have been a foaming torrent in the rainy season but was then a stream quietly winding its way from pool to pool. Presently it entered a gorge where one precipitous site was clothed with soft wind-blown sand. There we found a troop of baboons. At one or two prominent points they had posted look-outs, while below the young ones were playing. Like children they scampered up the sandy slope to take turns in leaping into the air to land on the soft sand below. So human was it that I felt like joining them in memory of my own sand-dune days. Instead we sat on the rocks making amiable noises which soon intrigued the juveniles who approached to within thirty yards, and then sat and made faces at us until an anxious adult appeared and sent them packing to join some playmates at a more discreet distance.

A few days later we were again up on the Ufipa and enjoyed a superb view over the northern end of the lake. The great sheet of water extended about eighty miles beyond its most northerly point in 1929, and even ten to fifteen miles beyond the highest point shown as under water in 1901. We came to the famous Zimba Mission and were quite appalled at the conditions.

A more disgusting place I can hardly imagine. We entered through lines of ruined and delapidated huts, the intervening areas strewn with indescribable refuse. The great brick church has fallen into disrepair and the awful brick hovels in which the natives live are truly unfit for human habitation. It is all very well for the natives to have their own latrines but they lose their point when unroofed, unwalled and unused! Needless to say the 'street' and the open spaces suffer instead.

It is a nasty thought to realize that the Mission villages are always fouler than the native ones. We had come from the beautifully kept village of Ngongo to this sink of filth. We had yet to meet the Mission Fathers, although we had seen a white-veiled nun trotting past our camp on a speedy donkey. It was a great sight for she went at a great pace down the hill with her habit blowing in the breeze. We thought how could these holy people live all their lives in such a world of grime and revolting refuse?

Although our camp was some distance from the village, our water had to be drawn from below the Mission. I therefore ensured that all the drinking water was boiled and chlorinated, even using potassium permanganate in the washing water.

As we continued along the low-lying west shore of the lake, we came to a village called Sangansilo where the mosquitoes were excep-

Mosquito refuge west of Lake Rukwa

tionally bad. The locals had devised an ingenious method of ameliorating the scourge which I had never seen elsewhere in Africa. They built structures each consisting of four long poles bearing a platform about twelve feet above the ground. On this a number of people could sleep under a conical grass roof to keep off the rain. On the ground below a smudge fire was lit so that the smoke rose gently up under the sleepers and kept mosquitoes at bay.

There too we found young people with skins the colour of milk chocolate and markedly European features. It transpired that a white man called Bwana Samaki (Fish) had lived there for twenty years and these were his progeny. He had apparently died some years before we came, and the eldest girl could hardly take her eyes off us for she had seemingly never seen a white man – she could not remember her father. Perhaps too he had been responsible for the idea behind the building of their mosquito platforms.

Pushing on, there was suddenly a great darkening of the sky ahead indicating a grass fire. Soon a black cloud obscured the sun, which reduced the glare and gave cooler conditions. Then the air became filled with increasingly large black and grey flakes, the remains of burning grass carried high into the sky. We walked for more than an hour through this 'black snow storm' as the smell of burning grew stronger. Then we heard fierce crackling like the sound of musketry while great columns of black smoke billowed into the sky obscuring everything ahead. Finally we saw the fire sweeping towards us at a great rate. We watched fascinated as an arm of flame swept through the tall grass and caught the trees outflanking us. In a moment we turned and were running back to a small clearing we had passed. Leaving the porters sitting safely on their loads, Katunge and I advanced again and were able to choose a moment when the flames near the track were less fierce, then we dashed through to the windward side. There among the smoking ruins of a thousand trees we watched great sheets of flame roaring forward through the ten-foot grass. It was an overwhelming experience to watch it all at such close quarters. In half-an-hour the fire had burnt its way back to the clearing where our porters had taken refuge, and we saw them sitting placidly in the choking smoke quite unperturbed.

That afternoon we came to Kapenta village and camped in a cleared patch. As we finished eating the sky again darkened and the crackling of fire could be heard. Soon our village was surrounded with a ring of flame often fifty feet high. So great was the heat that the updraught blew the leaves of the Borassus palms up towards the sky like skirts above the heads of the trees. That night the 3,000-foot Ufipa escarpment was a splendid sight as the fire swept up the gullies and astride the ridges in a complicated pattern of flame.

A few days later we climbed up those burnt-out slopes and camped by Lake Kwela at nearly 6,000 feet. It was then about one-and-a-half miles long and half-a-mile wide, but was clearly more extensive than usual because of the number of old termite nests standing up out of the water some fifty yards from the shore. What really surprised us was the existence of hippopotami in the lake. They could not have climbed the steep escarpment, and wherever they had come from it must have been a very long walk!

I found another unexpected inhabitant when I waded out to use the bushes on one of the termite nests as a photographic 'hide'. As I scrambled up the steep side, a large coiled python was suddenly gazing into my face a few feet away. Retreating hastily, but careful not to alarm it, I called for my rifle and shot it. Katunge waded in to collect it but the reflex writhing of the coils was too life-like and he fell into the water where the snake eventually sank. Now unable to see the 'monster', he fled, floundering and splashing his way to the safety of the shore. It was finally hooked out with a branch and found to be ten feet long with an excellent skin. We brought it home as a specimen.

We left the Rukwa area to begin the long trek back to Naivasha via Abercorn (now Mbala), Mbeya and Nairobi. Beset with the usual broken bridges and springs, we finally came to rest with a broken back axle for which we had no spares. The replacement had to come from Nairobi and we were delayed for two weeks. This gave us the opportunity to climb up to the Rungwe crater, where the highest point was over 10,000 feet. With the car going again, we set off for Kenya where we had to settle up our affairs and catch a boat in Mombasa to bring us home.

The expedition had been interesting, and we had made considerable collections of plants, insects, Mollusca and reptiles, but our main purpose, geology, had been disappointing. Since my interest had been to trace Pleistocene events and Donald MacInnes' fossil mammalia, we were both frustrated. Although we had examined extensive lake beds, they appeared to be entirely barren, not even yielding stone tools which we had been so used to finding in Kenya. Thus there was little evidence with which to date the deposits.

Chapter 9

The Second World War

In September 1938 I returned to England, and already the threat of war was in the air. Even during the voyage home Italy's attack on Abyssinia from Eritrea, together with Hitler's activities, had led to long discussions about the dangerous situation developing in Europe. Indeed, our ship was 'buzzed' by Italian aircraft in the Mediterranean. One of us strongly favoured joining the Navy on the grounds that 'you can be proud of a ship, but I'm damned if you can be proud of a trench.' I rather agreed.

It was great to get home and I was excited at the prospect of meeting my new daughter. She was a truly lovely baby, with fair curls and wonderfully deep blue eyes. But she lay endlessly quite still in her cot, doing none of the things that a six-month-old should be attempting. Completely unresponsive when I tried to play with her, she did not lift her head, and was not able to sit up without being propped on pillows. Feeding her took a very long time, and both Joyce and her nannie, who adored her, were beginning to wonder why she was so behind in everything – she did not even kick her little legs.

Before my return my father had already suggested that the child should be seen by the best consultant specialist we could find in Harley Street. So it was that Joyce and I took her down to London.

The doctor examined her alone for a long time and then invited me into his consulting room on my own. Gravely he told me that Rosalind was so severely spastic that there was absolutely no hope at all that she could ever be helped or trained towards making any sort of family relationships or becoming in any way independent. He pointed out what I had already observed – that the entire resources of the household would have to be centred on her care, and it would be virtually impossible for little Hilary to enjoy any normal nursery life in our circumstances. He emphasized that these would become increasingly tragic as the years went by. He further said that nearly all such children for whom nothing could be done had an expectation of only eight years of life, and he strongly advised me to consider putting her into the care of professional nurses. He then said briskly that his fee would be two guineas so would I please leave a cheque on his desk, and he left the room.

It was a knock-out blow – far worse that anything I had prepared myself for – and now I had to tell Joyce. My difficulty was enhanced by her early experience of a spastic child. Both her parents had died at an early age, and the family had placed Joyce and her elder sister Doris in the care of a couple named Moreland who had had an only child who was spastic. I thought this would make it doubly difficult for Joyce to accept the situation which now faced us with Rosalind. To my relief she took the news with fortitude, and in the next few days we were able to discuss the family future. It was an agonizing crisis. My parents were, as always, very supportive and, like the doctor, they felt strongly that our little daughter would be better off in a home with professional care. After much heart-searching and grief, that was the course we finally took.

We found a home near us where we were allowed to visit the baby as often as we wished, but sadly she grew into a pretty little girl who never recognized us, nor spoke, nor smiled. She could not walk or feed herself, nor even sit up in bed without support. Her nurses took tender care of her physical needs but none of us could reach her mentally. Mercifully, just before her eighth birthday, she quietly died. We could only feel happy for her.

Soon after my return I had applied to join the RNVR, but at thirty I was considered to be too old, and they turned me down. So a few days later I found myself in the Drill Hall in Cambridge, standing in a long line of volunteers for the Territorial Army. We stripped. A corporal put a tape round each chest in turn, inviting us to breathe deeply so that he could record the expansion. A sing-song repetitive patter developed between him and a very bored sergeant busy writing it all down.

'Three-and-a-half inches,' from the corporal.

'Three-and-a-half,' repeated the sergeant.

My turn came and to my embarrassment I became conspicuous.

'Six inches,' intoned the corporal.

'Do it again.'

'Six inches,' repeated the corporal, sticking to his guns.

'Three-and-a-half,' decreed the sergeant, pulling his rank and writing it down.

'Married?' enquired the sergeant.

'Yes,' I admitted.

'Got your certificate?'

I had never thought of it – and hadn't.

'Must have a Marriage Certificate,' admonished the sergeant. 'Bring it here next week.'

I retired abashed and went home to ask Joyce for her Marriage Lines. Her face went blank. Worse still – neither of us could remember the name of the church in which we had been married. After much concentration I visualized a long straight road with an avenue of trees in Hampstead, at the top of which stood a church.

I took the car down to London and began driving round and round Hampstead in ever-decreasing circles – and suddenly, there it was! The Vicar was somewhat surprised but most cooperative, and the following week I was back at the Drill Hall.

In the meantime Higher Authority had written to inform me that in view of my school OTC qualifications I should be applying for a commission. I produced this letter to a scathing sergeant who obviously thought the idea preposterous.

'All right. Got any children?' he intoned.

'Yes,' I admitted, 'two daughters.'

'Birth Certificates?' he demanded.

'Well no – but I've brought my Marriage Certificate,' I reported triumphantly.

'Don't need that now,' he crowed. 'Only soldiers have to have Marriage Certificates. Officers have to have Birth Certificates. Come back next week.'

It was getting harder than I had expected. It seemed a subtle distinction that apparently officers were allowed to father offspring indiscriminately, while soldiers' children were required to be legitimate. I went home again and we wrote to Somerset House. One week later I finally joined the Territorial Army and in June 1939 I was gazetted Second Lieutenant in the Cambridgeshire Regiment.

A staff-sergeant was placed in charge of a posse of about twenty of us. Once a week we began learning the military arts in a large field in Melbourne village. Here we were marched up and down and round and round, and taught how to 'throw our voices' — Communications Drill it was called — until we could shout loud enough to march each other around and end up roughly in the right place. We all rather enjoyed it. All, that is, except poor Harrison. He sadly never managed to develop the right vocal chords, no matter how hard he tried. One day, under his command, we set off across the field marching into the wind, and he lost us forever since he just couldn't produce enough noise to turn us about. Gleefully, we solemnly marched straight into a ditch and then into the hedge on the other side, where we subsided in general chaos. Later I learnt that poor Harrison had joined the RAF!

For the rest of us it was good fun in the fresh air, and our training bouts ended very pleasantly in the local pub where the staff sergeant cheerfully joined us.

At this time I had returned to the Sedgwick Museum to write up the results of the Lake Rukwa Expedition. I was also negotiating for a job in the Sudan, where I knew that the only geologist was about to retire. Suddenly all that changed, for war was declared on Germany in September 1939. Instead of prosecuting expeditions and researching the results I found myself in a new world, where quite different skills were needed. It was like going to school and university all over again, but I determined to dedicate myself to the new order and enjoy all I could of the experience.

As soon as we were called up in earnest, I became a desk wallah. As more and more men poured in, the battalions, brigades and divisions all rapidly sub-divided, spawning equivalent units, and the paperwork was unbelievable. On one day I found myself facing endless columns of names for enrolment which required my signature over 800 times.

The Second Battalion of the Cambridgeshires came into being with Headquarters at Wisbech, to which I was appointed Adjutant. We lived in requisitioned houses, and at eight o'clock each morning I found myself nervously bellowing orders at 800 men as the battalion paraded. A few months later I was thankful to be relieved by a regular officer, and welcomed an appointment to Brigade Headquarters as Transport Officer.

This was much more my field and I enjoyed it, though I was constantly amazed at how little the new citizen army, most of them from urban environments, knew about how to look after their vehicles and keep out of trouble. With zeal I began taking my own small section out and deliberately exposing them to awkward situations to see how they would tackle problems.

Once a driver backed his truck into a farmyard without taking account of a manure heap. He was soon stuck with wheels spinning madly.

'What about finding a rope and we'll pull it out,' I suggested tentatively.

'Oh no, Sir – we'll just hitch on another truck,' decreed my sergeant confidently.

I waited expectantly, and within minutes we had two trucks firmly bogged down, while the men prepared a third to send in after them. Finally I produced a rope, and there was general astonishment when they found that three men, aided by the spinning wheels, could pull a truck out quite easily. On these kinds of occasion no one ever admitted they had been wrong, of course, but by such small stratagems they quickly learnt useful lessons based on my African experience, and became first class 'expeditioners', taking pride in their skills.

All the available doctors were needed in hospitals, but day-to-day accidents happened in small units, too. I had taken my African medical kit with me, and soon found myself getting increasingly involved in small emergencies, until finally I was regarded as the unofficial 'witch doctor'. Indeed, the Brigadier encouraged me to take regular Sick Parades each morning!

What started as something of a joke often turned into a real thing. One day my sergeant rushed into my quarters in a panic. 'Could you see Private Butt, Sir? He's got blood spurting out a foot in front of his face.'

It sounded both bizarre and improbable, but I hurried out, to find the chap had scratched a pimple off the very tip of his nose, cutting a small artery. Blood was being pumped out with every heart beat and forming a sort of long comet's tail – it really looked most extraordinary. All I did was to stick a patch over the hole and, to his amazement (and my relief) it stopped!

Vivian Fuchs 1940

Winter was hard that year. Snow covered the country and there was no vehicle movement. One day a man was brought to me who I was sure was suffering from meningitis. I telephoned the nearest army hospital and requested an ambulance, but a young disbelieving doctor informed me that my story was most unlikely as the condition is very difficult to diagnose. Under pressure he finally said they could not send an ambulance, but 'If you can get him through, we'll admit him.'

My driver and I took the patient twelve miles through the blizzard. The following morning a very surprised doctor phoned, saying,

'Most extraordinary thing – but he *has* got meningitis.' Thereafter the 'witch doctor' had no more trouble in getting any drugs he asked for.

Young soldiers can be alarmingly careless with their firearms. The nearest I ever came to death was in my own office. It was on the first floor of a commandeered house. Engrossed in paperwork one morning, I suddenly decided I must answer a call of nature. I was away only about one minute, and returned to notice chips of wood on the floor and a hole in the seat of my chair, then another hole through the casement window. I thought a bullet must have come from an enemy aircraft which had flown over us, but suddenly I became petrified as I worked out from the broken wood on the floor that whatever it was must have come *up* through the chair on which I sat and *exited* through the window.

I shot down to the Guard Room below.

'Oh yes, Sir,' said the corporal cheerfully. 'Extraordinary, really. Private Higgs was just cleaning his rifle, Sir – and it just went off – just like that, Sir!'

Only by the grace of God not right through my bottom.

It is a Court Martial offence for officers or soldiers to strike each other; but one fine day I walked into the workshop and found a young driver with a lighted fag hanging from his mouth peering closely into his petrol tank. My reflexes were fast and to the point. I struck him across the face and sent the cigarette spinning away sideways. His were equally positive. He turned and socked me straight in the jaw. I don't know which of us was the more surprised, but suddenly the man realized either the enormity of his crime or the danger to which he had exposed himself, and turned very white. We tacitly agreed not to report the incident.

At this time the Brigade was stationed at Barton Mills, not far from Cambridge. One night there was a 'stand to' as it was reported that German parachutists could be landing. As part of the hurried scramble sentries were posted at strategic points with orders to challenge anyone moving. One of them saw a white 'billowing' form which he took to be a parachute and quite properly he challenged, not once but three times. Getting no answer in the dark he fired his rifle and the shape subsided to the ground. He had shot the farmer's white horse.

More memorable for me was the message received on 2 June 1940 saying that Joyce had had a son that day. Given compassionate leave, I raced home and was soon admiring the new baby. Although our unhappy experience with poor little Rosalind had inevitably made us anxious about having another child (and in those days there was no way of monitoring pregnancies by scans), we had categorically been advised that the chance of a repetition was so remote it could be ignored. Even so the previous months had been full of anxiety and sometimes dread for both of us; but the advice proved true, for Peter Ernest Kay Fuchs was to be a particularly robust baby and brought us great joy.

A few months later the Brigade was ordered to Galashiels, staging at Catterick Camp in Yorkshire. The rules laid down that convoys must move at thirty miles per hour, leaving a space of eighty yards between each vehicle, thus preventing enemy bombers from destroying more than one truck at a time. This also enabled civilian traffic to overtake safely. But of course if convoys meet when travelling in opposite directions, it produces vehicles on both sides of the road with only forty yards at most between each. This can turn into something of a 'bending race' for civilian motorists with the nerve to keep going.

I had learnt the theory, but there were no motorways, and towns could not be by-passed. Moving the Brigade, including the artillery, entailed a convoy covering twenty-two miles, our route passing through many small villages and towns like Stamford, Newark and Doncaster. My role was to organize the operation and then shepherd the flock along on a motor bike, and the farther north we travelled, the more icy the conditions became.

As the leading trucks entered a town they inevitably closed up and lost speed, the convoy getting slower and slower, until eventually the gunners who brought up the rear just stopped at some village café and enjoyed a tea-break. Once through a town, the leaders charged ahead once more, the centre of the column became attenuated and the artillery hastily paid their bills, wiped crumbs off their faces, and rushed to catch up. Whatever we did the blizzard blew, the whole grand progress being a very cold nightmare.

One of the last vehicles, which happened to be carrying my holdall of personal gear, produced an electrical fault and burnt out. No one was hurt, but some time later remnants were found by the civilian police who salvaged a burnt boot with 'Fuchs' written inside it. This led them to suspect that a German spy had been dropped, burnt his parachute on landing, and was now at large, which in turn led to a country-wide hunt. Months afterwards they had finally tracked me down, and paid me a visit in Scotland to find out the truth of the matter.

In Scotland we trained long and hard. The 18th Division, though we did not know it, was ear-marked for service in Singapore. After some months we were moved to Knutsford in Cheshire, our Headquarters in a beautiful stately home whence exciting exercises were planned to test the initiative of junior officers. In one such exercise my lot played the 'enemy' and we were told to get into and take complete control of the town of Stafford. Small parties went in by varied and ingenious ruses, one in a threshing machine, some sailed up the river in a barge, others in washing baskets and some with ice-cream barrows. My allotted target was the railway station, so the logical thing seemed to me to go by train.

... I led a party of 'German parachutists' to attack the railway station ... We stopped the Wolverhampton Express at Penkridge, and concealed in the engine and the guard's van ran straight into Stafford station, where we leapt out and tore over the railway lines and sidings to 'bomb' and 'smash up' the signal box ... I had an officer in civilian clothes as Fifth Column who had a wireless set in his suitcase and communicated HQ dispositions direct to us before we entered the town. Later he was caught by the police because he had no Identity Card, but after a lot of argument they let him go ... he was again caught and then they found a revolver on him, with the result that those who had let him go caught a tremendous rocket ...

A few weeks later I was detailed to go on a Staff Course at Worcester College, Oxford. Just after I arrived there the 18th Division was ordered overseas, and I was told that I would be rejoining them at the end of the Course. They arrived in Singapore just in time to be captured without ever firing a shot.

I was next posted to the 7th Suffolks, then in Poole as part of the defence system of the south coast. We laid minefields and erected barricades along the beaches, and then moved on to Westgate, a ghost town from which practically all civilians had been evacuated. My platoon was sent as an Advance Party to prepare for the Battalion's arrival. We took up quarters in a small empty hotel on the sea front, and began scrubbing out the indescribably filthy billets which had not been occupied for fifteen months, getting in forty tons of coal, ten tons of coke, two tons of anthracite, paraffin etc.

... suddenly comes this great scare; there are nine mines floating inshore ... While we are watching anxiously another one comes bobbing round the corner of the cliff ... We are not allowed to shoot at them to sink them as they are thought to be British – and are supposed to be immobilized on breaking loose. Presently the nearest one begins to bang against the sea wall ... Watching from an open window I saw a flash. My reaction was so quick that I was lying flat on the floor ... before the blast reached us.

On going out to see the damage we found that a great mass of the sea wall had been heaved up, the road was covered with fragments of iron, and both Pridhams and the Ingleton Hotels had been wrecked.

All the glass smashed, doors torn off their hinges, windows blown out, roofs lifted off and ceiling plaster lying on all the floors. The scenes of desolation are indescribable; as one goes through this empty town where no one lives one finds places where meals are still set on tables where people were eating when they left suddenly after Dunkirk ... gigantic kitchens left just as they were when the last meal was served ... I even collected a large lollipop some child had left uneaten. Today we have been hunting for suitable houses for cooking, dining and sleeping the 300 men who would have gone to the two hotels which have been destroyed ... more black-out is being made, gas stoves are being put into the new billets, glass has to be replaced, and water, gas and electricity laid on again ...

When the Battalion finally arrived, as a prelude to action overseas we were constantly sent on night exercises – a time when enemy aircraft were always overhead *en route* to their targets farther inland, so black-out regulations were very stringently observed. It was quite difficult driving around endless lanes by the glimmer which came from heavily masked headlights, and it soon transpired that not many officers were very good at reading maps in these conditions. The top brass became irate at so often finding themselves lost in some wet corner of nowhere which the subaltern in charge of their transport could not identify on his map. Our nocturnal wanderings sometimes ended in complete chaos.

... we came upon the most incredible tangles with tanks. In one village heavy tanks were advancing along a narrow lane when they met a tank obstacle of danaert wire defended by infantry. The wire was drawn up into the tanks together with some complete unrolled coils which were mashed up and torn to shreds. As the wire is high-tensile steel it did later stop two tanks and immobilized them ... Others charging through the smoke screen had smoke candles thrown on to them so that the periscopes were largely obscured ... an old scarecrow thrown on to a tank completely cut off all vision. The driver was mad and went straight on, and leaving the road charged through a fence, a ditch and somebody's garden. The one following ran down an Army lorry which was not really in the battle at all. Soon the village roads, all four of them, were completely blocked with Matildas. Then came twelve 40-tonners from the 'enemy' who, unable to get through the blocked roads, waddled through the cottage gardens and hedges, leaving a trail of destruction including a gaping hole in a 10-foot stone wall ... The streets were a sight to see – all covered in torn wire and broken bricks, clods of earth and torn up pavements ...

One night it fell to me to get the General himself, accompanied by my Brigadier, to an obscure temporary headquarters sited in a field 'some twelve miles outside the town. It was cold and very wet as I sat huddled in the front of our staff car, clutching a torch and poring over a map, my task to provide the driver with clear and incisive instructions *before* he overshot the turnings as we wove a tortuous route towards our objective. When we finally turned into the right field spot on and deposited our passengers at the encampment exactly on time, the driver never once having had to reverse, the General was pleased. And that is how, shortly afterwards, I was appointed Intelligence Officer, 25th Army Tank Brigade!

This job did not last for long because I had already volunteered for service in East Africa. I was one of the few people with knowledge of northern Kenya and the Ethiopian border, I spoke Swahili, and felt that perhaps I could make some worthwhile contribution to the war effort in an area where I had many native contacts.

It was a vain hope, for the desk wallah at the War Office handling our postings was obviously not much of a geographer, and must have filed my form under 'Speaks African'. For I was posted to *West* African Command Headquarters at Achimota in the Gold Coast – an area of which I had no experience and where the lingua franca was Hausa. I must confess to frustration and great disappointment.

With just time to spend two days with my parents at Heatherdene (it was to be the last time I saw my Mother), I made a Will, formed a Trust for the children, gave Joyce a Power of Attorney, saw the bank, and packed furiously in between whiles. All the family partings were painful.

I left home on 27 January 1942, travelling up to the Clyde where our troop ship proved to be the Polish s s *Sobiesky*, of 11,000 tons and built in Britain. With a Polish crew, she had put into a British port on her way back from America when Germany entered Poland. We ploughed off straight into bad weather until we were pitching and wallowing in enormous seas.

Soon the decks and saloons began to empty and pale-faced men stood nonchalantly or with introspective expressions close to the ship's rails. The inexperienced showed their ignorance by leaning upon the windward rail, only to realize too late why the lee side was the more crowded ... I was feeling squeamish and had a nasty pain in the top of my head, but managed to eat every course of every meal ...

By 1 February everyone was about again, the decks were crowded and there was little hope of a seat in the lounge. The officers' quarters were designed for sixty First Class passengers but we numbered 280. About 1,000 men lived in the holds. We also carried two Polish padres (one a Bishop), numerous civilian Masters whose ships had been torpedoed and who were now joining new ones, American steel men travelling to India, bankers for Cairo and technicians going to Gibraltar. We were guarded by H M S *California*, an armed merchant cruiser, and two destroyers.

Gibraltar appeared as a little gleaming jewel on the port horizon, with lighted houses, a strange scene to which we had become surprisingly unaccustomed after two-and-a-half years of war. Here we transhipped to the *Royal Waterman*, previously used for the Irish crossing, and waited for the convoy to load.

I am sitting in the lounge with about eighty other officers where a total of thirty should be. All are smoking, not only can one not see across the room but the eyes smart and the chest feels raw and constricted. God knows what it will be like in the tropics ... there are no fans, and all doors and windows have to be shut because of the black-out. We have been named the 'Hell Ship' or '*Altmark* the Second' ...

Fortunately we were finally removed from *Royal Waterman* to the *Batory*, another more comfortable Polish vessel which had accompanied *Sobiesky* from Glasgow. In her we sailed for Bathurst in the Gambia, calling at Freetown, Sierra Leone before disembarking at

Takoradi in the Gold Coast. From there we took the train to Accra where the Army Headquarters was in Achimota College. There I found that the 81st and 82nd West African Divisions were recruiting and training men from Nigeria, Gambia and Sierra Leone for service in the Burma campaign.

It was the end of the dry season and the countryside looked parched, but a few shrubs and trees somehow managed to remain clothed with a profusion of flowers. Every morning I walked to the office past a high hedge of brilliant red hibiscus, amongst which green trees covered with pendant yellow flowers like, but twice the size of, laburnums. Lilies forced their way through the iron-hard ground, and where householders had bothered to save their bath-water for their gardens, bougainvillaea cascaded over the walls.

Coming from beleagured Britain to a region virtually untouched by war was a strange experience. Food was good, with plenty of meat, sugar, eggs and every kind of fruit, but the pace of life was slow and inactive. I found the work uncongenial and boring, and was not happy stuck in an office dealing with personnel records. I began to learn Hausa from my African 'boy'.

Soon after I arrived there was considerable consternation when quite suddenly we found that the native desertion rate rocketed into something of a general exodus. However, it was short-lived for equally suddenly they all started coming back again. It transpired that it was all a question of priorities. The men had gone home for the rainy season to make sure their women had planted next year's crops properly. This ensured, they happily returned to draw their pay and get on with the war.

At Headquarters everyone was given one day a week off, and I used mine by acquiring first a bicycle, and later a motorbike and a surfboard, and spent my free time working hard until I really mastered the sport. The coast was notoriously dangerous and the authorities insisted that all bathing was done between two posts set up on the beach by the local Chief, who also supplied a rescue team and a surf boat for anyone in difficulties. Only too often their services were needed, for the nearby American air station had a constantly moving population of men on their way to the Middle East. Many of them anxious for a bathe got into trouble.

When the rains came in June, one noticed the extraordinary

prevalence of fungi. Books left unaired for a few days grew a light mould, shoes not in use, and even the linings of topis, became covered with a rich green growth. Some of us suffered fungus foot-rot, others developed fungal ear infections. Food was highly susceptible, and once opened nothing could be left lying around.

I took pains to relieve the austere decor of the 'A' Office by the introduction of a few fossils, large shells and beautiful local stones as paperweights, and encouraged my pet chameleons to climb around on the electric light and telephone cables. This foreign atmosphere was regarded with suspicion and disapproval at first,

But now everyone enquires daily after the health of Arabella who is expectant. Unfortunately my zoological knowledge has let me down, for I do not know whether to expect eggs or young chameleons.

Sadly Arabella died in an egg-bound condition, and my autopsy revealed that she contained forty-four large-sized eggs, which we then tried to hatch out – unfortunately without success.

One day I found a small African boy with a pigeon from which he had torn out the large wing feathers so that it could not fly. I asked what he wanted for it and he said, 'One and sixpence.' I gave him a box of matches instead and took the bird home. In a few days 'George' became quite tame and I began to put him on a bush outside the office for an airing. Each time, after an hour or two, he flopped to the ground, climbed the flight of stairs and came searching for me. Soon he was flying round the office, but he never tried to leave through the open windows. Once in my absence he disappeared and no one could find him, but when I returned two hours later he was roosting on the top of a window. Then a dreadful thing happened.

Yesterday George flew down from my room and swooped into the Mess hallway ahead of us ... frightened by a passing steward he flew down the passage and into the dining-room where he perched on a high wire which runs across the room. In a moment our Polish doctor leapt to his feet and seizing the wretched bird by the tail, pulled all his feathers out ... Now after six weeks recuperation and having regrown his pinions, George has to start all over again with his tail feathers after only one day of flying. I was *very* annoyed with that doctor.

However, George came to the office for his weekly Saturday afternoon outing, and much to my astonishment managed to fly up onto the roof where he crash-landed. Later he again proved he could still fly by visiting the office and coming to roost on my shoulder. But then, strutting about the table, he became very bold and showed signs of broodiness!

Indeed, we have now started calling him 'Georgina' as any advances made by dipping the hand like the bowing in courtship induces a trembling of 'her' wings and reciprocal bowing movements accompanied by evident signs of affection ... Today Georgina joined us in the outside loggia and went from table to table climbing all over everyone without the slightest fear ... She has become a great favourite in the Mess ...

Alas, the story ends unhappily, for one day she disappeared and I feared she had become too trusting with a strange African and gone into a stockpot. But after much searching I found her dead in the Mess kitchen, hidden behind two large boxes having sickened in some way.

About this time plans were being brewed to harass the German troops encamped some miles to the north, where they occupied French territory as a result of the capitulation in Paris. Small mounted parties were envisaged, trained to make night raids, cut communications, destroy ammunition dumps and generally keep the Germans on the *qui vive*. The possibility of some action at last! The only trouble was I couldn't ride – it was essential to remedy this quickly, and I arranged for a horse to be made available.

After an early lunch I was ready when the chap arrived with a rather large stallion with an extremely primitive saddle and two pieces of rope representing the reins. The animal seemed in high spirits and danced around, causing me some doubts as to my ability to stick on. After patting its neck and receiving what looked like several extremely dirty looks out of the corner of its eye I jumped astride. Being now for the first time on the back of a horse I found that the ground receded a lot. It felt rather like standing ready for a dive from a high board, except that the board was a movable factor. Not having a key, self-starter, clutch, gear or other instrument to make it go, I indicated to the syce that he should do something about it. Led by him we walked gently off towards the beach, but had to negotiate a steep and stony path down the cliffside. There the horse's head seemed to disappear as I sat sloping backwards expecting the animal to squat on its haunchs at any minute.

However, we arrived safely on the sands and my steed seemed inclined to linger. Suddenly I was horrified to hear the syce deliver two hard welts with a cane on his backside. The response was small, so – encouraged – I did the same, and we set off at a great pace straight into the sea.

With many Hoh Hohs! and much sawing with the bit, I managed to stop. Coming out of the sea we set off once more, this time attempting a trot, with disastrous results to myself and the horse, ending up with a right-hand turn into the sea. Pull as I might, I could not make him turn left. Then the horse suddenly turned round and bit my foot, and before I could recover myself he tore off down the beach at full gallop. Somehow I managed to stay on, but without any hope of stopping him, and the inevitable right-hand turn headed us straight for the cliffs. There my thrice-damned mount proceeded to career along the edge of the cliff where natives had dug innumerable holes in the sand looking for crabs. These were three to four feet wide and up to two feet deep. There being no hope of avoiding them, I left it to the horse – round, through, over and in he went, one after the other – I was terrified, but still in the saddle. Finally achieving a halt, I looked back to see a small black figure stumbling after us. He arrived in streams of sweat with the profound statement, 'He know you no know how!'

Next day I had another go with even less success. I let my steed thunder up and down the beach but nothing tired him, and finding I could not persuade him to stop, I turned him into the sea. This galvanized him into further action and I got a good sousing, which in fact was quite fun. He then took me back up the beach straight to a small pit containing a large palm tree stump. Over this he jumped at breakneck speed, and by the grace of God I went with him. Finally we came to a standstill and I dismounted stiffly – my legs were dithering like castanets and I was stiff for days.

In the event it was all a waste of time, for the exciting 'campaign' I was preparing myself for never took place.

On 20 August 1942 I received a cable saying that my mother had suddenly and quietly died of a heart attack, and had been found sitting peacefully in her chair in the conservatory. It was a dreadful shock and I felt devastated.

I have grown up with parents always quietly there, people to whom one has always looked for guidance and some appreciation of the small trials and triumphs of life ... I look back now and think of all the things I should have said and done, and how much more that will be in the future which would be nice to share with them both ... I only hope that they realized that I have always taken great account of what they said, and have been no less appreciative of the wonderful treatment I have always received.

My mother was always so uncomplaining of her physical disability and took such an interest in life, I could not get used to the idea that she had gone when I was so far away, and would remain far away for a long time more. I had never forgotten that when Hilary was born she had said to me, 'Now you and I have a stake in the future,' a true expression of the real meaning of heredity – that always something of the parent is passed on to live eternally in the generations that follow, generations for whose very future we were now fighting.

By the end of November the battle of Stalingrad was going in our favour, General Timoshenko's armies had already captured three Army Divisions and slaughtered many thousands. In Tunisia Montgomery was in touch with the enemy at El Ageila, there was at last light at the end of the tunnel. But for us the same routine went on. It was a depressed Command and we felt out of the war. By now my Hausa was quite good, and going round the native market I was struck by the number of witch doctors and 'Juju' shops. These displayed a great variety of objects used in African 'medicine' – dried flesh and bones like baboon skulls, birds' feet, lizard and crocodile skins, various claws and many unidentifiable fragments. I have little doubt that had one had the confidence of the owners and sufficient entrée, one would have found that certain human remains were also obtainable, though this was strictly against the law.

One day when I was Orderly Officer an African soldier came in to report sick, announcing, 'As I was lighting my pipe from the fire last night I was bending down when a loud explosion occurred and I felt a blow on the chest. I thought nothing more of it till this morning when I found my shirt covered in blood.' He then proudly pointed out a small round hole just below the right pectoral muscle and a slightly larger one two inches below and posterior to the axilla. The wounds had in fact been caused by a bullet which had passed right through his body. Evidently he or someone else must have been throwing live cartridges into the fire to hear them go bang! The wounded patient was quite happy about it all and said it would only hurt him 'small small'.

I was always interested in the methods by which the locals caught fish with seine-nets, some weighing up to thirty pounds. They included sting-rays, skates and parrot fish with four strong teeth for breaking up shellfish. These can inflate themselves to an enormous size by blowing out their speckled stomachs. The small boys would apply their mouths to those of the fish, forcibly distend them by blowing until the unfortunate creatures floated willy-nilly upside down. There were also fat fish, long fish, thin fish, and fish with the most peculiar faces. The sorting took place in an enormous crowd who shouted and yelled abuse at the tops of their voices. Each fresh outburst culminated in the indiscriminate throwing of handfuls of sand, to disperse the innumerable thieves, who, creeping into the crowd, would carry off an illicit prize at every opportunity.

One highlight of my life was the day I was taken on a trip out to sea in a surfboat by fishermen laying a seine-net. It was an honour, for I was invited to go despite rough weather. We fought our way out through the surf and once clear I seized a paddle from one of the men who was trying to lay out the net. The paddlers kept up a rhythmic sing-song to which they kept time, and when after a bit it became apparent that I knew how to paddle and was pulling my weight, they also let me set the timing – chanting 'Massa he savy, Massa he savy,' over and over again. This was a great compliment!

To my pleasure I had been recommended for the Camberley Staff Course, and on 30 June 1943 I was told that I had been chosen to fill one of the six highly coveted places allotted to the West African Command. While waiting to return home for this the two Divisions we had been training sailed for Burma under the command of General Gifford who, as is usual, took his personal Military Secretary with him. It was some weeks before the new General would arrive to take over. I was already DAAG and during this hiatus I also held the temporary appointment of Military Secretary. The two departments worked closely together, and this led to a situation where I spent the mornings wearing one hat and writing letters to myself in the other. After lunch I hurried across, put on my other hat and answered myself – all done by tea time. The Army seldom produced such quick decision-making!

There was one more adventure before I left the Command. At the beginning of July three of us left on a two-day trip to the River Volta. The Major whose car we were using was reputed to be the worst driver who ever handled a vehicle. In addition he was so short that he could only just see out of the windscreen and had the greatest difficulty in reaching the accelerator or the foot brake. We rose at 4.30 am and loaded our equipment, and as Deakin then insisted on bringing his 'boy' too, we were grossly overloaded. Ready to start, I noticed a smell of petrol, but investigation over a pit showed that the leak was not serious. On the other hand, I also noticed that his tyres were very soft so we pumped them all up. Once away the most terrifying drive of my life began. It started to rain, and soon the roads were wet and muddy, with skidding an imminent probability.

There we were, tearing along roads with four-foot-deep run-off ditches on either side and sharp bends around which we careered, free-wheeling in an ecstasy of mad judgement ... As the rain increased, the low-lying parts of the road flooded ... Crash! Splash! and amid a shower of muddy water, with three yards of visibility through the murky windscreen, we career on.

About this time our owner-driver informed us that the hood used to leak but in the proper manner of waterproofing ... he had spread this, that and the other on the roof – and wasn't it grand? But soon we were receiving a steady shower of water and had to cover ourselves with waterproof sheets – I used my gas cape.

Presently short sight, steaming glasses and the muddy windscreen caused our chauffeur to hit six inches of water so fast that the engine petered out as the ignition became soaked, and we were stranded.

We sat and did crossword puzzles in the rain with waterproof sheets stretched across our laps to catch the miniature cloud burst now penetrating the roof. I ended up with a pool five inches deep in my lap, and in trying to pour it away on the floor I allowed it to slip through a hole and fall straight on to the seat on which I was sitting. A six-wheel-drive Army lorry came towards us, and the driver stopped to tell us that the road ahead was now impassable for normal cars.

Still following the policy of waiting for the rain to stop, we went back to our puzzles, but presently Shaw wiped the rear window and on peering through it gave a sharp yelp – there behind us the whole countryside was flooded, the gathering water pouring across the road in a sheet two hundred yards wide, and already twelve to eighteen inches deep. Worse still, we could see small waterfalls forming as the road surface broke away.

Shaw and I bundled out and hurried our driver into a precipitate retreat to the far side of the torrent:

With the useless engine and the extreme need for speed (we had visions of the car being left cut off for a week or more) we pushed it slowly backwards, wading through the water for a quarter-of-a-mile. Once safely on the other side I dried out the distributor and we were off home, with only the mild hazards of wild down-hill plunges in a free-wheeling car guided by a semi-blind driver through deepening mud!

We reached home and I was back in the office by 11.30 am, my last effort to take a day's local leave over.

On 24 July three of us left GHQ and drove through 170 miles of forest and bush to Takoradi, where we joined the queue of about 1,200 men along the coast waiting for ships to get them home. I was one of only a handful who had been given 'priority passages' and after two weeks I finally sailed for Freetown. Here we transhipped to the Dutch *Dempo*, originally built for 400 first class passengers – now she carried 3,000 of us. It was an uneventful but tedious voyage, and as we finally moved into the damp chill waters of the Atlantic most of us went down with colds!

On the morning of 9 September we awoke to find ourselves anchored in the Clyde and began the hassle of securing landing papers, passes and ration cards from the harassed embarkation staff – suddenly we were at war again. Tenders took us ashore where a military band played a rousing welcome, but we were engrossed in heaving our luggage up the slope to Greenock station – and so home to a month's leave. It was good to be with the family again, but it was a very sad visit that I paid to my father, now living a lonely life on his own at Heatherdene. I found that his war effort was growing vegetables for the hospitals, including a quarter of a ton of tomatoes and scores of bunches of grapes.

At home the domestic scene had changed considerably. Our Nannie and the two indoor servants had been called up, and Joyce was now running a big house without help. Sensibly she had realized that Pajerkitok (our husky dog) needed the daily exercise which it had become impossible for her to give him, so she found him a happy home with a Norwegian officer who also loved and understood huskies. Our house was being shared by an army family, and a caravan stood on the front lawn housing a lady engaged in local war work. Joyce kept chickens in the garden and, of course, grew vegetables. Our gardener, Pratt, had volunteered for the RAF but failed his medical. He had a heart malfunction and was told to go home and keep on gardening. So at least she did not have to worry about maintaining our three acres of garden and cutting all the hedges.

My month's leave before going to Staff College enabled me to get to know the children once more, Hilary just eight years old and at her first school, Peter nearly four. It was great to get back to them for a bit.

The Staff Course at Camberley which normally lasted a year had now been reduced to four months of very concentrated work, late into each night. At the end of it I qualified and was posted to Second Army Headquarters in Victoria Street, London to work in Civil Affairs. My father had his own memories of the First World War, and so far throughout my war we had enjoyed burning much midnight oil during frequent weekend visits, discussing the progress of events and forecasting what the future might hold. But in Second Army I read the whole Invasion Plan, and at last felt part of the war effort – at which point I had to stop talking to my father about the war, since I knew so many of the answers to his theories, which till then we had pondered so agreeably.

Six weeks before D-Day (6 June 1944) Second Army left London and moved down to live under canvas in an old fort outside Portsmouth, where our offices were in a damp cellar some forty feet underground. The whole invasion force had moved into secret 'closed areas' spread across the south coast. Once in, no one was allowed leave and civilians were barred from entry. As the tempo increased with the build-up it was a truly awe-inspiring sight to watch the endless streams of ships and landing craft of every shape and size fill up the Solent – the whole country was tense with anticipation, and now everything depended on the weather.

On D+1 I began moving my MT convoy towards Portsmouth Hard. The shambles of that embarkation in the middle of the night, lit by a solitary floodlight, was unbelievable. All the heavy lorries and other vehicles had to back up into the craft. First they were driven backwards very slowly on a very steep slope, then through a water splash about two feet deep, then up a thirty-degree slope on slippery metal into the interior of the landing craft. There, according to their size, they were parked on the tank deck or sent by lift to the boat deck.

The extreme slipperiness of the ramp, combined with the very steep slope, made it impossible for some vehicles to get up. The difficulty could have been avoided had a permanent mobile wooden shore ramp been provided to bridge the gap of sea between the concrete Hard and the ship's ramp. Not only had no one thought of this, but even the wooden strips leading on to the ship's ramp were in no way bound together. In consequence many vehicle wheels fell between the boards, causing great delay while they were hauled out by an attendant tractor. Even the latter, though provided with a winch and drum as part of its equipment, had failed to bring a hawser. Thus it had to waste time using the vehicle's tow rope and could not be used to pull vehicles on to the ship.

My car, a four-seater Ford Utility, could not be waterproofed, and the distributor – almost the lowest portion of the engine – flooded when we were negotiating the water splash. By the time we had dried it out and got it going again the Loading Master would not accept any more smaller vehicles, and we had to leave behind a PU, a three-ton lorry and the Ford. Determined not to be left behind myself, I transferred my kit to another lorry, leaving my driver to get our abandoned vehicle over as soon as he could.

At 5.30 am we moved out into the roads near the Isle of Wight and lay there for twenty-four hours awaiting a convoy escort to take us across the Channel. The weather was cloudy, rainy and generally unpleasant.

The ship is crammed with vehicles of all kinds together with the troops riding in them. The quarters are very cramped. As many as possible sleep in the lorries and cars, for the rest of us there are a limited number of bunks along an extremely narrow passageway on the port side ... There too are the six wash basins and three lavatories, the latter a communal affair in one room where one is compelled to be seated inelegantly side by side. All this accommodation is used by officers and men alike – the scrum is something appalling. Personally I rise at 0100 hours in the night to make my various ablutions and toilet; then there is a period of about two hours when there are few people around. Perhaps I am over-fastidious!

Yesterday we finally left at 0700 and crossed in a calm sea with lovely blue sky, while convoy after convoy passed and repassed in both directions. As nearly all the ships have at least one barrage balloon, and many including ours have two, every convoy is shown up at a great distance by the cluster of shining silver sausages.

The sky was filled with innumerable planes as the RAF maintained an umbrella over the whole area as far as the eye could see, completely precluding any aerial enemy retaliation. As we anchored four miles off shore to spend our third night in our somewhat unsalubrious conditions, the whole scene resembled a great gathering together of ships for a regatta or review. Next morning we finally moved to within fifty yards of Gold Beach.

I clambered on to the first vehicle to take the plunge into four feet of water. Though waterproofed, the drop on to the bottom from the ramp was sufficient to upset the engine (or the driver) ... it stalled, and we remained water-logged in front of the LSTs exit entirely blocking all egress ... a waterproofed tank hauled us out, not without some alarming episodes, for the sea bottom was deeply pitted with holes from exploded mines and bombs. Into these we wallowed precariously, expecting any minute to turn right over.

However, we were soon on the sloping beach and were then towed away by a captured German tractor with enormous wheels to the Drowned Vehicle Park to dry ourselves out. All around lay the wastage of the original fighting when the first assault troops had established the bridgehead – broken ships and landing craft, lorries sunk in the sea, tanks burnt out on the shore, broken block houses and shattered buildings. Engineers were still blasting the west wall to pieces and clearing all the broken German defences away. Day and night the air was filled with the roar of hundreds of planes which never ceased, and always they were ours. Meanwhile the French civilians still tilled the fields and looked after their cows, sheep, goats, pigs and geese, as though the continued cannonade did not exist.

Throughout the campaign Civil Affairs moved in behind the tanks, to take cover and try to bring order out of the chaos left by the fighting and set up some form of civil administration. I was soon provided with a motorcycle and travelled all over the bridgehead, but it was not always the best form of transport.

The roads are crammed with thousands of vehicles travelling rapidly and purposefully towards objectives in every direction ... They are absurdly narrow and ill-metalled, and are being broken up in spite of gangs of army and civil labourers, and threaten to become impassable. The dust billows away in the wind so that a single car raises a cloud which can be seen for miles like a smoke screen. A convoy travels so thickly enveloped that it is impossible to see approaching vehicles and driving is a nightmare. Since the heavy rain mud has prevailed instead, making many routes almost impassable. For a motorcyclist either the deep dust-like sand makes it difficult to steer or the mud makes it well-nigh impossible to stay on ... and one cannot afford to fall off, for it is a certainty to be run over if you do. I don't! Occasionally we have a raid at night, but I have no fears as I have dug my bed into a hole in the ground on the floor of the tent. Thus nothing but a direct hit can get at me ...

How wrong I was, for the morning after writing this I found the nose-cone of an anti-aircraft shell lying beside me, with a tell-tale hole in the tent above.

On another occasion when trying to find Second Army Headquarters, thought to be in the vicinity of Bayeux, we dug shallow body trenches and lay down to sleep in the open. I awoke suddenly, concious that something else was sharing the bottom of my sleeping bag. It was pitch dark – and I do not like hungry rats! Cautiously I clambered out and found my torch, pondering the next move with some unease. And there he was – a furry little mole, terrified and desperate to dig himself out of trouble. My trench had cut straight through his underground tunnel system and he had unwittingly fallen in. Now he eyed me trembling. I helped him on to the surface and set him on his way.

Throughout the campaign I tried to keep in touch with my father, who preserved my letters. The following extracts from them perhaps give a more immediate account of our experiences than anything I could write looking back now after more than forty years. By the middle of July the battle for Caen was raging and the Germans were still shelling the town when we arrived.

16.7.44. I was there within twenty-four hours of our entry and saw a pretty bad mess ... Everything here is a great hustle and bustle with scarcely room for any more stores on the ground, the congestion of men is so great. The French seem very impressed with the quantity of stuff we have brought over. Their attitude to us changes as time goes on. At each place which is captured there are great welcomes and everyone comes forward to shake your hand, and to produce what gifts they can.

21.8.44. Things are moving fast now ... already over the Seine and Paris being evacuated by the Germans ... I was in Flers an hour after it fell and even Civil Affairs were still taking prisoners. They stood in a dejected group in the main street while British troops poured through, the vehicles decorated with hydrangeas and other blooms. Those who stopped like myself were handed glasses of cider and all was very cheery. One CA officer went round a corner on his motorcycle and found himself confronted by a Tiger tank. Wobbling to a standstill he drew his revolver for the crew were standing by their tank. They had run out of petrol so gave themselves up without trouble.

Flers was lucky in being only partly destroyed, but many of these towns are literally just heaps of rubble. Some of them have no walls standing at all and there are no roads until the bulldozers have cut a path through the shattered bricks and timber ... The villages and towns are all entirely deserted after the battle has passed over them, but in two or three days the people begin to drift back if they are allowed to. The trouble about letting them do that is that they find mines and booby traps all over the place, besides their houses in ruins, so that there is nowhere for them to go ... I'm sorry that these letters are so sketchy but I find that I'm so dead beat by midnight that I can hardly think consecutively.

4.9.44. Things are moving so quickly now that it is difficult to give any adequate description, or indeed to write at all for no sooner have I pitched my tent in one place than it is time to move on to the next. As I form the advance party and do the lay-out of the camp, I seem always to be on the move ... I went into Amiens yesterday, the fifth anniversary of the outbreak of war, and found little damage except that dating back to 1940, or possibly even to the last war. The roads here are much better than those we have been used to and motorcycling is not so bad. They are strewn with destroyed German cars, lorries and tanks, and in some places the destruction has been tremendous. One area we left behind us where the Germans had been caught in a valley, the whole area is strewn with dead. It will take three weeks to a month to bury them all – a very dreadful job which one of our officers, a Canadian, is having to deal with as the proper authorities can't cope with the amount of work.

As we go along the roads the French all stand in the streets waving, even days after the actual battle has passed on. Now we are moving rapidly through Belgium and I cannot see what can stop the move right into Germany.

Although I, too, had been through a war, perhaps only then did I begin to realize what it must have been like to be physically occupied by an enemy in control of every detail of one's daily personal life. It was a humbling experience to be with them on their day of triumphant liberation.

8.9.44. The latest move was a long one and for *at least 100 miles* we were cheered along the route by the entire population. In Belgium the people became absolutely frantic, waving and shouting, throwing plums, apples, pears into the vehicles – if one stopped out came tea, beer, eggs, souvenirs of flags, coloured ribbons, silver and other metal talismans. As one moved along the road all hands were stretched out to touch the driver or other person's extended hand as they passed. The scenes were often amazing in their enthusiasm – all Belgium turned out. The streets are decorated with the national colours from end to end, and all our cars and lorries bear Belgian flags and coloured ribbons.

In Brussels the scenes are wildest. As the convoys go through the people stand five and six deep in the streets shouting and waving; every shop and every window decorated ... When the vehicles stop one is handed from the car, everyone has to sign autograph albums wherever they go; you cannot look anywhere without finding everyone staring and smiling and making the V sign – one wears a perpetual grin and feels very self-conscious!

Today I was in Ghent and there things are calmer for the Germans are still in the south part of the town, but even so women came up to shake your hand in the street and say 'thank you for our liberation'. The Colonel and I were carried off to tea by one man who produced his whole family of six womenfolk plus children and tea and cognac. Everywhere are great signs saying 'Thanks to our allies for the liberation.' Pictures of Churchill, Roosevelt, even Stalin, have appeared twice life-size in some of the shops. All day long the Belgian forces of the interior bring in German prisoners so that there is no minor mopping up to do. There seems nothing lacking in the country, there is food and drink, sweets unrationed; all kinds of goods like wireless sets etc. which are almost unobtainable by us in England ... It may be that two weeks more will see it over in Europe. How are your tomatoes? I suppose by now that you will have picked the majority – and I have not had one this year yet!

23.10.44. As you rightly surmise, I am in Holland ... Things go more slowly now, but that is only natural for a period after so rapid an advance. Until about ten days ago we were living in the wet and mud, indeed in a real swampy patch of land where conditions were pretty awful. Now, however, we have managed to fetch up at a place where we can get billets, and conditions are not nearly so bad. The Dutch (they prefer to call themselves Netherlanders) are very concerned about the future of their land and of themselves, for there is the continual possibility of extensive flooding and they are already most terribly short of food and other necessities ... All the families here seem to be of such vast size – six, eight or ten children – perfectly astonishing. Perhaps because it is a Catholic part of the country ... It is very apparent that malnutrition during the last few years has had a very serious effect on the children, and so far it has not been possible for us to produce anything more than bare necessities, and then only in emergency. Everything in the way of transport and production must still go towards the prosecution of the war itself.

The battle in its present rather static state is again causing considerable destruction. Aachen of course is flat – only two or three hundred houses being habitable. As the front moves into Germany there is going to be a complete lack of regard for any property and I'm afraid the destruction will be terrible ... It may be that the war will cease before the entire razing of the Ruhr cities ... Most people seem all out to do as much damage as they possibly can, a sort of justified liberation of the destructive instinct common to everyone.

Once across the border and into Germany itself I witnessed the first released prisoners staggering out of the Belsen concentration camp, dirty tattered uniforms hanging off their emaciated frames, and hardly able to walk. The unbelievably terrible conditions found in the camps were being photographed and documented as evidence to be later submitted at the war criminal trials.

My unit, 218 Detachment Civil Affairs, moved up to the north into Schleswig-Holstein, passing through the total devastation of towns like Hamburg which Allied bombers had all but annihilated. There I found myself in a *Kreis* (an area equivalent to an English county) with Headquarters in the town of Plön.

In our sector a quarter of a million disarmed German troops lived in camps awaiting demobilization. Meanwhile we occupied them with community work such as painting, hedge cutting, road repairs and anything else that needed doing.

German refugees appeared in train-loads of hundreds, having been sent from the Russian front. There were no able-bodied men – only women or very old men and young children. They all had to be documented and dispersed wherever we could find an empty barn or a hall for them to sleep in. Sometimes I met the trains to dispatch people to various *Gemeinde* or parishes, which were under the control of local Burgomeisters. Most of them were passive and reasonably cooperative, usually small farmers just thankful to have got away from the Russians. Thus the 80,000 population of the *Kreis* was doubled almost overnight, much to the consternation of the locals.

At first I toured the *Kreis* in a car escorted by armoured vehicles in front and behind, but all the known Nazis were quickly rounded up and removed so the community was without leadership, and fairly soon they accepted us with increasing confidence. Soon I could walk about among them freely. Occasionally a man would appear with some request to his advantage phrased somewhat aggressively. Then the conversation became acrimonious, and invariably he was a political activist only too ready to remind us that stories of German atrocities had been invented by the British propaganda machine with absolutely no basis in truth. The Colonel soon discovered the antidote. The bottom drawer of his desk contained blown-up pictures of what we had found in the concentration camps. Spreading a few of these quietly on the desk could be counted on to silence the obstreperous visitor.

It was very difficult to set up a completely new education system, and even more of a challenge to reorganize the police force. Germans had never known policemen without revolvers and the new recruits could not understand the concept of policing by consent. But we gradually won through, and they quite liked it!

All our projects had to be carried out against the normal background of stifling bureaucracy and the paperwork this entails. Herr Schiller was put in charge of the local rebuilding programme. He was a nice but nondescript little man, trying hard to please but his materials all had to be ordered through our main Headquarters in Kiel, and he was far too scared to try beating the system. He came to see me in a terrible state asking to resign. My suggestion that he should go personally to Kiel to sort it out terrified him.

I told him to return next day in his best clothes and promised to take him in my car to meet the Brigadier A/Q himself. On arrival he was petrified with fear, but with some encouragement he spoke up bravely, and the Brigadier was astonished to learn what was going on in his own office. Very quickly indeed the whole system was eased and made to work. Lorries of bricks arrived and buildings started to go up.

Once a week I held Court, with power to impose sentences up to one year's imprisonment or fines up to 2,000 marks. When we first arrived in Plön a Judge Advocate General, a Major who was also a professional lawyer, had been sent for two weeks to teach us legal procedures and show us the ropes. After that we were on our own and I sat alone. It was a most interesting part of the job, from which I learnt much that was to be useful later in life.

I was greatly helped and supported by the Germans themselves, who were equally anxious that justice should be seen to have been done, and sometimes miscreants who had appeared before me and had served their time were not afraid later to come up to my office for legitimate reasons. In the eighteen months I was a Magistrate there was only one complaint from the German administration. Some felt I had been too severe on three women who came out from Hamburg and were caught digging up seed potatoes. They did not see this as a serious crime, but I gave the women two months' imprisonment, partly as a deterrent to others from surrounding towns who might continue to dig up next year's food crops, and we never had another such case.

A thriving black market in fish was discovered by the police, and tracked down to a trawler owner in the Baltic who worked a good racket from Kiel. When he appeared in Court I fined him 2,000 marks with a warning that if caught again he could have his ships confiscated. This was way above my own judicial powers, and probably untrue, but it ended the black market pretty smartly!

One day a bootmaker came to the office requesting a permit to buy leather to carry on his trade. I had to refuse because there just wasn't any for him to buy. 'Oh,' he said, 'So you want a backhander too?' I was so affronted and angry that my sergeant in the outer office was quite scared as I ordered that his books, his house and his belongings be investigated by Intelligence. In fact they uncovered a number of nefarious dealings and he was duly punished. A year later he reappeared, this time with great humility and full of apologies for his mistake, with a request for permission to buy something else he needed – and got his permit.

When the war ended British troops were repatriated on the principle of first in first out, but my turn had come just as the Unit was settling in at Plön and I had volunteered to remain on the job. Now I was offered promotion to Lieutenant Colonel and transfer to Kreis Flensburg on the Danish border. However, Military Government was gradually being replaced by Control Commission, staffed by civil servants sent out from England – the time seemed ripe for me to go home and pick up my life again.

In October 1946 I said goodbye with genuine regret. I had made many friends in helping to rebuild and re-establish this small agricultural community, and counted it a privilege to have lived among them. They presented me with a beautiful hand-crafted brass wall plaque depicting the Arms of Plön surrounded by the names of the three main towns, Plön, Preetz and Lütjenburg.

Around these are the embossed figures of foxes* representing 'Fuchs running round his *Kreis*', which adorns our sitting-room to this day and is a treasured souvenir.

*The German word for fox is *fuchs*.

Chapter 10

FIDS – Stonington Island

After demobilization it was good to be back with the family. Hilary was now ten and Peter six; both were healthy, well grown and lively, blessed with an unusual innate sense of tact. This saved us from the awkward questions or comments addressed to strangers which can be such an embarrassment to parents. I recognized that Joyce had done a marvellous, though lonely, job of bringing them up.

One advantage she had had was the extensive grounds where they could play under the friendly eye of our gardener, Pratt. It was a spring garden with successively flowering shrubs, heralded first by a spread of aconites under the trees (we had over 200), followed by snowdrops and crocuses before the swathes of countless thousands of daffodils lit the green swards. There were many trees to climb and we built a little house in the branches of a conveniently sloping yew. Once we sold a barrow-load of walnuts to a market trader and with the proceeds produced a firework display for the children's friends.

From one of their holidays by the sea they had brought back magical stories of an unseen character called 'Black Arrow'. It seemed to me appropriate that these manifestations should continue. First messages from Black Arrow were found in holes in old tree trunks. Then one day as we walked under a walnut tree to the big lawn, an unseen black thread was broken and a real black arrow fell from high amongst its branches. This revealed a message hidden elsewhere in the garden, and then another – the final one indicating that the finders would receive a present if it was taken to a village shop a mile away. Hastening off, they were each rewarded with an ice cream!

For a birthday party we had a gathering of twelve young. For this there were many of the usual diversions, but one which I invented, and which entailed the purchase of twelve balls of string, was original. At the starting point each child held a brass ring through which was threaded a string, which was in fact on the beginning of an unrolled ball. The game was to lead the ring along the string to its end, but this was not as simple as it sounds. Each string led round different trees, then in opposite directions through an open-ended barrel fixed on a grass slope. After that came the hazard of a tarpaulin pinned down over a foot of loose straw, beneath which the strings again led in varying directions, followed by other hazards. The confusion and pandemonium can be imagined, for they all knew there was to be a prize at the end. In fact there were prizes at the end of each ball, which tactfully ended at different places.

Behind such happy times there was always the question of what I could do next to earn a living – and where? I was thirty-eight and had never been employed except by the Army or working for expeditions. I thought of numerous jobs, at home and overseas, but none seemed right for me. Then quite unexpectedly my old friend Launcelot Fleming, later to become Bishop of Portsmouth and then Norwich, told me about a government organization which was recruiting scientists for work in the Antarctic. This perhaps was something I was competent to do, and I applied to the Colonial Office for a position as a geologist with the Falkland Islands Dependencies Survey (FIDS). There were then seven occupied bases in Antarctica, at Deception Island, Port Lockroy, Signy Island, Hope Bay, Admiralty Bay, the Argentine Islands and Stonington Island.

I was called for interview and all seemed to be going well, but as I was about to leave the building I was called back, and much to my astonishment was offered the job of overall Field Commander of all the bases, with headquarters at Stonington. Perhaps my age and expedition experience had influenced the Interviewing Board. The contract was for one year only since it was thought that the government was unlikely to continue the scientific work.

Accepting the post with alacrity, I set about trying to discover the whereabouts of the scientific specimens already collected by 'Fids'*. They seemed to be scattered throughout the country in various museums, but nothing had yet been published. When Britain was at

*The organization being known as FIDS, members of the Survey had nicknamed themselves *Fids*, referring to retired members as *ex-Fids*, and to new recruits on first arrival as *Fidlets*.

war the Antarctic was not forgotten. British claims to this sector of the continent were originally based on early exploration – South Georgia, the South Sandwich, South Shetland and South Orkney Islands, and Graham Land were all discovered by British expeditions, and for years no other nation challenged or even commented on the claim. In 1925 Argentina suddenly formulated claims to the South Orkney Islands and, more audaciously, in 1927 she extended such claims to include South Georgia. By 1937 she had claimed the right to all the Dependencies, based on geographical proximity and on the fact that a papal decree embodied in the 1494 Treaty of Tordesillas had allocated to Spain all new lands discovered west of a meridian thought to run from the southern tip of Greenland to the mouth of the Amazon – the title to which Argentina declared she had inherited.

The situation was further complicated when in 1940 Chile, unwilling to miss out on any pickings, also put forward a claim to a nearly identical area including the Falkland Islands Dependencies. Her grounds were based not only on geographical proximity, but also on the somewhat specious argument that geologically the Antarctic Peninsula is a continuation of the Andes, and therefore a concrete part of the motherland. This was the political background of events which led the British government, even in time of war, to take action to preserve the country's existing rights by occupying or re-occupying various sites within the Falkland Islands Dependencies. In 1943,

A small military force was therefore assembled under the direction of the Admiralty, acting on behalf of the Colonial Office. This force was known for security reasons as OPERATION TABARIN, the name of a well-known night club being thought eminently suitable for a detachment which was intended to winter in the Antarctic darkness. The original intention was for two bases to be established, one to guard Deception Island and the other to occupy a position on the peninsula* of Graham Land.

The detachment at Deception Island, while doing what it could to deny the use of the harbour to enemy commerce raiders, would be in a position to provide information on the activities of both enemy and neutral vessels (Hunter Christie, E W *The Antarctic Problem*. Allen & Unwin, 1951).

*Originally the peninsula was known to the British as Graham Land, to the Americans as Palmer Land. In 1964 it was agreed that the southern half should be called Palmer Land, the northern half Graham Land, and the whole feature became the Antarctic Peninsula.

At the end of the war the name was changed to FIDS when it was taken over by the Colonial Office.

My appointment dated from July 1947 and the relief parties were due to sail south in November in a boom defence ship from the United States then designated AN-76. This had been returned to the American Navy under the lease-lend agreement, having served during the war as HMS *Pretext*. Built of pitch pine, she displaced 1,015 tons, had a length of 194 feet, beam 34 feet, and draught 14 feet. Her twin diesel-electric engines developed 1,200 horsepower, giving a service speed of 12 knots. By the end of October she was in London refitting under the auspices of the Crown Agents, a task which took considerably longer than expected. She was renamed *John Biscoe*, after an early sealing skipper who had discovered and claimed Graham Land (now the Antarctic Peninsula) for the Crown in 1832.

I was given no directive about the general programme, nor the work to be undertaken. It was indicated that as much survey, geology and meteorology as possible should be done, and to this end I began collecting and reading past scientific papers. The upshot was that we went into the field with virtually a blank cheque to plan our own programme. Twenty-seven of us were scheduled to sail on 18 December 1947, and we went on board at Tilbury to a scene so chaotic that it is impossible to describe it adequately. It was half-past four, and dark. Crates, bales, half-opened boxes and miscellaneous paraphernalia of every kind strewed the decks, while we struggled helplessly with our luggage, seeking somewhere to put it down. We had not met each other before, and to add to the confusion it was an hour before the keys to the quarters aft could be found, which left the hopeful occupants wandering frustratedly about the ship cursing. I wondered how many might already be having second thoughts. When at last the keys were produced, we drew lots for the bunks.

There was one double cabin, the rest were to sleep on canvas strips slung in three tiers between steel uprights extending from deck to deckhead. Eighteen men occupied one closely packed space amidships, the remaining seven crawled into a similarly equipped cubby-hole entered through a hatch on the after deck.

Hundreds of cases, ship's stores and FIDS cargo all jumbled together, regardless of whether it was for the hold or deck stowage, had been dumped aboard by the dockers. Since they were paid by the ton, they cared little whether things were properly stowed. The sight was so appalling that in the evening some of the crew jumped ship, convinced that she would turn over once we left the river.

Without a full complement the Board of Trade refused us permission to sail, so the Captain hastily went ashore and press-ganged a number of unlikely looking characters standing about on the dockside, including a Latvian and a very large, fierce-looking Estonian – of whom more later.

On 20 December, by the grace of God and only five weeks later than originally hoped, we finally sailed down river and the Fids set to stowing the mountain of deck cargo. Our most dangerous job was extracting twenty-five crates of sulphuric acid from the aeroplane cases on the for'ard hatch. These had been stacked on their sides, upside down, even on edge balanced precariously among other boxes. We very gingerly moved them aft where, if any broke, acid would not, we hoped, be sprayed all over the ship by the wind.

Biscoe was not a passenger ship, so we were all officially signed on as 'supernumeraries' and quickly discovered the implications of this. As soon as some semblance of order was achieved and the decks scrubbed down, we began to play a regular part in the ship's routine. Daily I posted names for working parties in every department: to work in the galley, four men; bos'n's party, four men; Second Officer's Watch, two; watchkeepers, six; catering assistant, one; cleaning wash-place, two. So it went, and throughout the voyage the unofficial crew played their part in running the ship – only too often struggling against sea-sickness as well.

We hardly ever saw the Captain. The first evening he invited me to his quarters for a very stiff drink, assuring me that of course he never took a drop at sea, but this was only the river wasn't it? I reeled out of his cabin to make friends with the First Officer who turned out to be a very small and very charming Irish peer, Lord H. He had a large bald head, and a happy knack of handling men which was to surprise us all. He ran his polyglot and somewhat ruffianly company with consummate tact and soft words, always ready to turn away wrath and soothe down the drunks or the wild ones.

Of the twenty-seven Fids who made this first voyage, only Doc Slessor (ex-Stonington) had Antarctic experience. He had volunteered to come south for the trip to initiate me into my new responsibilities, and was indeed a great strength. His equable temperament suited admirably our rather strange conditions. Purposeful, sensible, helpful, never did he overplay his hand.

Our first port of call was St Vincent in the Cape Verde Islands, where we needed water and fuel. Needless to say we arrived on New Year's Eve, to be told that nothing could be done for us for twenty-four hours. So both the crew and the Fids were given shore leave, departing exuberantly in small boats to share local festivities. Perfect peace descended on the ship, where Slessor and I settled down to some quiet fishing over the stern. The officers, too, were ashore, only the Third condemned to sit out the jollifications in his lonely cabin.

It was a beautiful warm moonlit night, but presently he was disturbed from his contemplations by the totally unexpected arrival of the water boat, shortly followed by the oil barge. The latter managed to discharge a large quantity of diesel fuel on to the deck, which no one noticed in the darkness. Soon the shouting died away and once more peace reigned. Some time later we observed the bos'n and members of the crew returning – and suddenly there was an empty boat secured alongside.

Concerned to protect the belongings of those ashore, Slessor and I dashed down the companionway to hear loud laughter and female voices in the bos'n's quarters. Hastily summoning the Third Officer we opened the door, whereupon a number of black people rushed out and up to the deck. A very large woman suddenly decided she would not leave after all, but remained clinging like a limpet to the companionway rail, while the Third Officer pushed her broad backside upwards with all his might. Seeing that he was getting nowhere, I added a judicious judo grip, and up she went – straight into the bum boat. As the visitors rowed away, we began an argument with a very drunk bos'n who clearly resented our stuffy moralistic attitudes. We put him to bed, still swearing volubly.

So back to our fishing – but not for long. Soon we were interrupted by the arrival of a sailor who reported that we had now acquired a Canadian stowaway, and what should he do? The man turned out to be a tough-looking character. very drunk, very belligerent and demanding a job. Telling him that regretfully we had no vacancies just then, I realized that I was going to find myself in a fight fairly soon, so began edging him towards the rail.

Suddenly out of the dark little Lord H appeared. Immediately grasping the situation, he smiled warmly, shook our unwelcome visitor by the hand, and linking arms affectionately he led him gently back to the gangway. 'My dear fellow, how really nice to see you! Of course it isn't quite the moment to talk about jobs. But you get some sleep now and come back to see us in the morning. I'll see what can be done.' Totally confused by this friendly approach, the obstreperous Canadian meekly went over the side and disappeared in a rowing boat.

This story had sequels, for when we sailed next day we saw a great commotion going on on the top deck of an anchored American freighter, towering over us as we put to sea. Four men were swinging a body which they finally hurled expertly into space where, turning over and over, it fell fifty feet into the water with a mighty splash. It was our friend trying his luck with less courteous hosts.

The final sequel came seven years later when I was again in St Vincent in MV *Theron* carrying the Trans-Antarctic Expedition south. A stately bum boat rowed out ceremoniously, and sitting proudly in the stern, sheltered by a gigantic umbrella and smoking a cigar, was our Canadian stowaway. He had remained in the islands after all, and was now the prosperous boss of all the bum boats trading in the harbour!

To get back to New Year's Eve. Slessor and I returned to our fishing lines. Presently a boatload of happy Fids arrived out of the darkness singing gently. As they clambered nimbly enough up the side of the ship and over the rail, each in turn met the unseen oil slicks deposited earlier. The deck was suddenly a mass of very surprised slimy figures, picking themselves up off their hands and knees, now deeply suspicious of the potent qualities of the hooch they had enjoyed ashore.

Hardly had peace been restored than the air was shattered by blast after blast on the ship's siren – the New Year had arrived. The other nine ships in the harbour all joined in, vociferously sounding off on their hooters, firing rockets or Very pistols, and generally making the night hideous. *Biscoe*'s siren may have been weaker than some, but our searchlights, signalling lamps and rockets were more spectacular. The cacophony brought out all the Fids, and assembling on the monkey island we sang 'Auld Lang Syne', which swelled dramatically across the suddenly quiet harbour.

Thereafter activity languished until about three o'clock, when the Captain returned with a party of visitors, all in fancy dress. As the Mate went to receive him over the side someone pressed the fire alarm bell, which set off enough noise to wake the town. Unfortunately no one knew where to turn it off. Endless minutes passed and still *John Biscoe* made her presence felt, while frantic figures sped all over the ship turning or pressing every little knob and switch. The control was finally discovered on the aft mess deck, and suddenly we could talk again. It had been quite a night – and Slessor and I had not even one fish to show for it.

Next morning the last of our supplies came aboard and we sailed for Montevideo. Now our daily chores included painting the entire superstructure a pale blue-grey, a very great improvement. For entertainment we organized lectures and discussions, sessions of 'Twenty Questions', a ship's concert and a 'Crossing the Line' ceremony.

Once the engines stopped, and we found the ship turning in a swirling circle. The steering gear had failed. For different reasons this kept happening all day; first it was a fuse, then twice because of burnt-out contacts, and finally because a small metal spring one inch long broke – and of course there was no spare. This could have been bought anywhere for a penny, but now we had to set to and make one. It seemed ridiculous that the entire ship was controlled by so cheap and insignificant a vital part.

The night before we reached the River Plate I was sleeping on deck and was suddenly woken by someone falling over my bedding. Rubbing my eyes, I was astonished to find that our Estonian greaser was apparently chasing the ship's electrician with a large carving knife. Hastily setting off in pursuit, I lost him in the dark, so rushed off to find the First Officer. As I was speaking to him the huge Estonian appeared, still brandishing his weapon and towering menacingly over little Lord H.

'He calling me Estonian bastard,' he shouted. 'I kill him.'

With instant aplomb Lord H mastered the situation: 'But my dear old chap,' he smiled, 'you *are* an Estonian bastard. In England that is a term of endearment which we only use to our best friends. What more can he say to you?'

Confused by this direct and innocent approach the greaser wavered long enough to be led quietly away and to bed. The First

Officer had won again. But not for long. A few hours later our troublemaker was on the rampage once more, and this time had to be forcibly restrained until we reached harbour. Here he was handed over to the local police, and when last I saw him he was spread-eagled face downwards, being carried away by the gendarmerie, two to his arms, two to his legs, while a splendid officer with drawn sword marched solemnly ahead.

On 25 January 1948 we arrived in Stanley. The Governor himself was away, but the ship was to be officially welcomed by Mrs Clifford, who was waiting as we moved slowly in. Unfortunately in coming alongside we ran hard and fast on to the mud, and despite agonized cries of 'Hard-a-port' and 'Hard-a-starboard' from the bridge, the ship remained stuck just twelve feet from the end of the jetty. In the end a single plank was rather shamefacedly rigged across the intervening water, and the Governor's lady bravely made an assisted but rather perilous passage on board. Thus, a little ignominiously, ended the first voyage of the *John Biscoe*.

During our six days in Stanley the Governor returned, and swore in as magistrates those of us who were to become Base Leaders. This was to give us some political authority in the event of encountering Argentine or Chilean interlopers. In those days when the nationals of any of the three countries met, it was incumbent on them to exchange Notes of Protest at the presence of the other.

As this was our last visit to civilization for at least a year it was a busy time. We drew polar clothing from the FIDS store, checked equipment, and discussed affairs with the post office, the wireless station, the meteorological office and the ionospheric people – all very necessary as our only contact with them would be by wireless.

On 31 January we sailed for Antarctica amid mountainous seas. Abreast of Pembroke Lighthouse the Captain decided to turn back and shelter in Sparrow Cove. As we came about, *Biscoe* almost lost steerage way and, wallowing in the troughs, she rolled through more than ninety degrees. For some minutes the crashing of crockery and everything else that could move echoed round the ship. Even the normally stable pots and pans were dislodged and careered round the galley, leaving the cook wading about in a boiling swill of gravy, meat and vegetables.

On the fifth day we saw our first ice. Small icebergs about the size

Neptune's Bellows, Deception Island

of large houses shone a beautiful greeny-white in the occasional shafts of sunlight. Next day we came to Deception Island, its huge volcanic crater rising up out of the sea. As we sailed round its rocky coast a cleft about half-a-mile wide was suddenly revealed. Passing through this about one cable from the vertical cliff on the starboard side we were suddenly within a giant water-filled crater some six miles by four miles in extent. There, in a small embayment known as Whalers Bay, we could see the derelict remains of a whaling station which had been abandoned in 1931. Nearby was a large hut which served as the British base.

It seemed strange that at our first landing in cold Antarctica we should be greeted by clouds of steam blowing away from the beach at low tide. The volcano was only quiescent and, as it turned out, was biding its time before erupting again some twenty years later.

To reach the stores in the for'ard hold we had first to build a raft and put ashore the de Havilland Hornet Moth destined for Stonington. But sadly this aircraft never flew, for the boxes thought to contain its skis were found to be full of stove pipes for a hut!

The relief of the base took two days and then we sailed for Signy

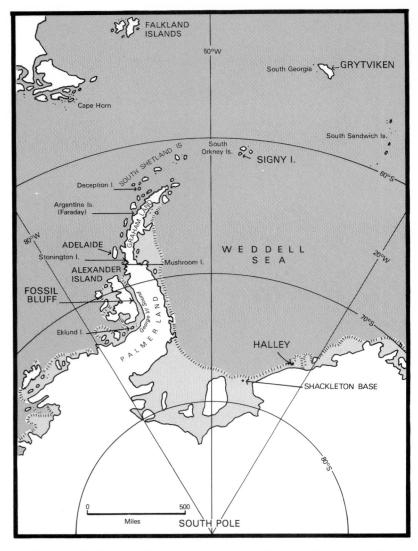

in the South Orkney Islands, some 500 miles north-east. At first a
very heavy following sea threatened to poop us, then we came to a
concentration of tabular icebergs which forced us off course. They
were a fine sight, the largest about six miles long and 100 feet high.
One which had turned over looked different, for its surface which
had been below water was smooth and rounded into a dome. This
shone bottle-green in the sun, unlike the flat snowy tops of the
others.

The Signy base was a small hut occupied by four men. Their Leader was Gordon Robin, later destined to become Director of the Scott Polar Research Institute. We relieved the station in twenty-four hours and replaced the personnel with three of the men in the ship. The new Base Leader was Dick Laws, who twenty-five years later was to succeed me as Director of the British Antarctic Survey – the new name given to FIDS in 1961. The station lay close to the mountains of neighbouring Coronation Island, a most attractive region where any one of us would have been glad to serve.

We were soon heading west for Admiralty Bay, King George Island where we were to erect a new hut to replace a temporary shelter which had been put up the year before. On arrival we found that the Argentinians had placed their small building only eighty feet from ours – their national flag flew provocatively. At once we exchanged our Notes of Protest at the other's presence, after which relations with our close neighbours were friendly enough. Two of us who visited their hut were warmly welcomed and regaled with a glass of wine. This was just one of many such occasions which followed routinely in later years when the governmental formalities were always followed by friendly relations between the men, who all found common ground in their battle with the harsh environment.

When the framework of the new hut was up we left the new wintering party to complete the building and sailed back to Deception. We secured alongside an Argentine mine-layer which was also watering from our well sunk into ground warmed by volcanic heat. During this operation there was a sudden flash, followed by a loud explosion near an old wooden whaling barge lying 300 yards along the beach. This was loaded with boxes of black powder once used by the whalers. It transpired that two Argentinian sailors had been amusing themselves by extracting some of the explosives and setting it alight. Both were badly burnt about the face and one man's clothes caught fire. He rushed into the sea, which extinguished the flames, but the cold was an additional shock on top of the explosion. Their ship carried no doctor but fortunately in *Biscoe* we then had three – Slessor, Bill Sladen destined for Hope Bay, and David Dalgliesh who was coming to Stonington with me. All of them went over to treat the injured men.

The previous year a private American expedition under Commander Finn Ronne had sailed to Stonington Island and frozen-in their ship, the *Port of Beaumont*, for the winter. This year ice conditions were very bad around Marguerite Bay and the ice had not gone out. The Americans had therefore sent two of their icebreakers to break out a passage for the *Port of Beaumont* and evacuate their expedition. On arrival at Deception I received an urgent message from the FIDS Commander, Ken Pierce-Butler, whom I was to relieve, suggesting that we make for ice-bound Stonington with all possible speed to take advantage of the channel which the icebreakers were then cutting to free the American ship.

We sailed that very evening, but hardly had we cleared Deception than the Captain arrived in my cabin to enquire if by chance I happened to have any charts of the Antarctic Peninsula area? Not having regarded this as my part of the ship, I shook my head in appalled dismay – apparently he had forgotten to provide himself with anything south of latitude 63°S. Something had to be done fast. We scoured our luggage until someone finally dug out a school atlas, while I found some small-scale maps of the land area. With only these rudimentary aids Second Officer Brown was to bring us safely through ice and shoals to Marguerite Bay. *Port of Beaumont* had been released and was lying alongside the icebreaker *Burton Island* at the Faure Islands. *Biscoe* in turn secured to *Beaumont*, handed over long-awaited mail to the American ships, and I went aboard to meet Ronne's outgoing party.

That evening dozens of curious American sailors invaded our little ship. Many of them were anxious to be on their way home, one in particular complaining bitterly at the length of their voyage. He turned out to be *Burton Island's* postman. He hadn't had a goddam letter to deliver for three months, and was being kidded daily by his companions for his failure to produce non-existent mail!

Next day we arrived at the channel cut through to Stonington Island, but discovered it filled with huge blocks of impenetrable ice already refrozen. As the United States were determined not to get involved in national disputes, the American ships were officially forbidden to assist us. But *Burton Island* had a friendly Captain who now found occasion to return to Stonington on his own affairs, and we most gratefully fell in behind him.

That evening we anchored in Back Bay, working frantically throughout the night to get our sixty-five tons of stores on to the sea ice by 6 am, which was as long as *Burton Island* could convincingly

Looking south over Stonington

remain. So it was that I took over from Pierce-Butler with all speed and few preliminaries. As we waved goodbye and watched *Biscoe* depart I noticed a fringe of splintered wood floating around her water-line, splinters up to two feet long weaving gently like seaweed along the length of her hull. This was the result of ice abrasion of the pitch pine hull which in places had cut in to a depth of two inches. Clearly she would require the protection of greenheart sheathing before she came south next season.

At Stonington we now numbered eleven: five old hands and six newcomers. Dave Jones (air fitter), Bernard Stonehouse (biologist), Terry Randall (radio operator) had already spent a year there. Ray Adie (geologist) had sledged down from Hope Bay, and John Huckle (general assistant) came with me after a year as Base Leader at Deception. The newcomers were Colin Brown (surveyor), Ken Blaiklock (surveyor), David Dalgliesh our doctor, Bob Spivey (general assistant) and Pat Toynbee (pilot). Nearly all of us had been recruited from the armed forces and still held our Service ranks. As I pondered my administrative duties I felt the time was appropriate to drop rank, and circulated a message to all bases that in future men would be placed in charge of projects, journeys or the home station according to their suitability and regardless of their Service seniority. The 1948 parties also brought down the expression 'radio' which had been introduced by our American allies, so we also dropped the term 'wireless' with our ranks.

For a time we continued to hope that *Biscoe* would return to Stonington with the aircraft and its skis, for the plane was to play a large part in the journeys we planned. The dogs also needed seal meat from the Argentine Islands if they were to be kept alive and healthy. But the ice situation precluded this and by 9 April we got a signal saying the ship was going back to Stanley for the winter. We were on our own.

There was much to learn at base. One day there was the dreaded cry of 'Fire', but our fortnightly practices stood up to this first test. Everyone seized extinguishers, axes and buckets of water as we tore down the smoke-filled passage to the bathroom, and in three minutes the fire was out. It had been caused by boxes and other inflammable material being pushed against the unlagged chimney pipe in the space above the ceiling.

Next Bob Spivey was caught out wearing the wrong footgear on a short trip during which the temperature dropped thirty degrees in two hours. He was severely frostbitten and nearly lost all his toes, their blackened appearance remaining an anxiety for many weeks.

Huckle and I learnt another lesson after making the mile-long crossing to Neny Island in a small boat. On our return two hours later there was a flat calm and a thin slush of ice crystals forming on the sea. The outboard motor would not start, so we rowed off in fine style for the first 200 yards. There the ice was thicker, in places over-rafted, and we were quickly in trouble. By the time we were halfway across the oars would no longer break it, yet it was not strong enough to bear our weight if we left the boat. We could have been held half-a-mile offshore indefinitely. Standing in the bows I spent nearly two hours smashing the ice ahead with a boat hook while Huckle rowed for dear life. As we at last approached the icefoot there was much jeering and applause from our unfeeling companions assembled on the shore, and happily betting on our progress. Lesson: never go boating in low temperatures.

We spent time hunting seal to feed the dogs and learning to drive the teams. We built a new generator house and tarred the roof of the hangar which had once housed an aeroplane that had crash landed the year before.

Transporting dogs to *John Biscoe*

This last task proved more formidable than expected. Firstly, of course, the forty gallons of tar were frozen solid and lay under some four inches of ice. We tried melting the surface with a blow-lamp, but in an hour only acquired about two gallons of tar mixed with water. Disgusted with this we cut off the top of the steel drum and dug and hacked out the tar, melting it in a sort of witch's cauldron suspended over a wood fire. All seemed well as we poured hot tar on to the seams and cracks in the roof. It rapidly congealed and long wisps and trailers were soon blowing about from our instruments. At the time this did not seem to matter as they were hard and brittle – as it was already dark we could not see what was happening. But as we went inside to the warmth of the hut we found we were all covered in festoons of melted tarry cobwebs!

We had already been caught when bringing stores ashore from the ship. Unrecognized, a case of twelve bottles of beer (it was before the days of tins) were left outside the hut. When we came to broach them the glass was shattered and we peeled pieces off like a banana skin – to be left with beer standing up by itself in the shape of bottles. Unhappily, in freezing it had expelled all the alcohol and the melted fluid was revolting.

I was the only Cambridge man among us, and had looked forward to listening to the Boat Race. My solicitous friends called me to the radio room where the commentator was already describing a very poor performance. Cambridge was nearly four lengths behind at Barnes Bridge. The speaker's voice was being drowned by the noise of the helicopter from which he worked, and the next thing we heard was an all-too-vivid description of the Cambridge boat sinking with all hands.

Suddenly realizing that my consternation was not being reflected in the faces around me, I became aware that they were all grinning and that Stonehouse was missing. In fact he was perpetrating the convincing commentary in the engine room, the generator providing the very realistic helicopter noises. Having had their fun in full measure, they put the clocks back to normal and half-an-hour later we reassembled to hear the real race – in which Cambridge won by five lengths. Oddly enough the real helicopter was grounded by engine trouble.

Every Fid who has served at a sledging base will spend the rest of his life recounting his dog stories, and on arrival a first priority is for the new men to learn to drive a team. 'Darkie' was leader of the team I took over, and I shall never forget his friendship and intelligent cooperation. Huskies are exuberant, rumbustious animals who fight each other with or without provocation, just for fun. However, they love humans and are always eager to be petted, fondled and made much of. Some are stupid but work hard, with their heads well down but never seeing the crevasses into which they inevitably fall; others are lazy and quickly learn to keep their traces just taut enough to fool an unsuspecting driver that they are pulling their weight. All are great characters, but only a few are sufficiently intelligent to use their wits, break trail, and keep a true course in a wilderness where there are no landmarks. These become the team leaders, not only

Sawing seal for dogs

willing and sensitive to a driver's commands, but ever alert and ready to look after both him and the team when, in his ignorance, he gives a wrong one.

When sledging parties are in the field, one of the first things drivers have to come to terms with is the ritual of the Evening Chorus. After camp is made and the dogs have been fed, one of them – usually a bitch – will point her nose to the sky and give a long-drawn-out h-o-w-l, which is immediately taken up by all the team. They sit, every nose pointing upwards, and 'sing' in unison. Suddenly it stops, then every ear is pricked awaiting an answer. The silence persists for about half a minute before they put on a repeat performance, which is again followed by an expectant pause. When yet another reprise fails to produce results they finally give up and, curling into balls, the teams sleep.

However, should another party be working in the same area and happen to make camp within a radius of, say, five to six miles, and there is no wind to drown sounds, it is a different story. As the first chorus dies away it will elicit an immediate response from 'over the hill', and when this in turn ends, the original teams will again take up the refrain. Chorus follows chorus, each 'silent' interval yielding a distant reply, and very soon exasperated drivers at both ends will be adding their infuriated cries to the general cacophony – but with no effect at all! The alternating howling will continue until at last the dogs themselves decide that enough is enough.

In my eyes Darkie was unique as a leading dog. He did not give friendship lightly and he never permitted liberties. Anyone trying to pet or fondle him was put in his place with dignity. When after many months of travelling together he had taught me many lessons, and saved me from disaster more than once, he would finally acknowledge the affection between us by standing quietly against my leg, pressing it gently and perhaps allowing me to stroke his ears – never more than this, and it was always a very private arrangement between us.

In every team there are two special dogs – the Leader and the King Dog. The Leader is appointed by the driver (and may sometimes be a bitch), but the King Dog has won his position by strength and cunning. Only rarely will another challenge him, and then only when he thinks he has a chance to oust him from the supreme position.

It is obviously preferable to have a Leader who is also the King Dog, for when the driver calls a halt the Leader stops, and none will dare to over-run him. If the King Dog is only one of the workers he, or the rest of the team, will all too often try to reach the Leader to settle an old score. Thus the Leader will be unwilling to stop, and the driver can have difficulty in bringing his sledge to rest.

A good driver must learn to be a real part of his team – the 'top dog' – and to establish that no one challenges his orders. But to achieve this he must understand things from the dogs' point of view, following their line of thought, even seeing the terrain ahead from their eye level.

Darkie was both Leader and King Dog but my first efforts to control the team were a dismal failure for, despite his high reputation, he completely ignored my commands. It was Stonehouse who finally suggested that my voice was much deeper than that of his previous driver; and indeed, as soon as I raised the pitch he began to respond intelligently. Sometimes too intelligently for my *amour propre*.

Once when I approached a line of small rocky islets, I knew that there was only one route between them for a sledge – but where? I decided to go round the last one but Darkie immediately objected, constantly looking round at me reproachfully as I persisted with my orders. As he turned the point we suddenly arrived at open water! Darkie just sat down and gazed at me disdainfully, clearly saying, 'I told you so'. Duly humbled, and feeling a little foolish, I stopped trying to be clever. 'Owk,' I cried, and without hesitation he turned back along the edge of the islets and without any command suddenly steered left. This took us up and through the gap which he had obviously known about all the time.

Lacking seals, dog feeding was a considerable problem. On 28 May we had for our animals only fifteen bales of stockfish, forty pounds of pemmican left behind by the Americans, one-and-a-half seals, three seal skins and blubber, together with fifteen gallons of seal oil which we had rendered down. There was also our dog pemmican, but this had to be conserved for travelling. We decided to feed them one pound of pemmican each on three consecutive days, the next day a stockfish soaked in seal oil and half-a-pound of pemmican, followed by a day on which they got nothing – then the cycle was repeated. Thus they lived through the winter until we were once more able to hunt seals.

In the Antarctic Christmas comes in the middle of summer when all the field parties are away from base. So it is Midwinter Day, 21 June, which provides the major annual celebration at all the bases. At Stonington the 20th was a day of preparation when everyone helped with the chores and the cooking was taken over by Bernard Stonehouse and Dave Jones who were the most experienced. Two weeks earlier they had prepared a gigantic 25-pound fruit cake, the marzipan being made from peanuts, almond essence and walnuts. Unfortunately it proved to be too big for the oven and the top five pounds had to be cut off. No matter – it proved to be an enormous success.

On Midwinter Day itself they also produced mince pies, jam tarts and caramel tart, the last improvised from sweetened condensed milk which had been boiled before baking.

That morning we found that the night before winds registered at 96 mph had blown numerous sledges through the dog lines. Likewise a number of 44-gallon fuel barrels had passed that way and could be seen far out on the sea ice up against an iceberg. A pile of timber had also been scattered far and wide, some of the pieces being 25 feet long. The only damage to our living hut was the disappearance of the top of the engine room ventilator, torn from its supports. Fortunately none of the dogs was injured.

All this entailed a lot of recovery work but this did not diminish the festivities. That night we all changed into uniform or collar and tie and sat down to a tremendous meal. At the end of it we were able to drink the King's health in a third of a bottle of South African medicinal brandy I had released for the purpose. After dinner we played liar dice for matches and had a singing bee round the stove.

Ten minutes after midnight we discovered that it had become John Huckle's twenty-second birthday, so we drank his health and presented him with the most enormous pair of fur gloves which had been left behind at the American base and which we knew he coveted. So ended our midwinter festivities.

On 27 July Adie, Huckle, Spivey, Stonehouse, Brown and I left for Alexander Island, with five dog teams and a total load of two-and-a-half tons, in order to lay a depot for the long summer journey we planned. The return distance was only 220 miles, but this proved the hardest traverse any of us was to make. For twenty-three days we struggled southwards in deep soft snow, driving drift and mists which obscured the coastline. Navigation was necessarily by dead-reckoning for it was impossible to see anything. Sometimes the surface was so bad that sledges were constantly overturning. On one day Adie righted his twenty-five times in one mile.

It was also gruelling work for the dogs, which were fed only one pound of pemmican each day. On 17 August I wrote,

Yet another day lying up – our third in succession ... Our tent is now deep in a wind-scoop but is itself set on a pinnacle of snow which the wind could not get at. This afternoon I went out early before feeding to dig the dogs out, and a big job it was for some of them could only get their noses out, others only their tails for they were held down by their traces into the drift. In the end I had to get Colin to help me as with John's team the drift was filling the trench I was digging to free the main trace faster than I could dig it. The dog feed itself was only half-a-pound per dog as I must save some food with all this delay, and it is better they have less while not working than after a hard day.

It was during these days that most of us gained our first experience of 'white-out'. This is a condition when no snow is falling, but with an overcast sky daylight is diffused by multiple reflection between snow and sky. Contrasts vanish, there are no shadows, and it is impossible to distinguish the horizon or any snow feature – although dark objects can be seen over long distances. I have even known my lead dog run head first into a snow bank which neither of us had seen.

After 110 miles 1,050 pounds of food and fuel were put down about three miles from the ice cliffs of Alexander Island and became known as Cape Nicholas Depot. I intended to return via Mushroom Island where we had left a small depot for the purpose, but Darkie now had quite other ideas. For the first five miles I had a really tough running battle with him, for he just would not keep the course I was steering. So determinedly did he pursue his own way before finally giving in and doing what I asked, that in our tent that evening I took the trouble to plot not only our actual journey but also the course which he had so persistently tried to follow. His was seven degrees off mine – and headed absolutely directly back to base still 110 miles away!

In marked contrast to the outward journey we returned in cold clear weather with surface hardened by constant wind, and took only six days.

On 16 September the Northern Party (Stonehouse, Blaiklock, Dalgliesh, Spivey) left with three teams in an attempt to reach Darbel Bay 100 miles to the north. The route led over the sea ice and through the narrow channels separating Adelaide Island from the mainland. Adie and I supported the first stages with two more teams, his towing two twelve-foot Nansen sledges, the last one carrying a flat-bottomed dory for use where open water was to be expected. When we reached The Gullet between Adelaide and the mainland we found it filled with thin ice or frozen slush, on which it was dangerous to travel even with an empty sledge, and it was impossible to launch the dory. Plans were therefore altered to include a survey of the east coast of Adelaide and the adjacent islands. Adie and I took back the redundant dory, making a sketchy geological reconnaissance of the coast *en route*.

On Jenny Island the Northern Party discovered a long bamboo pole iced into a raised beach, heavily eroded on its windward side

Returning to Stonington Island

and surrounded by rocks which had once formed a cairn. They believed it to be the cairn left by Gourdan of Charcot's *Pourquoi Pas?* expedition in 1908-10. Blaiklock computed the height to be sixty feet, very different from the ten metres quoted by Charcot. But their major discovery was a small emperor penguin rookery on the Dion Islands where 100 adult birds were found with seventy chicks. This was only the third such rookery known; both the others are on the other side of the continent.

While investigating the islands Spivey and Blaiklock with the leading sledge broke through some thin ice and began to sink slowly. Dalgliesh threw a rope, while Stonehouse, rushing up on skis to help, also fell through. Then a bridge of skis was made and the swimmers crawled out. Next a rope was fastened to the semi-floating sledge, the team cut free and, together with Dalgliesh's team, were exhorted to haul it out.

Suddenly Stonehouse's dogs realized that they were missing something and came pounding up to find out what. At the same moment Spivey and Dalgliesh's teams started a war until two of them fell through. One dog managed to escape and made off in pursuit of a penguin a few hundred yards away. By this time the sledge was almost water-logged but Spivey, working half immersed in the sea, frantically unloaded it and finally all the supplies were recovered. The only casualty was the poor unsuspecting penguin. This party returned to base after fifty-six days, having covered 500 miles, done much useful survey, and bringing back geological and biological collections.

Meanwhile on 22 October the Southern Party (Huckle, Brown, Adie, Fuchs), with three sledges had left for the Cape Nicholas Depot intending to make a geological reconnaissance, survey the northern coasts of Alexander Island, and select a suitable site for a proposed new station at its northern tip. But examination revealed that high unbroken ice cliffs precluded any possibility of establishing a station from the sea, so we turned south to continue survey and geology in George VI Sound. Dividing into two groups, Brown and Huckle concentrated on linking their survey with that of the British Graham Land Expedition at Ablation Point, while Adie and I carried the geological reconnaissance to the point we called Keystone Cliffs, south of Fossil Bluff. After journeys of 550 and 940 miles respectively, we were all back at base by 20 January awaiting the arrival of the ship.

At Stonington a wide pool had now appeared in Neny Fjord, and by the end of January this extended to the western end of Red Rock Ridge. Soon Neny Island was surrounded by water and we could launch the motor boat. Reconnoitring by sea we found a small, ice-covered, rocky island which looked like a low iceberg south of

Neny, and a rock lying only two feet beneath the surface. This had not been discovered previously because there had always been an iceberg grounded on it. Now these obstacles constituted real hazards, for they lay in the direct path of ships approaching Stonington.

Although our main interest was in the break-up, life was still very busy – painting the hut, maintaining engines, trawling for biological specimens, enlarging the hangar to accept the bigger plane which we still expected from Deception. On 11 February I climbed to the top of Roman Four Mountain and, from 3,000 feet, could see through binoculars a thin line of water stretching along the western horizon – but between this and Neny Fjord there still lay some forty miles of unbroken fast ice.

By the last week of March real doubts about our relief assailed us – particularly the five who faced the possibility of being the first men to experience a third consecutive Antarctic winter. We had rations for another year, but coal would be short, and if the same ice conditions prevailed again, who could know if the ship would be able to reach us even next season.

Biscoe, with the Governor on board, had arrived at the Argentine Islands 200 miles to the north, but sea ice, snowfall, mist and gales prevented her moving farther – she could not even get to Port Lockroy. On the 30th she made a final attempt to sail south, but after only eight miles reached impenetrable pack ice. On 1 April the Governor signalled that they could do no more, and the ship turned back for Stanley. At Stonington the sea was beginning to freeze, with temperatures already dropping to −30°F (−34.5°C). Our fate was confirmed – it would be another year before we saw a new face.

Chapter 11

The Lost Eleven
1949-50

We decided to improve our home comforts by converting the large workshop into a 'quiet room' to which anyone could retire from the general hurly-burly. This provided immediate action, and had a therapeutic value in diverting our thoughts from our disappointments, but once it was completed I never remember anybody going there to be quiet.

Early in April I submitted plans to the Governor for a geological and survey journey to the southern end of George VI Sound, and the establishment of a three-man party for six weeks (this ultimately turned into ten weeks) to observe the emperor penguin rookery discovered at the Dion Islands the previous summer. Since Sir Miles Clifford was taking no chances and proposed to obtain an aircraft to fly us out the next summer if this became necessary, all field parties had to be back at base by early January. In fact we did not expect a plane on floats to be able to land in Marguerite Bay until after the ice broke up, hopefully in late February.

Emperor penguins hatch their eggs during winter, so on 1 June Bernard Stonehouse, David Dalgliesh and Dave Jones, with Bob Spivey and me in support, left for the Dion Islands. Judging from Cherry-Garrard's account in *The Worst Journey in the World*, we believed that egg-laying would not begin before the second week. In three days we were at the rookery where, to our disappointment, we found many birds already carrying eggs on their feet as they slowly strutted about the bare ice. This was a serious blow, for Stonehouse hoped to collect a timed series of embryos throughout the incubation period – something which had never been done before. Its importance lay in the belief that emperors might be a particularly primitive bird and the embryos could reveal unusual stages of development. This idea was later found to be erroneous, but he wanted to prove the point one way or the other.

Stonington Island hut

The outstanding characteristic of the rookery seemed to be the peace and quiet prevailing: there were no squabbles going on, no bickering of any kind. Many birds seemed to be unpaired, but those that were kept together. Periodically the one without the egg would begin a croaking ululation, which was taken up by its mate who, at the same time displayed the egg by teetering back on its heels and raising the lower abdominal curtain of feathers. At this the 'enquirer' appeared satisfied, and both would settle down once more, standing quietly side by side.

Every bird had an overpowering desire to hold an egg, or indeed any object of similar size. On one occasion a Leica camera was found to be missing, the thief being discovered only when we saw a penguin waddling off with a leather strap trailing between its feet. Perhaps this innate urge to hatch something is valuable in preserving the species, for an unprotected egg or a newly hatched chick would quickly perish unless sheltered from the cold. A few eggs which had somehow been abandoned were frozen hard and cracked. However, they made excellent omelettes and we believed ourselves the first people ever to eat emperor penguin eggs.

Spivey and I spent two days mapping and geologizing around the islands, and then travelled some fifteen miles south to the Faure Islands for a one-day general reconnaissance. These proved to be an extensive group of perhaps fifty small islands and rocks, and we marvelled that Charcot's *Pourquoi Pas?* could have survived an involuntary storm-driven passage through them in 1908. In contrast to the Dions, where we had found numerous seals, penguins and blue-eyed shags, the Faures presented a desolate, eerie scene with no life of any kind. We turned for home, reaching base in time for the Midwinter celebrations.

By this time the British press, sensing a good story in our enforced extra year, had blown us up into 'heroes'. Headlines at home spoke of 'Trapped Men on Ice', 'Marooned Scientists' and more dramatically, 'The Lost Eleven', a name which stuck to us through many years. The BBC beamed special monthly programmes to us, on which our families were invited to send personal messages and choose a favourite piece of music.

As our plight became more and more exaggerated, another current radio cliff-hanger was keeping the nation enthralled each week. This was the heroic adventures of Duncan Carse as 'Dick Barton, Special Agent'. Becoming increasingly irritated with the absurd build-up about us, Carse got himself into trouble with the newspapers by stating publicly that all the fuss was totally out of proportion, and that we were perfectly all right – which indeed we were – but it spoilt the whole picture. As the controversy developed, the press scathingly suggested that it was time for this fictional hero to produce some real action himself. But in fact Carse, who had spent two years in the Antarctic with the British Graham Land Expedition, 1935-37, and was later to lead three expeditions to South Georgia, was well qualified to express an informed opinion on our situation.

Shortly after Midwinter I received a message from the Governor saying that because of the difficulties of access he had decided to close Stonington after our relief next season. To compensate for this, Port Lockroy was to be reopened. This was a bitter pill, for we all felt that we had opened up a valuable field of geological work on Alexander Island. I wrote in my journal:

Somehow it seems ... that all our efforts here are to bear no future fruit. In fact we have accomplished as much in our time as an expedition could be expected to do, but somehow in a concern of this nature it seems like the dying of a family through failure to produce a new generation to carry on the good work. I am desolate!

We put a brave face on it, but became stubbornly determined to use our last sledging season to advantage. The main journey could not begin until early September, but meanwhile there was still plenty to do. The Dions rookery party had to be brought back, we made soundings through the ice to find a new ship channel north of Neny Island, and numerous short journeys enabled us to complete the local survey and geological work.

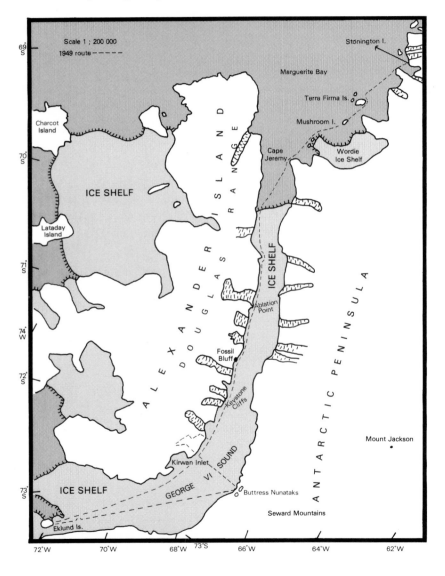

On 14 August Adie and I set off for the Dions with light sledges, for we hoped to bring back all the seal meat we could carry to nourish our dogs after their lean winter. To fatten them up we stayed at the islands for two weeks, our time well spent in survey and geology. My bitch 'Lizzie' was a great favourite but a headstrong girl who gave us plenty of trouble. She was very lovable but a real old trollop with no morals at all. When in season she always contrived to get off her span, and then went round visiting every dog she could before we caught up with the situation. We never had the faintest idea who was the father of her endless litters.

But on this occasion it was not love that was on her mind. She managed to get loose just for fun, and was found happily chasing penguins, who by now were all holding tiny chirruping chicks. A number lost their young in the scramble, and all of us spent a lot of time in the dark and a high wind trying to collect them. The live ones were brought back to the tents, to be kept warm until we could return them to the rookery next morning.

Settling down for the night, we had hardly got to sleep when a vociferous cheeping woke us, which was obviously going to continue indefinitely. At wit's end, we suddenly thought of feeding them with premasticated herrings in tomato sauce, the only fish we had. Soon we were all busy munching and dropping small, unsalubrious lumps into tiny ready-gaping beaks, after which silence prevailed. It was not long before we were to sympathize with penguin parents, for every two hours throughout that very long night the whole pantomime had to be repeated if we were to get any sleep. At dawn we thankfully relinquished our fostering, the chicks were returned to the rookery and immediately adopted by eager adult birds.

On the 28th the little winter camp was broken, and the five of us left for base carrying 550 pounds of seal meat and a large plywood box containing four emperors and three tiny chicks. They were intended for the London Zoo. The adults did not need to feed (they had not been observed to do so since 4 June), yet they were constantly able to regurgitate food for their young. Unhappily only one chick survived the journey, for the others were trampled on by their parents as the sledge swayed from side to side.

By the time we left for home six months later, the chick weighed 35 pounds, and our fishing commitment had become three fish per man per day, for the birds required thirty-three every twenty-four hours. We caught them by hand-line or in fish traps made from chicken wire. One stormy night the penguins' wire enclosure filled with so much drift that the three adults simply walked up and over the top. So in the end we brought back only two birds; sadly they did not have sufficient resistance to survive in England and died of aspergillosis.

Without an aircraft to lay depots, the long southern journey was a most complex operation. A four-sledge advance party (Huckle, Brown, Spivey, Toynbee) left on 8 September to establish depots at the Terra Firma Islands, Mushroom Island, and finally as far south as conditions would allow them to travel. At the appropriate time Spivey and Toynbee were to hand over their remaining loads and make a fast run home, leaving the other two to put in the final depot before carrying on the survey begun in George VI Sound the previous season.

According to the progress made by the advance party, Adie and I would leave two or three weeks later and travel as far south along the coast of Alexander Island as supplies would permit. In fact we set out on 1 October, knowing that bad conditions had so delayed the first depot-layers that we would be lucky to reach even the southern end of the Sound.

The previous year we had got as far as Keystone Cliffs, so named because it was there that we felt we had at last the key to the geological structure of the Sound. We planned therefore to travel as fast as possible to this point and continue work from there onwards. The main interest lay in the Jurassic and cretaceous sediments which form Alexander Island, which we already knew to be fossiliferous and heavily folded. Both the rocks and their structure were entirely different from the older dioritic rocks which formed the east side of the Sound only thirty miles away. In the interpretation of the relationships lay the answer to the origin of the Sound itself. In addition to geology, we also mapped the coast, made meteorological observations every three hours, and collected any botanical material (mosses and lichens) we encountered. They were busy days.

After three days we came to the deep, soft snow which had so hampered the advance party, and day after day were forced to 'relay', taking forward part-loads, returning for the rest – thus achieving only one mile forward for every three we travelled.

Seventeen days out, and 102 miles from base, we met the first support party returning.

That night we all camped together, and during the radio 'sched' with base learnt that Captain Harry Kirkwood had reported that *Biscoe* was already off Spain, and this time he was looking forward to reaching us. It all seemed very remote. We were only at the beginning of our journey and it would be another three months before we returned to the comforts of base, and perhaps mail from home.

Meanwhile Huckle and Brown still struggled south in appalling conditions. Speaking to them by radio on the 21st I agreed to their leaving our last depot at Ablation Point, seventy-five miles short of the planned position. It was essential that they should at least reach Ablation in order to tie in their survey with that of the British Graham Land Expedition (1934-37), where an astronomical fix had been made.

A week later we were at the ice cliff which marks the front of the floating ice shelf filling George VI Sound. Conditions at last improved, and on 2 November we reached Ablation Point, just missing the surveyors who had already crossed to the east coast. Once we thought we saw their sledges coming towards us and hastened forward to meet them, but about 400 yards farther on were astonished to find we had been deceived by some miraged empty dog pemmican tins left at one of their old camp sites.

As we travelled, the great Douglas Range to the west extended as far as we could see, the highest peak rising to 10,000 feet. At our halts we never tired of gazing at this magnificent panorama, with its peaks, spurs and great tumbling glaciers pouring down to the Sound. By the 6th we were at Keystone Cliffs and our real work began.

Soon we found ourselves among high ridges which were impossible to distinguish in the diffuse light condition of the 'whiteout'. Scouting about for a way through, I probed ahead with a six-foot ice chisel. Suddenly I felt nothing in front of me, and stopping rather hastily I became aware that my skis were projecting over an invisible but sharp edge. Retiring cautiously to firmer ground, we made camp to await better visibility. Next day when it cleared, my ski tracks could be seen ending at the edge of a fifteen-foot drop to a snow slope down to the bottom of a rift forty feet below.

Extricating ourselves from this confused area we followed the coast, expecting to find the ice promontory shown on the map as ending in 'Cape Stephenson'. Instead, the coast ran back into an embayment now known as Kirwan Inlet; thus on the map the area of Alexander Island was reduced by 300 square miles. We then set course for Eklund Island sixty miles distant.

Now forty-four days out from base, I was becoming increasingly worried about the dogs, who were clearly very tired. They were getting only one pound of pemmican each day, and the endless vista of snow provided nothing encouraging for them to run towards. The dejected state of these usually over-exuberant creatures even affected us, for it was both depressing and tiring to drive them when every ounce of pull seemed to be exerted by one's own will-power. At every slight rise or soft patch they had to be exhorted afresh while we also pushed, or the sledges stopped at once. As these occurred every few yards, the shouting was well-nigh continuous for hours on end. It certainly sapped our energy.

That night we decided to feed all the remaining blubber we had during the next two days, thereby giving each animal about half-a-pound extra in addition to the pemmican ration. Next morning the snow became increasingly deep and soft so we waxed our wooden sledge runners. There was also an astonishing improvement in the teams after their first blubber feed, and we began to feel that when it was finished we would just have to feed dog to dog if we were to get home.

As we travelled there was suddenly a black spot on the horizon, winking at intervals, then disappearing. Eklund Island, now thirty-seven miles off, was appearing and disappearing with the varying refraction of the atmosphere. As soon as it remained steady I tried unsuccessfully to get Darkie to hold course towards it, until bending down to his eye-level I realized he could not yet see it. It seemed incredible that an angle subtended by only three feet could make so much difference at so great a distance. But a mile farther on the whole team saw it and, pricking up their ears, broke into a rapid trot.

The surface was increasingly undulating with occasional rifts in the hollows. Halting on one of the ridges to rest the teams, the dogs suddenly jumped up, trying to turn back along our track. A quarter of a mile away, unbelievably, we saw eleven Adélie penguins plodding steadily across the ice shelf. Every now and then they stopped to look around as though getting their bearings. Our debilitated animals badly needed food. Hurriedly unloading Adie's sledge, we raced back in hot pursuit. Killing is never pleasant, but this providential gift was all the more extraordinary coming at such a crucial moment, for we never saw another penguin until we returned to Marguerite Bay one month later.

With the appetizing scent of the birds on the sledges being wafted over their heads by a following wind, the dogs perked up, and soon we came to the steeply drifted-up front of the ice shelf, separated from Eklund by sea ice. This was a surprise, for about thirty miles of the shelf must have broken up and drifted away since the Americans Finn Ronne and Carl Eklund had been there nine years earlier. Descending a steep drift-slope to the sea ice, we made for the nearest of nine small rocky islets which surround Ekland Island and camped.

There we cut up the penguins and each dog got half a bird, about five pounds of food. When they had finished feeding, just five tail feathers remained on the snow – beaks, claws, flippers, everything had been consumed.

During the four days spent at that camp we examined a number of the small islands, which proved to be granite or diorite, and were also able to climb to the top of Eklund itself. There are in fact two tops, the highest a snow ridge of 1,400 feet, the second a rock pinnacle 250 feet lower. To reach this we cut some 200 steps down the inside of the surrounding windscoop, and after a steep climb up the rock itself we stood beside a substantial cairn which had been built by the Americans.

Intent on finding the United States Claim Sheet which Ronne was reported to have left there, we began dismantling the cairn stone by stone, until at last, adhering to the underside of a boulder from the lowest layer, we found a specimen bag labelled FINDERS KEEPERS. Inside was a piece of paper letter-headed *United States Department of the Interior, Washington*, on which was written:

This peak in George VI Sound was climbed this day by the Southern Party of the United States Antarctic Expedition 1939-41.
Its base is in Marguerite Bay close to Neny Fjord.
Carl R Eklund Tomahawk, WISC. USA. Naturalist.
Finn Ronne Leader this party and Chief of Staff USAS.
Dec 14 1941

The date should have read 1940, for Ronne's party were evacuated by air from Stonington in early 1941. There was no other record, and this did not seem to us to constitute 'one of the Claim Sheets issued by the State Department'. Rebuilding the cairn, we left a note recording both the American visit and our own, taking the original with us.

Our intention to leave Eklund on 22 November was baulked by a rising wind and heavy drift, so we settled down in our tent to see out the storm. During our two years at Stonington Ray Adie and I had sledged many many miles together, and I always marvelled at his imperturbability and constant meticulous attention to detail. At the end of each day's long and often weary march he always gave me a written statement of exactly how far we had travelled, how much food and fuel we had left, and the actual weight carried by each sledge. Despite his youth he had already developed the habit of precise thinking which was later to make him one of the best scientific editors in the country.

By now our two books had been read and re-read, but Adie was not to be defeated. I was suddenly astounded to find myself listening to him expounding the virtues of a brand of sausages. With care and attention to proper emphasis he was reading aloud the label on the tin – every stop and comma. Next it was pea flour, then the tin of peaches we were keeping for Christmas Day. To such is one reduced when, during months of isolated travel, everything has been said, and each man knows every detail of the other's family life and the nooks and crannies of his home.

More profitably, we discussed the possible geology of the country beyond our logistic capacity to reach. This led us to thoughts of bigger and longer expeditions to the interior of the continent. So, in a snow storm, originated the idea of crossing Antarctica, and that evening I set to with a stub of pencil to outline the concept of such a journey. We even began working out logistics. Five years later it came true, and the betting fraternity at Stonington lost their wagers. But Adie, who had shared the first dreams, was not able to be one of my party. He had taught me to drive dogs – I would like to have returned the compliment in a Sno-Cat.

We finally left Eklund on our fifty-third day out, 420 miles from home base, although with the necessary relaying we had covered 620 miles. With eighteen days' food left before we would have to

The Douglas Range, George VI Sound

reach a depot put down in latitude 72°S, there was time to make for the rock bastions 123 miles away in the south-east corner of the Sound (now Buttress Nunataks). They had never been visited.

For seven days we suffered only head winds and low drift, but on the eighth we were in a field of enormous sastrugi (sharp irregular ridges – parallel to the direction of the prevailing wind – formed on the snow surface by wind erosion) where large crevasses, open and bridged, reduced our travel to six miles. That night we made camp two miles away from the 2,000-foot faces of the nunataks, and next day were able to reach two of them. Unlike the cretaceous sedimentary rocks of Alexander Island on the other side of the Sound, here they proved to be older, somewhat metamorphosed intrusives, which tied in with previous knowledge of the rocks on the east side. Continuous barometric readings showed that we were at the lowest level of the ice shelf – indeed at sea-level, which seemed remarkable. At Eklund I had sounded the sea depth near the ice front and found sixty fathoms, with a strong current running under the shelf. Now it seemed possible that the scour of the current in the bend of the Sound was sufficient to thin the ice from beneath.

Four days later we had crossed to the western side of the Sound and were camped at 1,250 feet on Alexander Island, among a group of three nunataks composed of fossiliferous shales and sandstones. A seventy-knot blizzard gusting to ninety knots hit us, and we hastily built a protective wall around the tent, remaining fully dressed all night, our backs supporting the bending tent poles. Fortunately the wind died in the morning and we spent three days working among some twenty nunataks in the area. One of them – Coal Nunatak – contained thin lenses of coal besides fossil remains.

On 8 December, with only one day's dog food left, we set off for the depot. Conditions were clear, with a bright midnight sun giving a distant scene of great grandeur. One hundred miles to the east-north-east, behind the heavily crevassed Goodenough Glacier, we could see Mount Jackson (13,750 feet), to the east lay the Buttress Nunataks, and beyond them the as yet unvisited Seward Mountains.

For some miles the dogs raced joyfully down the steep slopes. Then, after negotiating the ridges, pinnacles and walls of pressure ice at the edge of the Sound, we reached the ice shelf and soon found our depot. We now had six days' dog food to carry us the ninety miles north to Ablation point.

Biscoe was already in Stanley – it was time to head for home. We were determined to fit in all the work we could before the New Year deadline. The previous season we had tried to achieve more work by adopting a repetitive sequence of six hours' travel, followed by four hours' sleep, four hours' work, four hours' sleep, and six hours' travel. This was possible because the continuous daylight enabled us to ignore the time of day. But after some three days we had found this régime too much of a strain and had abandoned it. Therefore we realized that this time we could work only if we travelled for longer than the normal eight hours per day.

On the way back we stopped for a day at Ablation Point, and each spent twelve hours working separately in the hills. We thought there was tidal movement in the embayment, and if indeed there was a tide, the bay itself must be filled with sea ice, not ice shelf. This would provide a useful datum for survey purposes. But it would certainly be surprising, indicating that the adjacent ice shelf must thin out towards the coast at this point. (In 1970 this was proved correct.)

Leaving on 15 December the teams were soon involved in the crevassed zone which had caused us trouble the previous year. Then we had nearly lost Adie's 'Mutt' when his trace broke while crossing a crevasse. Peering into the depths we had seen him quietly standing on a bridge of ice twenty feet down.

'... we pushed the sledge back over the crevasse to act as a bridge ... about twenty feet down I came to rest on ice spanning the crevasse ... Mutt stood quietly without so much as looking round ... amidst a shower of tinkling icicles which plunged on past, and speaking gently to him I fixed the rope to his harness. Then Ray, who had tied my life line firmly to the sledge, began to haul the 100-pound dog slowly upward ... While this was going on I had the opportunity to study the magnificent sight of the narrow cavernous place in which I found myself. Everywhere there hung huge icicles ten to fifteen feet long, with bases as much as eighteen inches thick. Of these I had to be careful, for a piece could easily be dislodged and could have knocked me out ... The walls were hung with an amazing lace-like curtain of ice crystals, the individual crystals being an inch in diameter and linked together to form glittering pendants.

Remembering that experience, this time I tried to keep as far east as possible, but we were confined by great pressure ridges sweeping out into the Sound from Ablation Point. Thaw conditions are the worst possible for travel in crevassed areas and we soon found that where the bridges had not already fallen in, they did so immediately the sledges crossed.

It was interesting to observe Darkie's technique. He advanced cautiously, somewhat in the fashion of an heraldic lion or leopard, each paw extended as far as possible to test the surface in front of him, In this way he found every crevasse and successfully crossed the majority, whereas those behind went blundering into them in spite of the obvious holes he had made. Others would suddenly dash sideways to avoid an imaginary crevasse which was no more than a surface marking in the snow, which Darkie ignored. Indeed with him ahead, be it on glacier or thin sea ice, I can move forward with the greatest confidence.

On the seventy-ninth day of our journey we were once more back near the depot left on the edge of the ice shelf, with only one day's dog food left and still 150 miles to go. There we were shocked to find that the shelf had calved, and our supplies now lay on what was an iceberg, with sheer forty-foot walls descending to open water. Below us, and some 400 yards away on the sea ice, lay a seal we had killed and left for the return journey, separated from us by a belt of open water. I set off along the high front of the ice shelf seeking a way down on to the sea ice, and eventually recovered the seal, but it cost me eighteen miles to provide the dogs' dinner which had been lying so close to us.

After that we still had to recover the depot. With considerable relief we found a point where the iceberg was still only ten feet from the cliff on which we stood. This we bridged precariously with a twelve-foot sledge by building a snow mound on the very edge of the chasm, to act as a fulcrum, so that our combined weight could hold the sledge tilted in the air as it was pushed across. Once in position, we anchored it securely at both ends, and then laboriously brought across the second sledge to pick up the cache lying a few hundred yards away.

The last leg home led past Cape Jeremy, Mushroom Island, the Terra Firma Island and the Refuge Islands, clearing the depots as we went. During this period came high temperatures, mist and fog, and for a time we were all coated with white rime. Each black, doggy face looked distinctly odd through this white mask and the long hair on their backs and tails drooping with its weight seemed to be covered in delicate white lace.

Then the temperature dropped and we made better time, covering thirty-one miles on each of three successive days. Despite this, however, travelling was far from straighforward, for it was high summer and the ice was deteriorating fast. On 28 December we made our final run in, not a day too soon, for we were only just able to cross Neny Fjord. First we became involved in a series of diversions due to long tide cracks, and then found ourselves in a maze of melt pools, between which we had to drive with scarcely enough room for the sledge to balance on the ridges between them. The dogs, deeply suspicious of the water, refused to run through the pools, always trying to find a winding route which kept them on dry snow.

The inevitable happened. My sledge tipped sideways and turned over in a foot-deep pool, then Adie's did the same, then mine a second time. All our gear, and worse still our maps and notes, were sodden, while the wind blew across our course at thirty knots, with strong gusts which made the teams unwilling to run sideways to it. It was useless to try and keep clear of pools so I headed into the wind, but we made little progress despite throwing some of the dogs into the water hoping they would lose a disinclination to get wet. After a few hours of this we were very hot from our struggles, and decided to drop 660 pounds to be picked up later in more propitious conditions. Providentially we did this just in time, for within 400 yards I went straight through the bottom of a pool to the sea beneath. Adie perforce followed, and had he been heavily laden the remaining ice below could well have broken.

The wind increased, sometimes carrying clouds of flying ice particles, the teams hardly able to move against it, and skiing was out of the question. So we plodded on behind the sledges, pushing when necessary and caring nothing for the water. Presently the pools froze lightly, the dogs could step warily across although the sledges ploughed through, running on rotten ice below. When two miles from home we were seen, and Jones and Blaiklock came out to guide us in.

The base had laid out mile-long strips of a mixture compounded of soot, black diesel oil and sea water, aimed at hastening the melt so that a water strip would be available for the expected sea-plane. This had worked only too well, and now they led us along the only route past parallel lines of open water. So we arrived home, after covering 1,084 miles in ninety days. Steaming baths were ready, a considerate gesture extended to returning sledgers, made partly in self-defence for they never realize how evil they smell!

During our absence Jones and Blaiklock had sledged north to complete the survey work in Bourgeois Fjord, and had discovered that it was connected with Bigourdan Fjord by a channel filled by an ice shelf. This was probably the last remnant of a shelf which must have extended through all the fjords, and perhaps the whole of Marguerite Bay. Its presence supported the earlier deductions of Launcelot Fleming who had been both geologist and padre with the British Graham Land Expedition.

Even more important for us, the *Biscoe* had brought out two seaplanes, a de Havilland Norseman and an Auster. The former had been procured in Canada by the Governor himself who was determined on a successful relief – by air if necessary. This was the last Norseman ever built, for the type was soon to be replaced by the Beaver.

By early January 1950 the planes were at Deception and ready to fly, but it was planned that they would try to reach us from the Argentine Islands, over 200 miles nearer to Stonington. However, ice prevented *Biscoe* from getting there until the 28th. Meanwhile we too had our part to play in the operation. Appropriate flying loads were packed and weighed, regular radio 'scheds' and meteorological flying forecasts maintained, boats prepared to take us out to a plane if evacuation became necessary, ice conditions carefully observed, both locally and from the top of Neny Island as far as the horizon, and the base prepared for closure.

The first large pool of water, some 700 yards long, appeared in Neny Fjord, gradually extending to over a mile within two days. On the 28th Port Lockroy had been reopened, and two days later we were in hourly communication with the Governor, who despatched the Norseman on a reconnaissance flight. That afternoon the red and silver plane flew in from the north, soon it was circling base, dropping our mail and a welcome leg of lamb. Then Pilot Officer Pete St Louis RCAF flew off to investigate conditions in Neny Fjord. From base it looked as if the melt area had again been covered by jostling ice floes, and we were greatly astonished to hear that he was coming down.

What a scurry – everyone tearing hither and thither, dressing, loading a sledge, rushing off across the ice. John Huckle and I were first away to get the dory we had placed at Neny into the water. Then followed Stonehouse, Randall, Jones and Adie with the sledge. Looking back we saw that it had sunk, later it transpired that this happened a number of times, soaking the personal gear and records.

Meanwhile Huckle and I strode on, launched the boat and had it waiting for Randall and Stonehouse, the first to arrive. The aircraft seemed a long way off and we could see no open water, nothing but a heaving mass of brash and floes, but apparently decreasing in quantity farther out. It was clearly necessary to hasten, yet to avoid overloading the dory, which would have to be lifted in and out of the water to pass the heavy ice near shore. I therefore sent off Huckle, Stonehouse and Randall without waiting for the others or any of the gear to arrive. I hoped that Ken Butler, due to join us from the plane as relief radio operator, would be able to bring the boat back to the heavier ice where we could have gone out to help him. But conditions proved to be so bad farther on that this was impossible, indeed it took the boat nearly two hours to reach the plane. Rising wind and increasing overcast forced the pilot to take off immediately with Stonehouse and Randall, leaving Huckle who volunteered to return with Butler.

A southern Post Office

That evening we drank the last carefully preserved bottle of gin to celebrate Ken Butler's return to Stonington – the first new face we had seen in two years. There followed a further wait of eight days due to bad weather, but on 6 February the Norseman arrived, again piloted by St Louis, and this time able to land close to the ice edge, so loading was easy. The outgoing passengers were the last of the three-year men, Adie, Jones and Huckle, together with the penguins, and assorted specimens and records. It was a great relief to know that they at least would now get home come what may.

Meanwhile Flight Lieutenant John Lewis RAF was using the Auster to reconnoitre the ice situation for *Biscoe's* attempt to reach us, and three days later she was making good progress southward. That evening we paid our last visit to the observation point on Northeast Glacier. Through glasses we saw innumerable icebergs breaking the line of the darkening horizon, among them the intermittent winking of the ship's masthead light as she wove an erratic course through ice invisible to us. In a few hours she was gliding silently down Neny Fjord, past Neny Island, her dark hull twinkling with lights.

After the first greetings, final plans were made for embarkation during the next two days. Our most painful duty was the necessity to

Judy and her pups

put down all but thirty-seven dogs, the maximum number we could take out in the ship. It was something we had dreaded for they were our friends and had shared our lives. To them we owed our achievements, sometimes even our survival, and now we were going to break the mutual trust which had built up between us. Quietly, in the still of the night, a few of us steeled ourselves for the inevitable, our only comfort lying in the knowledge that as each animal in turn enjoyed his last meal isolated from his companions, none of them knew what was about to happen. It was a terrible thing to have to do.

Of the remainder, most went to live at other bases. A team of nine came back to England, to play their part in the Polar Pavilion during the Festival of Britain in Battersea Park. There Darkie and his followers gave over 2,000 sledging performances for the public, living isolated in the grounds under special quarantine conditions. They were a great draw. Two drivers lived with them, and each morning the team was exercised in harness, hauling a sledge around the grounds before the public were admitted.

When, after six months, the Festival ended, Darkie came to live with us in Cambridge where he became a well-known figure. He always wove a careful course through the traffic as he hauled me on a bicycle, ever punctilious in obeying commands regarding the lights. But it took a long time to teach him not to jump the white lines, which *he* knew to be 'crevasses' in the tarmac!

By the evening of 11 February, 1950 my forty-second birthday, the chimneys, windows and doors had all been boarded up and we said goodbye to Stonington. It seemed extraordinary but we were truly sad at leaving – the beginning of a nostalgia which has remained with the Lost Eleven ever since.

Leaving Marguerite Bay was much easier than we had expected for nearly all the ice had blown out to the west. Two days later we called at Port Lockroy and then the Argentine Islands to pick up Fids who were returning home, where we left a number of the Stonington dogs. Next we sailed to Deception Island where we met HMS *Bigbury Bay* to which the Governor and eight Stonington men transferred on their way to Stanley. Three of us remained in *Biscoe* to pay the season's final visits to the bases at Admiralty Bay and Signy Island.

We spent five days at Signy unloading many tons of stores and timber for new building, all of which had to be carried by hand up seventy feet of a rocky slope. On 2 March *Biscoe* finally brought us to Stanley, where I stayed with Stewart Slessor, the Senior Medical Officer who had accompanied me to Stonington two years earlier.

During the next three weeks we were royally entertained by the Stanley community, and on 22 March sailed in *Bigbury Bay* for Brazil to connect with RMS *Andes*. Seven days later we docked in Santos which, from the sea, seemed to resemble Freetown on the other side of the Atlantic. From a distance one saw a number of skycrapers, but as we approached the planned nature of the town became apparent. Even towards the docks the red-roofed bunga-lows were well spaced along wide, stony roads, and there was much greenery around all the buildings.

Sailing up the wide river for some miles we finally berthed as it were behind the city as seen from the sea. As soon as we secured the Naval Attaché, the British Consul and the Port Captain came aboard accompanied by numerous reporters. The latter showed little interest in our Antarctic adventures except to ask whether we had seen any Flying Saucers in the south. It seemed incredible that such stories which had been in full swing before we left England in

1947, should still be in the news. Next morning the papers were full of my denials!

The days following provided a long succession of official or private parties and receptions until the time we sailed in the *Andes* for Lisbon and Southampton. The voyage was a relaxed period when the Lost Eleven found themselves organizing sports competitions in which large numbers of the South American passengers happily took part. The only problem arose from the large number of totally undisciplined children on board. Their main pleasure seemed to be the interruption of adult games by repeatedly throwing the deck tennis quoits or shuffle-board discs overboard. Since they spoke no English, they learnt discipline and good manners the hard way! There were no complaints from the parents, so either they welcomed our corrective actions or we were sufficiently surreptitious for them to be unaware of what was going on.

About 200 miles off the coast of Portugal we came upon a small Portuguese fishing-boat flying a white shirt as a distress signal from its topmast. They had no radio, so our Captain brought the ship round in a five-mile arc to lie alongside her. It transpired that the crew were short of water and had no idea where they were. It was a coastal vessel which had been blown off course, and they had no navigational instruments. After providing water and fixing their position, we sailed on to Lisbon.

There we spent two days sight-seeing and then left on the last leg to Southampton where we dispersed to our various family homes – I to join Joyce and the children at my father's house at Heatherdene. Hilary was now fourteen and Peter ten, and when we went back to Barton Cottage in Cambridge I was able to get to know them again during the months of leave which had accumulated during my two-and-a-half years' absence.

I was once again considering where my future lay, for it was essential to find employment without too much delay. Fortunately the Scientific Advisory Committee's proposals for the establishment of an office to handle the increasing mass of scientific material then returning from the Antarctic were approved by the Colonial Office, and I was offered the initial post with the task of setting it up. This new organization was given the cumbersome title of the Falkland Islands Dependencies Scientific Bureau (FIDSC Bureau) and came into being on 19 June 1950 at Queen Anne's Chambers, Broadway in London. It consisted of two bare rooms, two wooden trestle tables and two steel cupboards crammed with some hundreds of field reports.

My instructions were to buy a typewriter, some stationery, and an armchair for visitors. Later it was hoped that I might be able to employ a typist and even look forward to a time when I could acquire an assistant. My brief was to interview the returning scientists and decide where, and for how long, they should write up their results. I was also charged with making arrangements for the publication of the scientific work, and to act as the centre for the distribution of specimens and information.

Inevitably it was not long before I was widely exceeding these instructions as I began to deal with the innumerable queries on Antarctic matters which were already arriving from the public. The Colonial Office recognized this and wrote,

The Bureau has, whether by design or not, gathered unto itself various functions, some of them of considerable importance, not set out in its terms of reference.

This was an acceptance of reality which could not be avoided since there was no one else able to perform those functions.

After about a year I recruited my Assistant, Evelyn Todd, a Geography graduate from Cambridge, and a typist whose name was also Evelyn. To avoid confusion I arbitrarily decided that the former should be called 'Anne' Todd – and thus she became known to successive generations of Fids for the next thirty-five years. We were in business – and this time it was for keeps.

Chapter 12

Bids and Counter Bids

At first the formation of the Scientific Bureau occupied all my time, but I had not forgotten the idea of a trans-Antarctic journey. On my return home I had talked about it to Wordie, who was then Senior Tutor at St John's College and a member of the Colonial Office Polar Committee, but he advised that the time was not propitious to submit such a proposal to the Colonial Office and ask for three years leave of absence to lead the venture. Wordie gave me his full support and promised to tell me when the right moment came.

In Stanley, on our way home from Stonington, I had also told the Governor, Sir Miles Clifford, that I had these plans in mind. He had immediately grasped the idea that such a journey was of potential scientific value and could add to British Antarctic prestige. Within a very short time he sent Ken Pierce-Butler, who was then Secretary FIDS (SECFIDS) to ask me to give him my plans. The Governor also asked Ken to prepare plans of his own for a journey from Stonington Island to McMurdo Sound on the Ross Sea, to be mounted within FIDS resources and under FIDS control. I was flabbergasted by this attempted poaching, and after refusing to discuss the matter with Ken we sailed for home.

By 24 March Sir Miles was writing to James Griffiths, then Secretary of State for the Colonies:

One of the greatest areas of unexplored territory still remaining in the British sector of the Antarctic continent lies at the head of the Weddell Sea ...

It has been held that the Antarctic continent may, in fact be sub-divided by an ice-filled depression linking the Weddell Sea and the Ross Sea; geographically this is entirely possible.

My object then would be to form a special expedition within FIDS to undertake the investigation of this theory, using Stonington Island as the main base for it ... It would be desirable, indeed necessary, to enlist the active cooperation of the New Zealand Government ...

There then followed details of the proposed plan (presumably put together by Pierce-Butler) and the statement that although the cost of the expedition could not be accurately computed at that stage he considered that the FIDS share of the venture would be £45,000 for the whole period of 1951 to 1954. The balance could be expected to be found by New Zealand, and the RAF from its own resources.

By 16 May the Governor was again writing to the Colonial Secretary submitting the outline of an abridged programme should the major project of a trans-continental journey fail to enlist sufficient support. This time his letter said:

I desire at this stage to recommend that whichever of the two projects be decided upon, the leadership should be entrusted to Lieut.-Colonel Pierce-Butler; familiarity with the area, proved sledging ability and leadership qualities are required and are combined in this officer. I also recommend the appointment of Mr R J Adie as principal scientific officer and second-in-command.

The Colonial Office was cautiously interested, but the proposals bristled with difficulties. Did either project provide a desirable use of FIDS resources, and would the FIDS organization be able to carry out such a major undertaking? Somewhat lengthy exchanges went to and fro between London and Stanley, and the situation was not improved by the dearth of mailing opportunities – then only ten each year. No decision emerged, and by December Sir Miles was sending cables pressing for an answer. On 12 December the Colonial Office cabled:

Way is not yet clear for decision your proposals. In any event long period of preparation would be necessary. You therefore can assume that in any case project could not be put in hand early enough to affect your plans for season 1951-52.

The matter was shelved.

Meanwhile at the Bureau Anne Todd and I had, among other things, been busy with the distribution of material to various workers in universities, and drafting the introductory issue of the *Falkland Islands Dependencies Scientific Reports: No. 1.* Sometimes our routine was enlivened by unusual events. During the late Antarctic winter of 1950 one of the men at a small base became increasingly withdrawn, spending most of his time sharpening a knife for no apparent reason. When questioned by his Base Leader he was unable to explain this, but volunteered the information that he did not really feel responsible for his actions – even suggesting that it might be safer if his companions tied him up. So they lashed him to his bunk, and for some weeks until the relief ship arrived he remained happily under restraint, only being released for meals. The *Biscoe* was specially diverted to fetch him out to be sent home for treatment.

At Montevideo the shipping company refused to carry him unless accompanied. So another Fid was detailed to travel home with him, and as soon as they arrived in England the escort reported to me at the Bureau. I learnt that on one occasion during the voyage the patient had woken up and asked his friend to please lend him his soul in order to fetch back his own which, he alleged, had left the cabin. 'What did you do?' I asked with considerable curiosity. 'Well, I hardly liked to lend him mine,' was the bizarre reply, 'I wasn't sure I'd get it back.' The trouble seemed contagious!

In the summer of 1951 Sir Miles Clifford returned home on leave, still persisting with his plans for a trans-continental Antarctic journey. This, and the alternative idea of investigating the southern coast of the Weddell Sea, were discussed at a Colonial Office meeting in July. Both were vetoed as impracticable. The official Minutes recorded:

> It was agreed that the transcontinental expedition from Graham Land to the Ross Sea was not a project suitable to be undertaken by the Falkland Islands Dependencies Survey in present circumstances, and should be left in abeyance.

In 1953 James Wordie said he thought the right moment had come for me to produce my plans for a privately organized Trans-Antarctic Expedition and ask for government backing. He added that Dr Gordon Robin (ex-Signy), who had been a member of the Norwegian-British-Swedish Antarctic Expedition 1949-52, was also thinking about a trans-continental journey, and he suggested we should meet to discuss the matter.

This we did and Gordon assured me that he was not planning a rival expedition. Later on he generously joined my expedition's General and Scientific Committees, where his advice was based on his experience at Maudheim (the NBSAE base) when he led a successful 1,200 kilometre mechanized scientific traverse to the polar plateau and back in 1951-52.

Thus reassured, I set to work on detailed proposals, the whole idea remaining strictly confidential except for the few people in the government who were being asked for approval. Hoping that he would be able to help in New Zealand, I also sent a copy to Professor Noel Odell of Otago University, but he inadvertently released the news to the New Zealand press. Immediately it was taken up in Britain, and soon I was having to sit by my phone in Cambridge most of the day to answer the unending stream of questions which resulted from this unsought publicity.

Suddenly it was apparently also the main talking point in the entire polar community, with everyone feeling free to express opinions as to the value of such a journey, and even questioning the leadership in the harshest terms. I was soon aware that there was a solid body of opinion against my project. This seemed to be headed by Dr Brian Roberts, who worked at the Polar Desk of the Foreign Office and also at the Scott Polar Research Institute. His views were supported by Dr Colin Bertram, Director of the Institute and Sir Lawrence Kirwan, Director and Secretary of the Royal Geographical Society. They were the three big guns with most influence on opinion, and their opposition was apparently based on the possible embarrassment for Britain if the project failed. They preferred to 'leave such a journey to the Americans.' There were other side issues as well, and the Geographical Society faction decided that the journey ought more properly to be led by Sir Edmund Hillary of Everest fame – who at that time had never even seen sea ice. While my opponents argued and made impracticable suggestions, I withdrew from polar contacts and continued work on my plans.

I reckoned that the expedition would need £500,000 and the chief problem, apart from getting permission for leave of absence, was how to raise the money. I did not know the right sort of people – but Wordie supported me strongly, and he did. Through his good offices I was introduced to Marshal of the Royal Air Force Sir John Slessor who knew everyone in the right places, and he kindly agreed to become Chairman of the Committee of Management which was to be formed to put the expedition into the field.

I envisaged a 'Commonwealth' expedition, and the Commonwealth Prime Ministers were then meeting in London. Through Sir John's influence I was given the opportunity of addressing them on my plans and seeking their help with funds. I had already been in discussion with the British Treasury about financial support, but it was only after this meeting that Sir Winston Churchill approved a grant of £100,000, and New Zealand, Australia and South Africa all agreed to help.

It was enough to begin with, and we found a small suite of offices at 64 Victoria Street (just near where Captain Scott had established the office from which he ran his 1910-13 expedition). The Colonial Office approved my secondment on full pay to organize the expedition, and soon I was joined by Rear Admiral Cecil Parry who was appointed Secretary.

Together we began to recruit office staff and a number of girls presented themselves for interview. Among them was Mrs Eleanor Honnywill. The name was familiar to the Admiral who immediately said did she know 'R B' Honnywill, one of his old naval chums? But of course – he was her husband! He then discovered that her country address was in a Dorset village where the Admiral had close friends. Yes – she knew them too. The interview turned into a social event. And so they conversed for about twenty minutes. The Navy being a very good club, it turned out that Eleanor knew many of the Admiral's cronies, and he promptly arranged for her to come temporarily on a month's trial and start a filing system – the cupboards also needed scrubbing out. She got up to leave and as she reached the door the Admiral said rather shamefacedly, 'Er – I suppose you *can* type?' Fortunately she could do that too! Her position in the office was never confirmed, and is the longest temporary job she ever held – to date she has worked for me for thirty-five years.

We set up the office in April 1955 and Sir Miles Clifford was again at home on leave. On the principle of joining those one can't beat he generously forgot his prejudices, and on Sir John Slessor's invitation became an enthusiastic and hard-working member of my Committee of Management.

About this time the Royal Geographical Society had their own machinations going on and circulated a note 'to all Fellows who are members of Dr Fuchs' Committee' warning that the President, Sir

James Marshall-Cornwall, wished to raise a number of matters at the next expedition General Committee 'including the question of the expedition's leadership'. As I too was a Fellow I received this prior warning that the knives were out, so I promptly invited the Treasury to send a delegation to the meeting to speak in my support if this became necessary. After all it was to *my* expedition that they had made a financial grant. They were good enough to send three representatives, but we had reckoned without Sir John Slessor who was now very angry. In the event it all turned into a build-up to a terrible let-down. None of us know what Sir John said to General Marshall-Cornwall on the telephone the evening before, but when he arrived at the meeting he looked a very sorry man, and his prepared script had obviously been torn up. Indeed there was nothing in his statement to discuss, and it was all very embarrassing. So ended the second take-over bid.

After that débâcle the hectic preparations for the expedition went fairly smoothly. It became clear that I had to abandon my position at the Scientific Bureau, and the problem was who should take it over. This was solved by Wordie who suggested Sir Raymond Priestley. He had been south with both Scott and Shackleton, and had recently retired as Vice-Chancellor of the University of Birmingham. Happily he agreed to come out of retirement 'for the duration' and took over the Bureau. Having acquired so eminent a replacement the Colonial Office and the Governor agreed that he should become Director of FIDS. So the Stanley Office, the representatives in the Crown Agents and the Bureau itself all came under one central control. Relieved of responsibility, I was able to concentrate on the expedition.

Briefly the plan was for a small Advance Party of eight to build a base on the shores of the Filchner Ice Shelf in the Weddell Sea. The following season this would be occupied by the main Crossing Party which, after spending a winter of preparation there, would attempt the journey the following summer.

We needed a reception base in McMurdo Sound whence depots would be laid out towards the South Pole to support the last stages of the crossing. This was in territory claimed by New Zealand, and the New Zealand government generously undertook responsibility for establishing and occupying a station to be known as Scott Base.

They formed their own Ross Sea Committee and did their own recruiting except for two experienced men, Dr George Marsh and Lieutenant-Commander Richard Brooke, whom we sent out from England. Rather naturally they chose Sir Edmund Hillary to lead the New Zealand contingent. New Zealand also provided HMNZS *Endeavour* to carry their party south. The New Zealand Air Force provided four men and an Auster aircraft, and the New Zealand Post Office gave all the radio equipment and communication facilities.

Together the four Commonwealth governments contributed £187,000 in cash, but this still left £300,000 of the estimated cost to be found from private sources. Besides industry, various Trusts and Societies generously supported us, and the first gift of all, £1,000, to my surprise came from the Geographical Society – which was invaluable as concrete evidence of their interest in our fortunes. When Sir Anthony Eden succeeded Churchill as Prime Minister he agreed to launch an appeal recommending our cause to the public. The response was generous and some 480 firms made major contributions in cash or kind. I was also delighted that schools began to take an increasing interest, and nearly 4,000 of them contributed to the cost, raising money for us in many ingenious ways.

The expedition itself was formed as a Limited Liability Company and granted the status of a Charity. This enabled it to earn money by the sale of press, book, broadcasting and other rights. In the end the income from these sources amounted to about one fifth of the total required which came to £750,000 – far beyond my original estimates.

We were soon in the throes of selecting the men who were to take part. Applications poured in, mainly from Britain, but including offers from Canada, Australia, South Africa, various European countries and even from Nigeria, Pakistan, India and Ceylon. Certain guiding principles controlled selection and occasionally these were found to conflict. For such an enterprise each successful candidate had to be physically fit and have that equable nature so necessary to the vicissitudes of polar travel. He had to be qualified in his own subject and at the same time able to carry out duties in other fields should the necessity arise. He also had to be prepared to take his turn at cooking or scrubbing and cleaning, and indeed any of the heavy work or unpleasant duties around the base. The Selection Committee had also to take into account nationality, for we wanted representatives of all the participating nations to be included in the Crossing Party.

Previous polar experience was naturally a great advantage, as it would have been inadvisable to attempt such a venture without a large proportion of experienced men. Those who had no scientific or technical knowledge had inevitably to be left out, as our numbers would be too small to include anyone who had no more than enthusiasm to contribute. In this way we lost a great many potentially excellent polar travellers, for by far the greatest number of applicants were untrained in the necessary fields.

As individuals were selected they joined the office and assisted in the procurement and preparation of the materials required in their particular field. Thus the men who were to use the equipment were themselves responsible for its provision.

The first to arrive was twenty-eight year-old David Stratton, who was to become my second-in-command. To him fell the immense task of preparing stores lists and co-ordinating the whole complex of material with the Crown Agents for packing and shipping. He was shortly followed by David Pratt, aged thirty, who took over the engineering section and became responsible for our transport and fuel requirements. Full of ideas, he had the happy knack of persuading unsuspecting manufacturers into doing far more than they had intended when first confronted with a 'Pratt Scheme', and it was due to his untiring and relentless energy that the enormous amount of work on our vehicles, in England, Norway and the Antarctic, was completed in the short periods of time available.

The Royal Air Force agreed to provide very considerable assistance – four men, two specially prepared Auster aircraft, the main radio communication equipment, and the radio beacons. A de Havilland Otter which was flown to England from Canada was handed over to the RAF for operational purposes. All this took a tremendous load off the shoulders of the London Committee.

Squadron Leader John Lewis joined us as chief pilot, and it was his task to act as liaison between the expedition and the Air Ministry. He co-ordinated the provision of aircraft, spares, radio equipment and the variety of stores required. Aged thirty-three, he had had experience of Antarctic flying when he had helped to evacuate us after the enforced extra year the Lost Eleven spent at Stonington. He was unfailingly cheerful and delighted when, being measured for his windproofs, he discovered his vital statistics and announced gleefully, 'I'm 42-44-46 – call me Pear'! When flying the Auster on floats it seemed incredible that the small plane could become airborne bearing his large frame and a passenger as well. When there was little water available he sometimes flew alone to avoid any risk of running into the ice at the end of a pool.

The second pilot was Gordon Haslop, a New Zealander serving in the RAF. We were soon to gain complete confidence in his handling of a plane in really uncomfortable situations, for nearly everything happened to Gordon. Another of the RAF contingent was Peter Weston, who at thirty-four had already had experience of maintaining aircraft in the Antarctic with the Norwegian-British-Swedish Expedition. With unruffled calm he bore the whole responsibility for the maintenance of our aircraft in very difficult circumstances, and they never failed us.

The Air Ministry also seconded 'Taffy' Williams who was to be the radio operator with the Advance Party and then remain for the second season as part of the main party. Aged thirty-five he was responsible for all communications, keeping our bases and field units in touch besides maintaining our contacts with the outside world. Perpetually smoking a cigarette, except when in process of losing a bet that he could give them up, his lilting Welsh accents and characteristic way of introducing the base over the air to London became renowned, and his opening gambits were eagerly awaited at the other end. He was a great asset to our life, and finally flew across the continent with the rest of the RAF men.

Another New Zealander was George Lowe, aged thirty-one. Originally a school teacher and later a member of the Cho Oyu and successful Everest Expeditions, his ability with cameras won him a place as our official photographer. He and Gordon Haslop singing Maori songs in parts were a favourite double act when they could be persuaded to perform.

Our offices consisted of five small, sparsely furnished rooms. With sometimes as many as nineteen members of the expedition working from them, they were overcrowded and congested to the point of standing room only, and almost never empty, for work went on late into the night and continued throughout a great many weekends. Gradually they filled up with all kinds of paraphernalia – skis, dog whips, samples of windproofs, sleeping bags and every sort of survival ration sent to us to test. The latter often proved their worth by keeping the weekend workers alive till the shops opened on Monday. The one larger room referred to as the Palm Court was occupied by the Admiral and myself and used for Committee Meetings. The walls of the smaller rooms became covered with cartoons, press-cuttings, engineering graphs and photographs, and on the outside of David Stratton's door was a large bow made of red tape!

To our delight the Admiral's first action was to hang over his door the Duke of Wellington's famous dictum:

IF I ATTEMPTED TO ANSWER THE MASS OF FUTILE CORRESPONDENCE THAT SURROUNDS ME I SHOULD BE DEBARRED FROM ALL SERIOUS BUSINESS OF CAMPAIGNING.

From the beginning we were magnificently supported by the enthusiasm, capacity for concentrated hard work and bubbling high spirits of the girls who joined us, and who endured with patience and good humour a constant pressure and telephone barrage which would have daunted many.

On one occasion the phone rang and an aggressive man demanded peremptorily to be put straight through to me quickly – refusing when asked to give his name. With tact and patience Eleanor gently explained that we were receiving so many strange calls that it was impossible for me to take them all, and she was only putting through calls from those who were prepared to identify themselves. For this she got an unpleasant dressing down and the caller slammed down his phone. At lunch time, four hours later, he rang again, apologized profusely for his bad manners and in the most honeyed tones said, 'My dear you were perfectly right to behave as you did. Actually I am the Managing Director of Rolls Royce in Derby, and I only want to offer Dr Fuchs all the facilities of this factory if there is anything he would like done!'

The Committee of Management met every two weeks, and as our

plans progressed I asked Sir John Slessor if he thought it would be appropriate to invite Her Majesty The Queen to become Patron of the expedition. The idea was welcomed by the Committee and the Chairman promised to write to her Private Secretary.

A few days later a phone call came through for me from Commander Michael Parker, then on the Duke of Edinburgh's staff. Eleanor announced him and put it through, and then heard a completely different voice say, 'What's all this I hear about it being a very bad thing that this expedition is being promoted?' Apparently my opponents too had access to the Palace. Rather unusually for me I exploded, and worked up a real tirade explaining exactly what the expedition was all about. Eleanor was horrified and hastily rushed into my office with a bit of paper on which was written, 'I think you are talking to Prince Philip'. I glanced at it but it was too late – I was well and truly launched and it was impossible to repair the situation. I continued in full flood as if talking to Parker; my caller thanked me for putting the record straight so succinctly and rang off. At least Prince Philip had got a straight answer; and two days later a letter arrived saying that Her Majesty had graciously consented to become our Patron. In later years I was to meet the Duke of Edinburgh on a number of occasions – neither of us has ever mentioned this unfortunate occurrence!

Ken Blaiklock, aged twenty-seven and with four winters' experience in the Antarctic, was appointed Leader of the Advance Party. He had of course been with me at Stonington and had all the necessary experience. Although appreciating the necessity for vehicles, his heart was with the dogs. With them he was to survey the Shackleton Range, and finally he and Jon Stephenson, our Australian geologist, were to drive the only teams to reach the Pole since Amundsen in 1911.

Ken's deputy was Ralph Lenton, aged thirty-two, who had already spent five winters at various bases. He was primarily responsible for the construction of the base we were to call Shackleton, but his ability to turn his hand to anything was an enormous asset.

To maintain observations around the clock there were three meteorologists with the Advance Party. Tony Stewart, aged thirty-two, took charge of the programme, joining us from the Nautical

College, Pangbourne where he was an instructor in physics, having already had experience with upper-air balloon work in the Atlantic weather ships. Peter Jeffries was lent by the Air Ministry Meteorological Office. Aged twenty-four, his service in Atlantic weather ships had given him experience of life in small isolated communities. South Africa sent us 'Hannes' la Grange, aged twenty-eight, who came from the Weather Bureau in Pretoria. He was a 'blind date' but we need not have worried, for his service at South Africa's Meteorological Station on Marion Island had prepared him for our way of life and, being meticulous and painstaking in all he did, he took the work in his stride.

'Roy' Homard, seconded by REME, was going as the Advance Party engineer. Aged thirty-four, he had spent a year with the British North Greenland Expedition in 1953-54, where he proved himself an adept at vehicle maintenance in very low temperatures. The eighth member was Dr Rainer Goldsmith, aged twenty-eight, who as medical officer not only cared for the health of the wintering party but also started a physiological programme of his own using his companions as guinea pigs.

By the beginning of November 1955, stores were pouring into the hands of the Crown Agents for loading into the Canadian sealer *Theron* (Captain Harald Marø) chartered to carry the expedition to the Weddell Sea. Now our months of thought, persuasion, listing and letter writing took concrete form in thousands of packing cases that began to fill her holds. Her deck space was taken up with hundreds of barrels of fuel, two aeroplanes, a Sno-Cat, twenty-four dogs, oxygen and acetylene cylinders, stove pipes and a hundred other items. Moving from one end of the vessel to the other entailed climbing over all this assortment, while every cabin bulged with personal belongings.

It was time to say goodbye – to our families and to 'No. 64' where everyone had laboured so hard to see us fully equipped. We hoped that for them there would be some relaxation. So closely had we all worked together that it seemed as though a part of the expedition itself was being left behind, and indeed the strong unity of purpose which had been forged between the field parties and the office at home was to prove a great strength in times of unforeseen stress during the next three years.

Chapter 13

The Commonwealth
Trans-Antarctic Expedition
1955-58

As *Theron* moved down the Thames from Millwall Docks on 14 November 1955, isolated groups and small crowds waved and shouted good luck from wharves and jetties, while tugs and steamers hooted their good wishes. When our astonished Captain understood what was happening, our siren began to reply. It was then, I think, that all of us, expedition and crew alike, realized that we had the goodwill of the country, and in return owed a debt we could only repay by our utmost endeavour.

We sailed for St Vincent in the Cape Verde Islands to take on fresh water before the long trip across the equator to Montevideo. There we were joined by Sir Edmund Hillary and 'Bob' Miller who was to be his second-in-command, and Squadron Leader John Claydon, the New Zealand party's chief pilot. They were accompanying us to obtain a summer's experience of Antarctic conditions, before setting about their own tasks on the far side of the continent.

Our next call was Grytviken, South Georgia, where wings were fitted to one of the Auster aircraft and the plane was successfully test-flown.

On 22 December we entered a belt of brash growlers and bergy bits that lay scattered over the water. (A bergy bit is a piece of floating ice less than fifteen feet above water and not wider than thirty feet. Growlers are smaller, and almost awash.) A few hours later we encountered the beginning of the Weddell Sea pack ice. It was four to six feet thick, and as we took a winding course along open leads it gradually consolidated – the floes were more extensive, some of them several miles across.

From time to time we killed seals to provide food for our dogs during the coming winter, and frequently we encountered emperor and Adélie penguins, curious about our every move. In four days we reached an area of large, old hummocked floes through which it became increasingly difficult to penetrate as upended pieces of ice were forced alongside and beneath the ship. Slowly we fought a way to a small pool ahead from which John Lewis managed to take off, and after an hour's reconnaissance he reported a series of open pools connected by leads through which Captain Marø worked his ship. At first we made progress, but soon *Theron* was halted by really heavy ice and the weather became overcast, making it difficult to see ahead. From this time the story of our progress was repetitive – momentary opening of the ice, movement of some fifty yards, then suddenly we were held tight again.

Day after day, time after time, for hours on end everyone was over the side with axes, shovels, boards and boat-hooks, to clear ice from the side of the ship. Some would hack at the huge piled up floes and prise them free with crowbars, others poled the loosened pieces back into the wash of the propeller, thus clearing them into the small pool of water which always lay astern.

With our voluntary movement measured in yards per day, and the short summer season rapidly passing, patience was a virtue hard to retain. Yet every day we were busy not only in moving ice but in bringing at least a ton on board to maintain our dwindling water supply. We became accustomed to the noise of steel on ice and of the propeller thundering against the floes. It seemed impossible that blades or shaft, or indeed the engine, could stand the strain when, from full speed, the spinning propeller was stopped in two turns and the whole ship canted, turning about the shaft.

An extract from my journal reads:

It is impossible to describe adequately this forceful butting of the ice. The ship runs up through crowded brash forcing three- or four-foot plates of ice many yards in extent beneath the keel, or upending them alongside the hull. Then with a shuddering bump the bows rise on a floe – up and up we seem to go – when suddenly she subsides and cracks go shooting across the ice. Other times she hangs there with her bows up and we go astern to try once more. Over and over again the process is repeated, gradually breaking away the obstruction, while the ship jars, twists and shudders till one feels she will fall apart. The most frightening noises are when the propeller strikes the ice and a thundering hammering shakes us from stem to stern, or when going astern the rudder butts a heavy floe and the hydraulic release valve screeches in apparent agony.

We were beset for thirty-three days. Work on the ice continued night and day, and when eventually we got into easier conditions the rudder was so much twisted that the ship answered to only about six degrees of port helm. The Captain found it impossible to navigate and late one night he decided he must take a course once adopted by his father in a much smaller vessel many years before. This was to attempt bending the rudder back into position by purposely going astern against a solid floe. Three times he gently tried this manoeuvre without effect. Then risking all, he forced her hard into the ice. Looking back, one realizes that this was one of the occasions when the fate of the whole expedition hung in the balance. But his courage was rewarded by the rudder being returned to an almost normal position (actually over-corrected five degrees to starboard), enabling him to reach the first pool of water we had seen for three weeks. This was about 350 yards long, only just enough for the Auster to take off, and with a dog-leg in the middle. It was John Claydon's turn to fly, and he told us that he would make a dummy run to find out how the plane would behave on the curving take-off.

As we watched him, it suddenly became apparent that he was going to make the real attempt. The wash from the floats curved out across the water, and nearer and nearer the little plane approached the ice at the end of the pool. The airmen among us hardly dared to breathe, but at the very last moment, feet rather than yards from the ice edge, she lifted and John was airborne. Afterwards he told us, 'I had to make it on the first run as I would never have dared to have another go!'

For three hours Claydon flew at 5,000 feet and all the time his radio reports were plotted. Fifty miles north of us he found light open pack with a belt of navigable ice extending south towards our destination. Soon he came in to land, sharing the available water with a number of whales that rose to 'blow' in apparent protest at this visitor from another world.

Immediately the plane had been taken aboard we started working towards the promise of easier conditions. Although successful, it was another week before we reached the Filchner Ice Shelf at the head of the Weddell Sea. To try and make up so much lost time we worked in shifts round the clock to unload the stores before the sea froze over and trapped the ship for the winter. Shackleton Base was established on the Filchner Ice Shelf up a steep slope one mile from the edge of the ice cliffs. With two Ferguson tractors and a Weasel we hauled as much as we could up to the base site, including, of course, all the timbers for the hut. But nearly 300 tons of stores, including the coal and much of the food and fuel, was left stacked on the sea ice at the foot of the slope.

While this was going on the three pilots took turns in flying Stratton, Blaiklock or me on inland reconnaissance flights, for it was of the greatest importance for our future journeys that we should determine the topographical situation. So it was that we discovered the Theron Mountains some 120 miles south-east of base, and could see another range about 100 miles farther south.

Soon the sea around the ship began to freeze and the new ice to over-raft under pressure from wind-blown pack ice. It was fascinating, but ominous, to see the ice breaking into many tongued plates which slid silently one over the other like loose playing cards, somehow animated to rebuild themselves into a pack. Ever moving, always thickening, buckling, advancing on the ship, it seemed that the ice was alive and moving with the silent purpose of our destruction. Presently it was twelve inches thick around the ship, and away to the east we could see a tongue of pack ice approaching the coast, threatening to close our escape route. Captain Marø decided that the ship must move within an hour. It was time to say a hasty farewell to the eight members of the Advance Party who were to winter. We knew that they had an enormous task ahead of them, which had become far greater than had been intended owing to the lateness of our arrival. We had expected to complete at least the framework of the living hut before the ship left. As it was, all that had been done was to re-erect the Sno-Cat's packing case which would serve as an emergency shelter until the main hut could be built. We little knew that it was to provide quarters for the entire party throughout the Antarctic winter.

We all congregated on the ice to say our goodbyes. Handshakes and badinage, some laughter and a little awkwardness, all played their part. No one liked to feel that the expedition was dividing into two, and many of those going home to prepare the next stage must have felt that in some way they were leaving their companions in the lurch.

Theron slid slowly away from the ice edge while three long blasts of the siren drowned the final shouts of farewell, and we found ourselves silently waving to the tiny cluster of men quickly dwindling in size until individual figures could no longer be distinguished.

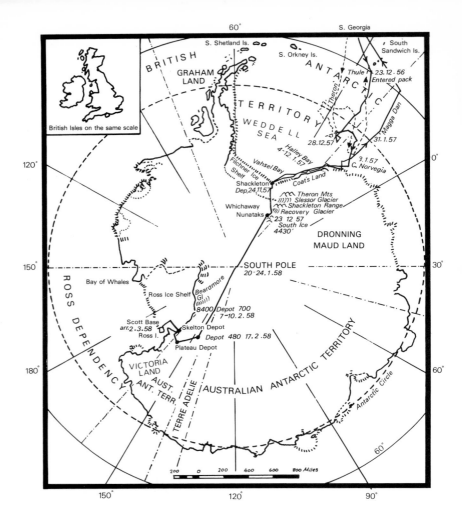

On 10 February we were in the open sea and the following message was sent to Her Majesty The Queen:

Expedition vessel *Theron* now clear of Weddell Sea ice on return voyage having established Shackleton Base in latitude 77°57'S, 37°17'W. Wintering party will examine mountains discovered to the south-east. Loyal greeting to our Queen and Patron. Fuchs.

The following reply was received:

Thank you for your message. I have been following your adventure with great interest and we are all delighted at your success. Please send my best wishes to all members of your expedition. Elizabeth R.

During March the weather deteriorated at Shackleton. Blinding drift obliterated everything and strong winds broke up the sea ice on which a large amount of stores still remained stacked. When the blizzard was over the men found only open water – all their coal and much of their food and fuel had disappeared. As a result our Advance Party spent perhaps the hardest winter endured by anyone since Scott's Northern Party at the beginning of the century.

Wind was the great enemy. Relentless, unremitting wind, driving a torrent of snow like a horizontal waterfall, to fill every nook and cranny, burying everything in its path. Fortunately on 4 March, before the blizzard that blew the sea ice away, they had carried out 'Operation Dog-span' to move the huskies from the sea ice up to the base. To walk each animal individually would have taken much time and effort, and they were not yet trained to run in teams. So Ken Blaiklock decided to leave them chained to their steel wire spans, and attaching a vehicle to each end, they drove gaily up to the top of the ice shelf, bringing the dogs to Shackleton in a chorus of excitement. There they were picketed close to the building site.

On 1 March regular meteorological observations were started and by the 19th the main framework of the hut was up, the gable ends were completed. By this time they had settled down to a routine in the confined space available. The crate measured 21 × 9 × 8 feet and at one end a small kitchen bench had been built on which were three Primus stoves used for cooking. Down the centre was a table with forms on either side, while at the other end near the door was a work bench and the radio equipment.

There was always an inch of ice on the floor, while condensation from the cooking and their breath froze into stalactites which hung down from the ceiling. An ingenius 'oven' was improvised from an empty oil drum insulated with fibreglass. In time it became a challenge to the cooks' ingenuity and they learnt how to bake bread and cakes. If at first standards were not very high, appetites were keen and burnt offerings were overlooked. Occasionally a bright idea enhanced the menu, as when Roy Homard surprised them by providing tinned peas with a pleasant flavour of mint. He had achieved this by adding half an inch of Mentasol toothpaste to the boiling pot!

They slept in two-man tents, but comfortable sleep was a rare thing, for the temperature ranged down to as low as $-65°F$ ($-53°C$)

and the sleeping bags were becoming heavy with frozen condensation, cracking and creaking as the men crept into them.

At last on 26 March the wind died down and they were able to move about and survey the changed scene around them. The tents were nearly buried and had to be dug out and re-pitched. On the north side of the hut a huge drift seventy yards long stood fifteen feet above the surface, and under it lay buried all the wall panels which had so laboriously been dug out the day before the blizzard began. In the old days when parties got into serious trouble, they had no choice but to endure their hardships; but our Advance Party had a radio, sledging rations and fresh dogs. An Argentine station, Belgrano, where they could have taken refuge, was only fifty miles away. They chose to remain, and despite continual struggles against the weather, the hut was slowly built.

On 20 April the sun set for the last time for four months, but work on the hut continued by the light of Tilley lamps, each man setting out to his roof panelling or tunnelling for the buried cases carrying his own lantern. Aurora appeared as curtains of wavering light, changing their form, intensity and colour from minute to minute. Usually the displays were white, but sometimes they were tinged with red and green, colours that pulsated against the dark background of the polar night.

May was the coldest month. The mean was $-35°F$ ($-37°C$), which meant that on many days it was in the minus fifties and sixties. Another blizzard lasting ten days stopped all but essential work outside. The dogs had to be fed, meteorological observations were continued, and food and fuel had to be brought into the crate, but building work was impossible. On the 7th, twelve weeks after the ship had left them, Ralph Lenton at last succeeded in making his first radio contact with the FIDS base on Horseshoe Island. Everyone was spellbound with excitement and they sent a message to us in London reporting that they were all well. From then on communication was maintained with them at regular intervals.

So they dug their way into June as the drift poured over the hut almost as fast as they could remove it. On the 6th the wind blew at seventy knots and there was much snow. By the time they had cleared eighty tons from the east end of the hut, another forty tons had filled the west end – it was hard, gruelling work.

On Midwinter Day Taffy Williams produced all the radio messages which had accumulated for the occasion, while Ralph prepared a special meal of turtle soup, ham with brussels sprouts, followed by strawberry shortcake. Their table was graced with a cloth and decorated with crackers, while a small clockwork train ran on rails round and round a Dundee cake in the centre. Above it two angels revolved endlessly in the warmth of the candles, merrily tinkling tiny bells. They had made each other presents, and Peter Jeffries, who was never seen without a book, received a bookmarker inscribed, 'Here you were interrupted ...'

On 2 August they recorded their lowest temperature, −63°F or ninety-five degrees Fahrenheit of frost (−53°C). In London it was David Stratton's wedding day and the Advance Party were determined to share in the celebrations, but their toast was considerably delayed because the carefully conserved whisky was frozen and even the paraffin had turned into a thick jelly.

On 7 August, six months after the departure of *Theron*, Blaiklock and Rhino Goldsmith slept in the hut. Many of the bunks had now been completed, but there was some disinclination to move in as it was still easier to warm the tents than the two-man cabins. On the 23rd the sun returned to Shackleton.

Meanwhile in London and Wellington final preparations were being made for the main parties to sail south. There were factories to be visited all over Britain, Sno-Cats to be tested in the snows of Norway, an Otter aircraft to be flown from Canada, and presently an endless stream of stores was once more pouring into the hands of the Crown Agents.

During the summer the last four members of the expedition joined the office. Dr Hal Lister, aged thirty-three, had spent two years with the British North Greenland Expedition as glaciologist, and this practical experience was to be put to excellent use in the Antarctic. Allan Rogers, aged thirty-eight, was a physiologist who was to replace Rhino Goldsmith as medical officer for the second season. He joined from Bristol University, where he was a lecturer. With little medical work to do, he was able to concentrate on his scientific programme. His services were also constantly in demand for dental treatment, and many a tooth was to be saved by his meticulous and careful work. Jon Stephenson was the Australian representative. Aged twenty-six, he was a geologist completing his thesis at London University. He quickly and enthusiastically took to dog driving, was never happy out of the sight of mountains, and was constantly thinking of ways to reach new rocks, however inaccessible they might appear to be. Lastly the British Petroleum Company, who had generously agreed to provide all our fuel requirements for ships, aircraft and vehicles, also lent us Geoffrey Pratt, a geophysicist aged thirty-one. He had worked in Iraq, Papua, Kuwait and Canada, and now became responsible for our seismic work and the gravity traverse across the continent.

All through the summer and autumn the tempo increased until, at the beginning of November, the newly built Danish polar vessel *Magga Dan*, which had been launched by Joyce in Denmark, arrived to load at Butler's Wharf, Tower Bridge. On the 13th Her Majesty The Queen visited the ship and all members of the expedition were presented. Captain Petersen then presented eleven specially chosen members of his crew – all of whom had the surname Petersen! Her Majesty was kind enough to stay and have tea with us in a marquee put up alongside the ship. This was a particularly poignant moment for my German-born father with his unhappy memories of his treatment during the First World War. He watched all the proceedings with great pride and afterwards said to me, 'In my wildest dreams I could never have imagined a son of mine having tea with the Queen of England!' The following day the ship sailed from Tower Bridge, again with the good wishes of the river traffic and the crowds lining the bridge.

A month later Hillary's party sailed from Wellington in HMNZS *Endeavour* to set up Scott Base at Pram Point in McMurdo Sound, and to begin their exploratory journeys inland.

On 23 January Shackleton was relieved, and the hard-pressed Advance Party received their first mail for a year. Now all our energies were directed to finding a suitable site for a small inland station 300 miles towards the Pole.

This advance base was named South Ice, and was to be a meteorological and glaciological observatory during the winter. It was established entirely by air, our single-engined Otter making twenty flights carrying one ton of material at a time. A small prefabricated hut was built in a specially dug pit where it quickly became buried, the snow providing good insulation against the winter temperatures which fell to $-76°F$ $(-60°C)$. For seven months Hal Lister, Ken Blaiklock and Jon Stephenson lived there carrying out glaciological studies and maintaining four-hourly meteorological observations. The base finally became the last depot through which the Crossing Party passed on their way to the Pole.

At all three expedition stations winter was a busy time, both for the scientists and for the engineers who were preparing tractors for their challenging summer journeys.

It was on 24 July that I learnt that my father had died of cancer on the previous day. When the *Magga Dan* sailed he had seemed reasonably fit. Yet I had known that after our departure he had been taken to hospital, and by July I knew his death was not unexpected. To me it was doubly painful because I had not been with him in his last months.

Today I have received the sad news that Dad died yesterday morning. Although recent messages from Joyce and from the hospital had warned me that there seemed little hope, it has come as a horrid finality, a closing of a chapter in life.

A wiser father no one could have had, not in the matter of learning – he was not learned – but in understanding and patience. He has always been a quiet source of encouragement and, as it were, a bystander providing gentle approval of anything that may have seemed worthwhile in my life. I am glad to think that he was proud of any success that may have come to me from time to time. I shall miss him and his almost 'enquiring' advice which was so often very pertinent.

He was good to my mother – they were devoted – and he was good to me. No one could have done better by any child, youth or man. Sometimes I have tried to express my appreciation. I hope and believe he understood.

When the sun returned to Shackleton, field parties with dog teams were flown out to examine the newly discovered mountain areas seen during the flights to South Ice, and in particular the Shackleton Range.

At the same time the New Zealanders set out from Scott Base to lay depots towards the Pole. With dog teams and two modified Ferguson farm tractors, the ground party found suitable vehicle routes and chose the sites. Their Beaver aircraft then flew in the supplies to establish the depots.

From Shackleton four of us set out with three Weasels and a

Sno-Cat on a route-finding reconnaissance journey to South Ice. It proved to be the most nerve-racking experience. Huge crevassed areas had to be crossed, and with heart-breaking regularity the fragile snow bridges collapsed under the weight of the roped vehicles. Deep chasms opened up and tractors fell in, each time posing a new problem of how they could be extricated. The recoveries were dangerous, highly skilled operations, and it was often five or six hours before a vehicle was safely back on the surface.

We invented a technique of probing the way ahead on skis. Every yard two men working the width of a vehicle apart plunged long aluminium poles into the snow to their full length. If a pole broke through the surface, the crevasse beneath was opened up and examined. By discovering the direction in which it ran, it was possible to flag a safe passage through to the next one. Laboriously we marked out a tortuous path. At one point my journal reflects our anxiety:

The next ten miles are going to make or break the expedition for we may lose vehicles ... with crash helmets, safety straps and roped vehicles we have taken all the precautions we can.

It took us thirty-seven days to reach South Ice. Leaving the tractors there, we flew back to Shackleton in two-and-a-half hours. Nine days later we started all over again.

At base packing had begun, and on 22 November we began loading the sledges with twenty tons of food, fuel and other material. Two days later the trans-continental journey began. All the vehicles had been nicknamed by their drivers, and we left in the order Sno-Cat 'Rock'n'Roll' (a characteristic of all the species), then Sno-Cat 'Able' named by David Pratt, followed by two Weasels, 'Rumble' and 'Wrack and Ruin', belonging to Allan Rogers and George Lowe respectively. Next came Muskeg tractor 'Hopalong' bearing the emblem of a jumping kangaroo, named by Jon Stephenson, with Sno-Cat 'County of Kent', named by Roy Homard because of his Kentish origins, bringing up the rear.

The first two days we passed over filled chasms safely, and after fourteen miles thought that we were well on the way for a long run. Then, in a twinkling, a snow bridge fell away beneath 'Rock'n'Roll' leaving David Stratton and me suspended in mid-air over an impressive hole, some fifteen feet wide and sixty feet deep to the first step in the walls of the crevasse below. Peering out of the right-hand side the situation looked distinctly uncomfortable, for it was impossible to tell how firmly we were wedged against the sides, and in any case there was nothing to step out on to – even the pontoons were inaccessible. On his side David found that he could reach the rear pontoon and I followed him out, crawling over the ladder-like track as it hung in space.

Recovery seemed impossible, but David Pratt and Roy then moved the other two 'Cats' into position side by side behind 'Rock'n'Roll' and attached them to the rear towing hook. Next, after careful prospecting along the length of the crevasse, a point was found where George and Allan could take the two Weasels over and then bring them round in front of 'Rock'n'Roll'. There they were joined in tandem and attached by steel cable to the Sno-Cat's front axle. In this way they formed an anchor, preventing the front of the vehicle from falling vertically into the crevasse when an attempt was made to pull it out backwards. On a Sno-Cat each pontoon is able to swivel freely about its axle, hence it was extremely difficult for us to move the left front pontoon into the correct position to rise over the edge of the crevasse as the vehicle was hauled out.

This was accomplished by lowering David Stratton on a rope into the crevasse, where he cut a suitable ledge. Then, using the Muskeg as a fifth recovery vehicle, we pulled the recalcitrant pontoon into position, and 'Rock'n'Roll' was drawn slowly backwards.

The necessarily simultaneous movement of the five recovery vehicles was a complex manoeuvre, and it is doubtful if we should have succeeded had we not had the immense power of the other two Sno-Cats using their emergency low gear, known to us as 'Grandma'. On this occasion it showed what it could do when we discovered, at the end of the recovery, that 'Rock'n'Roll' had been left in forward gear the whole time! The operation had taken five hours.

From then onwards the trek to South Ice was a sorry repetition of our first experience. Each vehicle hauled two sledges and our highest speed when roped together was three-and-a-half miles an hour. For hours on end we ground along at one mph in bottom gear. The warmer summer temperatures had further weakened the snow bridges crossed during the reconnaissance journey, and often whole areas had to be probed all over again. At the end of one particularly bad day Jon Stephenson walked to his tent, and the snow gave way leaving him hanging by one elbow over a dark cavern which appeared to be bottomless.

9 December was another near disastrous day. To preserve the Sno-Cats we now sent the two Weasels and the Muskeg ahead, roped together, the leading Weasel to act as a crevasse detector. Moving forward in this new order over a section of the probed route, David Stratton, who was skiing ahead to guide my leading Weasel over the prepared track, suddenly pointed back. There behind us we could see two loaded sledges but no third Sno-Cat. At first I feared that David Pratt had dropped right into a crevasse, but then I could just make out a part of the vehicle standing up in front of the sledges. Figures were moving about gesticulating to recall us.

As we skied back Hal Lister met us to say that all the vehicles would be needed for the recovery, so we unhitched from our various sledges, probed a turning place for each tractor, and started back over a course like a switch-back, where the numerous smaller crevasse bridges had sunk or broken through.

We found 'Able' resting in the crevasse with only the very tips of the front pontoons on the surface, the main weight of the vehicle being supported by the back of the body, and the rear pontoons hanging free. It would be necessary to support the rear pontoons from below when the Sno-Cat was drawn forwards, for there was no possibility of hauling it out backwards.

Happily there was a local closure of the crevasse walls about twenty-five feet down, and after some discussion we all set to with shovels to fill in the entire crevasse below the 'Cat' until it was possible for me to stand on the snow filling and set our crevasse bridging units in place beneath the pontoons. To secure them, ledges were cut into the walls of the crevasse, upon which the aluminium spans could rest at a sloping angle beneath the tracks. These had been specially constructed in fourteen-foot lengths, each weighing 125 pounds and stressed to carry four tons.

It was impossible to put the bridging into position on both sides at the same angle, thus the whole structure looked even more precarious than it really was, and we were particularly concerned about the strength of the ledges at the lower end. On them the whole weight of the body would be bound to fall suddenly as the back dropped free from the side of the crevasse. So as to make the structure more secure, steel rope slings were placed round the ends of the bridging pieces and fastened to 'dead-men' set in the snow above.

When all was ready, two Sno-Cats began slowly to pull ahead, while two Weasels acting as anchors gradually gave way at the back. As 'Able' started to move we held our breath. There was a loud crunch as the ledges under the bridging gave way and the vehicle lurched sideways to sink momentarily deeper, but the 'dead-men' held. Then like some monster rising from the deep, it appeared to heave and wallow its way to the surface, finally to come safely clear.

When the reloading of 'Able' was completed, and all the tools, steel cables, shackles, boards, bridging, ropes and other equipment had been returned to the various vehicles, we all set off for the third time over the broken and sagging crevasse bridges along the trail we had already made. With a few diversions, and great care in driving, everyone reached the sledges, hooked up and continued safely to the end of the probed route:

... the last mile was the worst, but the tortuous course was gay with coloured flags, stakes and ski sticks – ninety-eight of them in one mile, each marking a particularly hazardous point, for minor crevasses we now crossed without concern. In the bright sunlight the scene was suggestive of a course prepared for some nightmare 'bending race' ...

With worn nerves – but all the tractors intact – we finally reached South Ice on 21 December. We remained there four days, overhauling the battered vehicles and restowing the sledges for the longest leg of the journey – 550 miles to the Pole, and then another 500 miles to our first supply dump at Depot 700.

On the other side of the continent the New Zealanders had made unexpectedly fast progress in good weather conditions. By 20 December all the depots were laid, and it was clear that it would be some time before the two groups met. Ed Hillary decided on a quick dash to the Pole, as he put it 'for the Hell of it'. His two Ferguson farm tractors had done much more than had been expected in getting to Depot 700. But now the soft surfaces and high altitude proved almost too much for them. The party jettisoned every unnecessary ounce, and with much coaxing from devoted mechanics, the tractors struggled to Amundsen/Scott, the American Pole station. It was 4 January 1958, and they were the first party to arrive there overland since Scott himself, for all the men and material for the station had been flown in.

At South Ice there was still much to do. David Stratton levelled a line of pegs over the snow for three-and-a-half kilometres for Geoffrey Pratt's seismic refraction shots, and another line of fifty stakes extending over a mile for Hal Lister's glaciological work. Ralph Lenton removed the transmitter from the hut and installed it in the 'County of Kent', leaving behind the less powerful equipment which would meet the needs of the RAF party during their brief stay at the station before they flew across to Scott Base. We scrubbed out and tidied the hut itself, and dug out from the snow the aviation fuel which would be needed for the Otter, and lashed down on top of the sledge loads the tents, skis, crevasse flags, probes and other items required immediately to hand when travelling.

At five minutes to three on Christmas afternoon we were all congregated in the tiny living room to hear The Queen's speech. Bulky forms filled every chair, sat on bunks and table or leaned against the walls. To us, who were perhaps her most isolated listeners, there seemed to be special encouragement, not only because we were proud that Her Majesty was our Patron, but because we were engaged upon a Commonwealth enterprise.

Two dog teams driven by Ken Blaiklock and Jon Stephenson were already running ahead to reconnoitre the route. When we finally left on Christmas evening the tractors were loaded with twenty-one tons of fuel and half a ton of explosives for the seismic work, besides the scientific equipment, food and personal gear.

In order to discover the depths of ice on the polar plateau a seismic shot was fired every thirty miles. This entailed drilling a thirty-foot hole, at the bottom of which an explosive charge was fired, the shock waves 'bouncing' back to the surface from the rock below. The time interval between the explosion and the return of the waves was recorded in 'Haywire', Geoffrey Pratt's Sno-Cat. Since the speed at which they travelled through the ice was known, it was possible to calculate its depth, and as the series of shots took place right across the continent, the undulations of the land beneath the ice cap were also discovered.

The dog drivers marked the route up to the plateau by building a snow cairn every five miles. As time went on they became ambitious and produced increasingly complicated structures. The final work of art which met our astonished eyes as we followed them was a miniature 'Snowhenge'!

We now travelled at night to take advantage of harder surfaces when temperatures were lowest. At one point we found ourselves in an enormous field of sastrugi, where for sixty-five miles each driver had to judge the best course for his own vehicle. Soon the tractors were scattered a mile or two apart, working and weaving their way among hard ridges four or five feet high. The Sno-Cats were driven at less than half-a-mile an hour over vertical drops. Climbing to the top of sharp-tongued ridges, they would tilt up then suddenly dip violently forward, followed by the plunging sledges completely out of control.

Every 200 miles we stopped to service the vehicles, and always the scientific work continued. Each evening two to three hours were spent in drilling the hole for the seismic shot. The core which came from it was laid along the surface, and by examining this Hal Lister was able to determine the age of the different horizons and also the annual snowfall.

Thermometers were left at different depths in the bore hole all night. From the temperatures recorded at the various levels it was possible to calculate how much of the sun's heat penetrates into the ice cap and what effect it has on ice crystallization.

The following morning a bell rang warning everyone to switch off engines and remain utterly still while the seismic shot was fired. Then our whole cavalcade moved off, stopping at regular intervals to make gravity measurements, to take rammsonde soundings, and to record the meteorological observations. The gravity measurements varied according to the amount of snow lying on top of the rock, and so filled in the gaps between the seismic shots in obtaining a profile of the land lying under the ice. The rammsonde was a complicated measuring device whereby a rod with a steel cone at the end of it was hammered down to a given depth of snow by a block of known weight dropped from a known height. The number of blows taken to reach a particular depth gave the density of the snow at that point. All this work, which included measurements of the sun's radiation, contributed to an understanding of the structure and behaviour of the great Antarctic ice sheet.

All day on 3 January we travelled over the most vicious sastrugi, the vehicles making very heavy weather and the sledges suffering severely. More and more tow bars were getting damaged, so that most of the towing was now by steel wire rope, which was very hard on the transmissions. We had taken to travelling by sun compass, for the magnetic compass was already showing some sluggishness. As the altitude increased it was necessary for the sake of efficiency and economy to change the carburettor jets on all the vehicles. This we did every 2,000 feet above 4,000 feet, not of course to increase the power of the engines in any way, but as an economy measure. As we gained altitude our unsupercharged engines were continually losing power, though such was their reserve that no loss was yet apparent, and the Sno-Cats continued to haul their maximum loads without trouble.

That evening I received a message from Hillary suggesting that as we were so delayed I should consider stopping at the South Pole and flying the party out with the assistance of the Americans. To this I was unable to agree, and replied explaining the situation. The messages we exchanged were as follows:

Dear Bunny. I am very concerned about the serious delay in your plans. It's about 1,250 miles from the Pole to Scott Base, much of the travelling north from D.700 being somewhat slow and laborious, with rough hard sastrugi. Leaving the Pole late in January, you will head into increasing bad weather and winter temperatures, plus vehicles that are showing signs of strain. Both of my mechanics regard such a late journey as an unjustifiable risk and are not prepared to wait and travel with your party. I agree with their view and think you should seriously consider splitting your journey over two years. You still probably have a major journey in front of you to reach the Pole. Why not winter your vehicles at the Pole, fly out to Scott Base with American aircraft, return to civilization for the winter, and then fly back into the Pole station next November and complete your journey? This plan would enable you to do a far more satisfactory job of your seismic work, and I feel fairly confident that Admiral Dufek would assist with such a flying programme. Personally I feel the need for a break from the plateau after nearly four months of tractor travel, and there is a lot to do. I prefer not to wait at the Pole station, but will get evacuated to Scott Base as soon as possible. If you decide to continue on from the Pole, I'll join you at D.700. Sorry to strike such a sombre note, but it would be unfortunate if the sterling work you've put into making your route through to South Ice and the Pole should all be wasted by the party foundering somewhere on the 1,250 miles to Scott Base. I will go ahead with the stocking of D.700 and I will leave at the Pole station full details plus maps of the route from Scott to the Pole.

Hillary.

Hillary Pole Station. Appreciate your concern, but there can be no question of abandoning journey at this stage. Innumerable reasons make it impracticable to remount the expedition after wintering outside Antarctic. Our vehicles can be and have been operated at minus 60°F but I do not expect such temperatures by March. Whiteout and drift will be our chief concern. I understand your mechanics' reluctance to undertake further travel, and in view of your opinion that late season travel is unjustifiable risk I do not feel able to ask you to join us at D.700, in spite of your valuable local knowledge. We will therefore have to wend our way using the traverse you leave at the Pole. The present field of giant sastrugi has extended 57 miles so far, and continues with ridges up to four feet. Are we to expect similar fields north of D.700 and approx how many miles *in toto*? Main damage is to sledge tow bars, which have to be electrically welded causing delay. Am shortly abandoning second vehicle as planned, leaving us four Cats and two Weasels. Max interval seismic stations 30 miles, gravity stations 15 miles, rammsonde once or twice daily, meteorology includes fluxplate and radiation measurements. Present position 84°43'S, altitude 7,000 feet.

Bunny.

Unfortunately this private exchange was leaked to the press in New Zealand – and so to the world. Although we were quietly getting on with our own work, it gradually became apparent that the media had turned the matter into a *cause célèbre*. It was not until we reached the Pole station that I began to realize the amount of publicity which the expedition had suddenly acquired. For the next fortnight our plans were argued and debated in newspapers and journals, and much well-meant but ignorant advice was offered to the Committee at home. Our small office staff took the brunt of a press onslaught none of us had ever visualized.

Meanwhile I had received encouraging support from the Committee who told me to take any decisions that might be necessary in the light of the situation in the field. As I, and all my party, had complete confidence in our ability to carry the journey through, and were considerably surprised at the turn of events; there was virtually no decision to take.

On 6 January we caught up with the dog teams and after that they ran with the vehicles, of which we abandoned two more at predetermined intervals as the fuel and supplies they carried were used up. The dogs began to feel the strain of maintaining an average of twenty miles each day at high altitude, but on 19 January their ears pricked. A cluster of huts and radio masts had come into their view. It was the South Pole station.

In contrast to Scott's heartbreaking words when he reached 'this awful place', my journal tells a happier story:

> The dogs were tiring, and the convoy moved slowly so that they could keep up and arrive together with the vehicles. The day was a brilliant one, without a cloud and only a light wind ... As the party moved towards the Pole I looked back and thought our convoy a brave sight; the orange Cats and Weasel, together with the loaded sledges, bearing many fluttering flags of different colours ... the great condensation plumes streamed away from the high open exhausts of the Sno-Cats ... As we approached nearer we could see quite a crowd ... all armed with cameras ... Our reception has been a most warm one and we have been invited to sleep and eat in the base instead of our tents ...

The Americans had flown in Ed Hillary from Scott Base, and a plane load of reporters sent from all over the world to witness our arrival. We gave a press conference, and found that many of our audience seemed genuinely amazed that the journey was to continue as planned. That evening the reporters were all flown out again, which relieved pressure on the station, and we were offered every hospitality.

At an evening party in our honour each of us was presented with a fine coloured testimonial stating that we had been round the world on our feet. For this one only had to walk a few yards round the flag marking the site of the Pole itself! We in turn presented the station with the expedition pennant in memory of our visit, and were proud to display Her Majesty's signed portrait which we had carried with us all the way from Shackleton. Another item of interest was Captain Scott's watch which I had worn on a leather thong round my neck since starting the journey. This had been entrusted to me by the makers, Smith's Instruments, to take back to the South Pole and on to Scott Base.

We spent four very crowded days at the Pole, for there was much to do. The loads all had to be unlashed and restowed, which relieved

Vivian Fuchs at the South Pole

us of nineteen empty fuel drums. Our electric welder was set up in 'Haywire', which had been taken into the station workshop, where work went ahead on repairing our broken tow bars and battery heating equipment.

While we were still on our way to the Pole the RAF contingent had the task of closing down Shackleton and then flying up to South Ice. This short trip provided the opportunity for checking the aircraft itself, the navigational equipment and the radio under actual flying conditions. As navigation would be of paramount importance, here in John Lewis' words is an account of the equipment and methods to be used:

An astro-compass was mounted on the cockpit combing in front of the second pilot's position, and with this the true course could be checked using the sun. It was made easy at this time of the year because the sun was well above the horizon for the whole twenty-four hours. A Bendix polar-path gyro acted as the master direction indicator, checked for heading precession every twenty minutes with the astro-compass. An ordinary directional gyro calibrated for 80°S acted as a standby gyro; a drift sight mounted on the inside of the cockpit door, used in conjunction with a radio altimeter, gave drift and ground-speed. True course, drift and ground-speed are all that is required to navigate, but obtaining these depends on the weather. Clear skies to see the sun and a visible surface to pick up features by which to measure the aircraft's drift and ground-speed are essential.

In fact their first attempt had to be aborted after seven hours due to bad weather conditions, but on 6 January 1958 they tried again. This time a following wind helped to eke out their fuel. They headed straight for the Pole (9,200 feet), circling it several times before setting course for the Beardmore Glacier, up which the early explorers had so painfully manhauled their sledges. From here, as John put it, it was 'down hill all the way'. A few hours later Ross Island loomed ahead, and new friendly voices came over the air as Scott Base prepared their reception. Gordon Haslop was delighted to be back 'in the right quadrant of the world', and helpful tail winds caused them to revise their time of arrival to eleven o'clock. Passing the message, Taffy Williams took the opportunity of ordering 'four bottles of very cold beer please'.

They were met by an aerial reception committee. Two United States Navy Otters from the base at McMurdo Sound flew out to greet them, both crammed with Americans and New Zealanders, as Gordon put it, 'packed like quills on a porcupine, and every one of them with a camera trained on us'. There was much waving and gesturing, but as the aircraft were controlled on different frequencies by the two stations at McMurdo the ribald messages they were anxious to exchange had to be relayed through Scott Base, and lost something of their originality in the process.

The escorting planes took station on either side of them as they approached the base. Ted Gawn, the radio operator, could not bear to miss the party when they landed. So shouting excitedly, 'There you are! You can see the landing strip now. I'm off to be there when you get down,' he abruptly went off the air and raced for the runway.

As they circled the base more American aircraft – Dakotas and

Otters – came up to meet them and described exuberant circuits of welcome. The Otter went down, with the two original American planes flying slightly ahead on either side to guide them in. Then from almost ground level, as the Otter triumphantly touched down, the escorting aircraft roared upwards to join their compatriots in the air – much to the chagrin of all the enthusiastic photographers now borne out of range. After a flight of exactly eleven hours and 1,430 statute miles our little aircraft had made it.

That evening, through the radio operators at the Pole station, we heard that the flight had been successful. John was famous for the comment he invariably made on any kind of good news. 'Jolly good,' he would say, 'Jolly good, bloody good, first class.' We were all delighted to know that they had done it, and our message of congratulation was simple and direct: 'JOLLY GOOD, BLOODY GOOD, FIRST CLASS!' – and indeed it was.

Since our route from the Pole had been proved by Hillary's party, the dog teams were no longer required. Through the kindness of the Americans they were flown out to Scott Base. There they remained to work for successive New Zealand parties who occupied the station after the expedition was over.

On 24 January 1958, two months after our departure from Shackleton, we left the South Pole on our way north to the other side of the world. The distance to Scott Base was 1,250 miles. By no means had we reached the halfway point in our journey, but now we had fewer vehicles to maintain, when we dropped the last Weasel we should be able to increase our speed, and the seismic soundings would be spaced more widely.

It was slightly confusing to find that when we turned north on to our course the compasses became increasingly useless. For on leaving the Geographical Pole every direction was 'north', and we had to travel some fifteen miles before stopping to take sights and decide which way north we wanted to go. Since the Magnetic Pole was still 1,250 miles 'south' of us, according to the compass, 'east' had become 'west' and *vice versa*. The nearer we got to the Magnetic Pole the less responsive our compasses, and attempts to use the sun compass were constantly frustrated by the generally overcast sky.

On 27 January we began the seismic shoot as usual, but the charge failed to explode; and almost immediately David Stratton came over to tell me that he had found Geoffrey Pratt unconscious on the floor of 'Haywire'. His face was unhealthily pink, his eyes closed and his limbs twitching – altogether an alarming sight. Allan Rogers diagnosed carbon monoxide poisoning and hastily improvised a crude mask from a handkerchief on which he administered oxygen from a bottle used for the gas welding equipment. When he had come round, Geoffrey was carried to his tent where more oxygen was given, but we had at most only five hours' supply, which was insufficient to ensure his complete recovery at 10,000 feet.

It was established that Geoffrey and Hannes la Grange had been keeping the windows of 'Haywire' closed. Exhaust gas leaking into the compartment had been pumped by a heater fan between the two windscreens to de-ice them, and thence into the cab. Over a period of days Geoffrey's blood had been increasingly affected, until at last his life was threatened by the destruction of so many corpuscles. We were at the extreme range of our Otter from Scott Base, and even if the plane came out to us it would probably be unable to take off again at our altitude. I therefore signalled Ed Hillary asking him to approach Admiral Dufek for help. By eight o'clock that night two American Neptunes had taken off from McMurdo Sound. When they reached us the sky was completely overcast and the two pilots performed a fine feat of navigation in coming in to us on the first run, to parachute bottles of oxygen and breathing apparatus. Soon Geoffrey was receiving a three-hourly dose of pure oxygen, followed by many further hours at a strength equivalent to the atmosphere at sea level. In the three days he was off work, the seismic soundings were carried out by Allan Rogers.

Then one after the other the Sno-Cat tracks began to give trouble. These had gradually become looser, until a point was reached when they jumped the lower guide-rail and jammed solid with a nasty jarring noise. To tighten all four tracks 592 steel links had to be bent by hand with a special tool. This was a long job taking an hour for each track and requiring considerable judgement, for it was essential to make, by eye, an equal adjustment all round and yet arrive at the correct degree of tension at the end. The fact that there was no means of bending the links back if one should go too far, tended to make the operator over-careful, and he would end his task only to find that the track was still too loose. Then the whole operation would have to be begun all over again.

1.   *Theron* beset

2.   Sno-Cats on Polar Plateau

3. Crevasse trouble!

4. Solar halo

The 4 February was a maintenance day. Such days occurred after every 200 miles and involved much work. On the tracks of each 'Cat' 296 points had to be greased, and the two gearboxes and two differentials topped up. All this, besides other greasing and maintenance work, was an unpleasant task with the temperature at $-20°F$ ($-30°C$) and the wind blowing at twenty-five miles per hour. Filling grease guns was a slimy, slippery process, and the waste grease exuding from the nipples in thin worm-like threads blew about in the wind, to become mixed with snow and finally to adhere to the unfortunate who was humping his way to and fro like a seal between the tracks.

On this occasion the trials of maintenance day were added to by the discovery that the main steering attachment for the front pontoons was loose on three of the Cats. Metal locking tags had therefore to be made like one already fitted to 'Rock'n'Roll'. As a result of all this work we did not start travelling until half-past eight that night, but I was determined to cover a reasonable distance each day when the weather was suitable, since we should have enough trouble when we had to travel in bad conditions. For thirty-three miles we ran over hard sastrugi, but fortunately these were fairly low and it was possible to drive round the isolated groups of higher ridges and deep hollows. That night bed-time was again at four o'clock in the morning. During these days of relatively good going our fuel consumption improved from the very low figure of 0.9 miles per gallon to 1 3/4 miles per gallon.

On 5 February we again had to stop suddenly with the front pontoons of 'Rock'n'Roll' only just short of a sunken crevasse bridge twelve feet wide. Skiing on ahead for a quarter of a mile to climb a high ice hummock, I crossed nine more wide crevasses before reaching it. From there at least two more miles of crevasses were visible stretching at right-angles across the path. To east and west they could be seen extending into the indefinite distance.

Next morning a number of us began probing and flagging a way across, while Geoffrey in 'Haywire' remained behind to organize his seismic shoot. When the charge went off from the three shallow pits which had been dug, three gigantic but perfect smoke rings shot whirring into the air for several hundred feet. Thereafter Hannes, who had dug the pits, amused himself by devising bigger and better pits, purely to obtain greater and more perfect smoke rings!

The flagging party, who were now well ahead, were probing the edges of great clefts that varied in width from twelve to seventy-five feet. So sunken were the bridges, and so parallel the sides, that they seemed like a series of parallel canals. As we started to drive slowly over I was more concerned with the side-swing of the trailing sledges than with the strength of the bridges we were crossing, for many of the wider ones had steep slopes leading down for as much as four or five feet to the sunken level of the bridges. When at last we arrived at the far side of these obstacles, we had crossed fifty major crevasses in three-and-a-half miles.

After another twenty-five miles we again came upon a crevasse belt, and cautiously crossing this the 'County of Kent' suffered damage when the large cast-aluminium rear steering platform was badly cracked. Then, in making a sharp turn, 'Able' sheared the pin linking the forward steering arm with the steering platform, and a new part had to be fitted. These constant mechanical faults all delayed our passage, and at the end of our journey we found that from the Pole to Scott Base we had averaged only five hours of sleep per night.

On 7 February at nine in the evening we finally reached Depot 700. We had arrived at the end of the supply line laid out to meet us from the other side of the continent. Bad weather at Scott Base precluded flying until the 9th when the Beaver, flown by John Claydon, brought Ed Hillary out to join us. While waiting for this flight we had pumped 405 gallons of petrol into the Sno-Cat tanks and drums which had already been emptied, and extra food supplies were loaded on to the sledges.

A tooth of mine had been giving considerable trouble ever since we had left the Pole, and now there was time for Allan Rogers to attend to it. Dentistry in a small pyramid tent is necessarily a primitive manoeuvre, the patient reclining with his head on a box or between the operator's knees, the latter's legs doubled up beneath him, and instruments inconveniently disposed in precarious positions. At least on this occasion Allan had the advantage of electric light derived from one of the Cats, and he did an excellent job which relieved me of much pain and probably saved the tooth.

The Beaver had brought up mail which had been accumulating for us at Scott Base, and we were amazed to receive a present of caviar from the Management of the Savoy, together with an

Antarctic traffic accident

invitation for Joyce and myself to stay at the hotel as their guests when we first got home.

Ed joined David Stratton and me in 'Rock'n'Roll' and thus, with ever-recurring mechanical problems, we drove towards Midway Depot on the 10th. During the next day, which was my fiftieth birthday, we covered fifty-three miles to reach the depot. News of the occasion seemed to have been put around by the media, for I received numerous cables from home and elsewhere, including an unexpected one from the Prime Minister of New Zealand, Walter Nash.

Four days later, when travelling to Depot 480 over a very rough and hummocky surface, I found it increasingly difficult to steer, but put it down to the side-pull of the sledges sliding off the ice swells. Then, when we had covered thirteen miles, 'Rock'n'Roll' took charge and described an 'S' bend over which I had no control. On climbing out I saw that the front and rear pontoons were pointing in quite different directions. Investigation showed that the same welds had given way as had failed on 'Able'. Having no more spares the only thing to do was to re-weld the broken parts. David Pratt and Roy Homard inspected the same welds on the other Cats and found that the break had gone almost as far on 'Haywire', though it had not yet affected the steering.

Now our special Terylene travelling tent for work on the vehicles really came into its own. A brisk breeze and a temperature down to −38°F (−38.8°C) made it essential to have cover for the preheating and prolonged cooling of the heavy metal parts, quite apart from the actual electric welding. This preheating and after-cooling was carried out with blow torches over a period of some hours and then we had to reassemble the Cats.

We reached Depot 480 on the 17th and again topped up with fuel, lubricating oil, gear oil, grease and food. Next morning there was complete whiteout, and the magnetic compasses were so sluggish that their rate of response made it impractical to use them. It is normally foolhardy to travel in such conditions, but the *Endeavour* was waiting at Scott Base, the season was advancing, and soon she might be forced to leave for New Zealand if the sea began to freeze. We felt it was essential to keep going at all costs.

After one or two experiments we finally invented a singularly uncomfortable but effective technique. Three stakes were planted along a line carefully orientated by compass. The driver of the leading Sno-Cat then drove forward while looking backwards out of the open door along the stake line, steering with his right hand behind him. Forward vision and accelerator control were provided by the passenger. As the Cats began to move cautiously, a man from the leading tractor placed more and more stakes in line with the first three thereby extending the course, while a man from the last vehicle collected them in again for use farther on.

This certainly speeded things up, but the strain on the driver's arms and neck was considerable, especially as his left hand had constantly to grip the window-frame to ensure that the lurching did not precipitate him through the open door and beneath the rear tracks of the Cat. By changing drivers every two hours we managed to move forty-two miles in a day, and felt that we had found a way in which we could travel satisfactorily in whiteout.

So it went on − maintenance on the 20th followed by twenty-five miles of route flagging, another thirty-nine miles flagged on the 21st, then relief the next day when slight visibility made it possible to see surface irregularities, and for fifteen miles we went 'sastrugi-hopping' − that is, driving from one selected ridge to the next, thereby maintaining a reasonable course.

We passed through Plateau Depot and reached the top of the Skelton Glacier. On 24 February we began the long, steep descent to the Ross Ice Shelf. Here we were harassed by strong katabatic winds which poured down from the plateau to displace the warmer air rising from the Ice Shelf. These had scoured the steeper inclines so smooth and hard that the sledges slid from side to side completely out of control. Sometimes they smashed into the rear pontoons of the towing vehicles till we had to stop and fit heavy rope brakes under the runners to check them.

At the bottom of the glacier was our last depot. Here we carried out our final maintenance on the tractors. We were happy to think that it would be some time before we would have to fill a grease gun again or become covered in a mixture of oil and drift.

Just as we were setting off on the morning of 1 March we saw an American Otter flying towards us, then as it circled the vehicles and we were climbing into the cabs we fired a 'two-star-red' as a gesture of *joie de vivre* before starting. In consequence various things happened which nearly resulted in a serious traffic accident. Unknown to us, the Americans took our signal to mean that we needed something, so they made a circuit and came in to land. Looking back from 'Rock'n'Roll' I saw them touch down and told David Stratton who was driving that we had better stop. In a moment the following Cat, whose driver was also looking behind him, began to climb up over the top of our rear sledge. When we went back to look at the damage done by the pontoons which were resting on top of our load, we found that not only was the sledge wheel badly damaged, but a box containing many hundreds of detonators had been smashed into small splinters. The metal containers were themselves crushed almost flat, revealing detonators in profusion. Had they exploded it certainly would have been the end of the 'climbing' Sno-Cat. Fortunately nothing happened and we were able to tow it slowly backwards off the sledge without further damage. In all the excitement we forgot about the plane, which had taxied across the snow only to take off again without stopping!

That evening once more the Sno-Cats were decorated with all available flags and pennants. The next morning we broke camp for the last time and prepared for the run in to Scott Base. At Castle Rock a fuel drum marked the start of a line of pennants leading to a route bulldozed through the pressure ridges by the Americans. Soon Weasels, Ferguson tractors and even Bren-gun Carriers came streaming along the track to meet us. As the Sno-Cats thundered and wove between the ridges they were escorted in front and behind by every variety of vehicle, while scores of figures stood, camera in hand, at every vantage point.

At precisely three minutes to two on 2 March 1958 our long journey was over. We had travelled 2,158 statute miles from 'Shackleton to Scott Base via the South Pole. In my original plan I had estimated that the journey would take 100 days and that our average speed would be about twenty miles a day. We found that we had completed the trip in ninety-nine days (ninety-eight if it is remembered that we crossed the date line at the Pole), and had averaged twenty-two miles a day.

In front of Scott Base the Cats assembled on the sea ice, and confusion reigned as scores of photographers had their way with the somewhat astonished new arrivals. Then we all congregated around the flagstaff and listened to speeches of welcome from our own people and the Americans.

An improvised American band from 'over the hill' did their worst with our national airs, ending up with what we were told was God Save The Queen. It had been formed the night before by calling for all who thought they could play an instrument. The edict went forth, 'it don't matter if you can't play – but you gotta be able to play LOUD' – and this they certainly did!

During the expedition coal seams had been discovered in the Theron Mountains, though no mineral ores were found. Fossil plants taken from a number of different localities showed the rocks to be over 300 million years old, and the seismic and gravity work revealed that mountain ranges lie buried in the ice cap. It was also proved that despite the different nature of the rocks in East and West Antarctica, the landmass is one continent. The physiological work included studies of the food and oxygen consumed by the men in relation to the cold they experienced and the work they did. Later the scientific results were published under the title *Trans-Antarctic Expedition Scientific Reports*. The physiological results were published separately by Allan Rogers at the University of Bristol Medical School.

Three days later, on 5 March, we sailed north over the ice-free waters of McMurdo Sound on our way to New Zealand. Although the Antarctic let us go without even a floe in sight, the Southern Ocean took its toll as *Endeavour* pitched and rolled in the heavy seas. Twelve days later in brilliant sunshine we sailed into Wellington Harbour.

It happened that the *Magga Dan* had arrived a few days before, and we were delighted to see her red-painted hull coming out to meet us early in the morning carrying our families and friends. We were given a most vociferous welcome by the many ships lying in the harbour while a flight of RNZAF Vampires roared overhead, and an unforgettable reception by the generous people of New Zealand.

We had crossed the continent at speeds of two to three miles an hour – eight to ten when the going was good. Suddenly being driven with Ed Hillary through the cheering crowds of Wellington at thirty miles an hour was one of the most frightening experiences of my life!

Emperor penguin and chick

Chapter 14

Aftermath

In order to close the financial gap in the expedition's affairs I was under contract to Cassells to write the story for publication, and great pressure was put on me to do this as quickly as possible in order that the book could be out by August, and thus be in time to catch the Australasian Christmas market. The publishers wanted to fly me home from New Zealand to expedite things, but I refused to come home ahead of the expedition, and they were not willing to bring us all back by air. Joyce had come out to meet us in Wellington, and we all spent a few very happy days being generously entertained, officially and unofficially, by kind New Zealanders.

We finally embarked in the s s *Rangitoto* on 5 May, and had the most enjoyable voyage home. At Southampton where we docked, the Mayor himself came down to the ship to greet us, and the school children had been given a holiday to welcome us back. It just poured with rain, but nothing seemed to dampen their high spirits as they waved us through the streets to a civic reception at the Town Hall.

A special train from London had brought all our families and members of the Committees down to share the party, after which it took us all back to Waterloo where we were officially welcomed by Sir Alec Douglas Home who was then Commonwealth Secretary.

Dick Honnywill, Eleanor's husband, was a veteran car enthusiast, and he had offered the loan of his beautiful open Phantom II Rolls Royce for use on what for us turned into a great occasion. Rolls had taken it up to their Derby factory where it was re-sprayed, and they then replaced each side-light by two tiny flagstaffs on which there now flew the flags of the four countries which had taken part in the expedition. The car carried George Lowe from New Zealand, Hannes la Grange from South Africa, Jon Stephenson from Australia and me. The remainder of the expedition followed in a line of smaller open cars lent by the Rootes Company, two men in the back

Expedition leaving Waterloo station for the Royal Geographical Society

of each. As we were driven slowly through the streets to a press conference held at the Royal Geographical Society we passed New Zealand House where we got a particularly vociferous welcome from the staff crowded at every window. That evening Joyce and I gratefully went to stay at the Savoy Hotel for two weeks, by courtesy of the Management. This enabled us to fulfil the many engagements which had been arranged by the office.

Two days after our arrival The Queen graciously received us with our wives privately at the Palace, when I received my knighthood and every member of the expedition was invested with the Polar Medal. This invitation had not included children. I was therefore astonished to see my schoolboy son among our number. It transpired that he had had the initiative (and the temerity!) to ring up the Palace and ask Colonel Charteris if he could attend too – a ploy which had been successful.

This private audience was followed by a lunch held at the Fishmongers Livery Company in the City, hosted by members of all the expedition committees in our honour. Sir John Slessor presided over the festivities, and in conversation I thanked him for the full support and confidence the Management Committee had given when it had been suggested that we should stop at the Pole and abandon the expedition until the following season. They had been put under enormous pressure by the world's press to tell us to fly out with the Americans. He asked me what would have happened if their decision had gone the other way and they had ordered me to come out leaving the vehicles at the Pole? I told him that radio conditions would have unfortunately deteriorated so badly that I would never have received such a message. He ruefully smiled his approval of such a tactful stratagem!

My first lecture was given jointly with David Stratton, supported by the whole expedition, at the Royal Geographical Society, and for me it was an outstanding occasion because the Duchess of Kent, then the Honorary President, presented me with the Society's Special Gold Medal. It was the fourth to be awarded in 128 years. Happily each expedition member was later presented with a bronze replica. So it was that relations with the Society were finally healed. The Scott Polar Research Institute also let bygones be bygones and presented us all with gold cuff links engraved with our initials, saying 'From the SPRI' and bearing the token 'TAE Crossing'.

This hectic first fortnight in London included an invitation to an evening Government Reception at Lancaster House. It was a very formal occasion hosted by the Prime Minister, then Sir Harold Macmillan, at which we wore white ties and the ladies their long gloves. As the guests circulated music was provided by a regimental orchestra from the Guards. Soon after eleven o'clock a number of people, particularly the older ones, began to go home. As the ranks thinned out Rainer Goldsmith's young bride, Sally, who was talking to Lord Mountbatten, said wouldn't it be fun if we could now dance? He thought it a splendid idea and promptly went off to put the suggestion to the Prime Minister. Sir Harold, too, was enthusiastic, and among the first to start rolling the carpets back, and asking the orchestra to change the music. They demurred a little because they did not have their sheet music or the right instruments, but very sportingly they broke into a waltz and everyone took their partners. All formality was abandoned. Lady Mountbatten, dancing with Rainer Goldsmith, meeting Sally dancing with her husband, said as they passed, 'My dear, you will go down in history as having made one of these stuffy functions bearable!'

Successful as the evening turned out to be, there were unhappy consequences. The next time I met Mr Macmillan he told me ruefully that I had got him into a lot of trouble – apparently the General Secretary of the Musicians' Union had read about the evening's goings-on in the morning newspapers. He was furious and had rushed off to see the Prime Minister personally and register a very strong protest. Apparently we had broken all union rules, and if we had wanted to dance the government should have provided a professional dance band to replace the orchestra for the second part of the evening! It seemed a very churlish and sour note on which to end a happy and innocent evening. For me it was a curious claim to fame, for I am non-musical and an incompetent dancer!

Her Majesty The Queen, Prince Philip and Princess Margaret were good enough to come to the first public lecture at the Royal Festival Hall, which David Stratton and I again gave jointly supported by the whole expedition. I was only just beginning to get used to the cult of autograph hunting, and after it I was quite daunted by the crowd awaiting me outside for this purpose. However, children are a good antidote to a swollen head. Eleanor was also waiting for me to come out into the crowd, and standing next to two school girls she overheard one little madam saying to the other, 'Yes, well I particularly want this one because I've already got Sir John Hunt, and if I can get Sir Vivian Fuchs I can swop them both for Sir Edmund Hillary!

After two weeks of being entertained somewhere for lunch and dinner every day we all split up and went our own ways. For me the pressure was now on to write the book and meet the very tight deadline. Dick Honnywill had retired from the Navy and had begun to work for the Ottoman Bank. Fortuitously they were sending him on a six-week tour of all their branches in the Middle East, so Eleanor was free of family obligations. She came up to Cambridge with us and as I wrote she typed, all day and every day, while Joyce provided food at regular intervals to keep us going. As each chapter was written it was rushed to the station literally hot from the typewriter, where it was handed to the guard of the London train to be met by a representative from Cassells at Waterloo.

Soon the galley proofs were arriving back to us, and as we got to the later chapters we received the earliest ones in page proof, the more recent ones in galleys all at the same time. No time for second thoughts or revision, it was confusing to say the least. To make sure we were not slacking George Greenfield, our literary agent, came to stay and Cassells too paid us a visit. An added complication was the fact that four chapters written by Ed Hillary had to come from New Zealand to be incorporated into the rest of the text.

After six weeks Dick Honnywill returned from his travels looking forward to a reunion with his wife. But we had not finished, so this time I went back to London with her and stayed in their flat where the work continued – with the added pressure that Eleanor now had to cook the dinner as well as type the last chapters. After eight weeks the whole operation was over, in the very nick of time for the books to catch the boat to Australia for Christmas. It was an experience that neither of us wants to repeat!

Later the book was translated into fourteen languages, including Hebrew and Japanese, and made a lot of money for the expedition. The irony of the situation was that when John Lewis and his RAF crew had made the transpolar flight, John had been invited to dine at the American station over the hill from Scott Base. The occasion had turned into quite a riotous party, and next morning the office in London had received the following message,

Sold the Otter aircraft to the Americans last night for $30,000. Hope OK? – Lewis

This sum was sufficient to close our financial gap, and therefore had there not been a contract, I need never have written the book!

In the end the book sold very well world wide and the expedition found itself with a large profit. The problem was what to do with it? When the TAE office closed down we formed the Trans-Antarctic Association with the surplus money, and this Trust now makes annual awards to individuals or organizations to promote further Antarctic work.

British Petroleum, which had supported the expedition so generously, now made a film entitled *The Crossing of Antarctica*. This followed a much shorter twenty-minute film called *Foothold on Antarctica* which they had earlier made recording the adventures of the Advance Party in 1955-56. Both these were the property of the Company, and in their interests they were translated into eighteen languages including Hebrew, Japanese and Vietnamese. I found *Foothold* most useful when lecturing in foreign countries.

In the months after finishing the book the insatiable demand for lectures and our attendance at various functions continued until May in the following year. Since officially I had returned to the FIDS as Director on 1 January 1959, I owed much to the Colonial Office and the Governor of the Falkland Islands for allowing me to continue to attend functions in the aftermath of the expedition. So it was that Joyce and I visited Oslo, Amsterdam, Copenhagen and Paris, where I gave lectures and met a number of Heads of State. A particular surprise was the interest that General de Gaulle showed in the Antarctic when he received me privately.

In February 1959 we visited the United States and Canada, where I lectured in Washington, New York, Indianapolis, Chicago, Toronto and Montreal. The highlight of this series was a visit to the White House to receive the National Geographic Society's Hubbard Medal from President Eisenhower. There was one disappointment when as a result of my timetable I had to refuse an invitation to go to sea in the nuclear submarine USS *Nautilus*, which had just made the first trans-Arctic voyage under the ice via the North Pole. However, it seemed appropriate when the stories of that voyage and our crossing of the Antarctic were published in the same issue of the *National Geographic Magazine*.

Before embarking on this tour across the water I had been made aware of the very high temperatures maintained in American hotels, and was somewhat apprehensive. To ease my situation Eleanor rang up the hotel in Washington and asked them to shut off the central heating in our suite. On arrival the manager personally conducted us to our rooms, and ignoring the spark of static electricity which leapt from the door handle to his hand, proudly flung it open. The curtains on the far side blew inwards with the snow-cooled wind from the open window. The central heating was off, and we never had to turn it on, for with the window closed the walls were still so warm they gave sufficient heat during the next days.

This episode must have got around for when three reporters were ushered in for an interview they were all muffled up in overcoats. Furthermore, during the interview there was a knock on the door and a man in a white boiler suit entered. Asked why he had come, he said with a splendid accent, 'I jus' came along to see how the little ole iceberg were gettin' along.' Thereafter we were left in peace to enjoy our micro-climate.

Peter Fuchs with Darkie, and Hilary Fuchs

During this visit I was asked to give a number of television and radio interviews. At one of these early-morning breakfast shows the theme was the recent publication of the expedition book in the States. The lady interviewer began by asking me, 'Would you tell us about this map – we all know that north is at the top of the page and south at the bottom, but ...' Since in fact the South Pole was in the middle of the map I could not resist saying, 'No, no – north is all around the page.' She was disconcerted and bemused, and I found we were suddenly hearing an advertisement for gas cookers. On returning to the interview she was unwise enough to dispute my statement because north was *always* at the top of the page, and we were into quite an argument. At a party that evening I met several people who had been driving in to work with their car radios on, and who had been vastly amused at my fruitless efforts to teach the lady some simple geography. Perhaps it enlivened what might otherwise have been rather a dull event.

When we got back home from America it became apparent that there was a great discrepancy in the fees being offered to different members of the expedition. We all undertook many local lectures in our own districts for which no charge was made, but in addition a number of public lectures in large halls throughout the country were promoted by commercial organizations and brought in a lot of money. Since we all gave virtually the same lecture and showed the same slides, this seemed to me rather unjust. I therefore formed a joint 'lecture fund' into which all the money was paid. At the end of the programmes fifty per cent of the proceeds went into expedition funds, and the remainder was equally divided between everyone who had lectured.

In the intervals between all these activities I had been able to catch up on family affairs. For the first time I met Hilary's husband, Howard Brooks, whose stable outlook on life very much appealed to me. He was a lecturer in a Teachers' Training College whom she had met when he was ill in hospital, for since 1954 Hilary had been training as a nurse. She had left nursing to get married, and was now soon to present us with our first grandson, David.

Peter was still at Sedbergh School when I returned home. Then in 1959 he secured himself a place at St John's, Cambridge – my old college. There he took a degree in Natural Sciences with geology as the main subject. It was during this period that he had his first taste of adventure by working for four months for British Petroleum in Alaska. Unplanned though it was, like father like son, we both became geologists and had our first field experience in the Arctic.

Chapter 15

Towards Retirement and After

When I had returned to FIDS as Director on 1 January 1959 I had taken over from Sir Raymond Priestley, and although officially I was responsible to the Governor of the Falkland Islands it was found to be more practical for me to deal directly with the Colonial Office in London. In those days before teleprinters there were still only ten mailing opportunities to the Islands in a year, and it took a minimum of six weeks to get a reply to a letter. Our day-to-day communication with the bases and the Stanley office were therefore conducted by telegram.

I had been fortunate in persuading Eleanor Honnywill to come with me as my Personal Assistant, for there were still all the TAE scientific publications to come out. Anne Todd and I taught her how to edit, and she quickly learnt to deal with printers. This was a major task for the series of *Trans-Antarctic Expedition Scientific Reports* covered a wide range of subjects from survey, geology, palaeontology and glaciology to tides, gravity, seismic sounding and meteorology. Fortunately for her she was not concerned with some forty other books and papers published about the scientific work of the expedition. Another advantage that Eleanor brought with her was her ability to handle awkward people or situations and this smoothed many a difficult path, while her sharp mind has contributed much to my books and other activities.

During the 1959-60 Antarctic summer season I went south to visit all the bases, taking as my guest Alfred Stephenson who had been a surveyor with the British Graham Land Expedition twenty-six years earlier. We flew to Montevideo to join the Danish ice vessel *Kista Dan* which had been chartered to assist *John Biscoe* with the annual relief. Our flight ended in Buenos Aires, where we heard that the ship would be arriving late owing to engine trouble, so we delayed our onward flight to Montevideo. Through the Embassy we were introduced to Don Juan Alberto Harriet who invited us to visit his extensive *estancias*. His father had been a Basque immigrant, and as a young man Don Juan had started on his own with the equivalent of £10 in his pocket. With this he went south to Patagonia, where he bought some cattle which he drove north to sell. He did this for some time, through the years always improving his financial position.

Now we found that the scale of his operations were so astonishing that it seems worth recording the statistics. He farmed over 1,000 square miles in Pampa Province, and owned twenty-three aeroplanes, most of which were used for spraying the crops of rye and alfalfa on which his cattle fed. Apparently his final annual product was 23,000 head on the hoof or as beef. The scale of his operations was enormous, and we were fascinated to learn that 5,000 acres of rye were being harvested each day while some 3,500 acres were being ploughed at the same time. It was equally astonishing to learn that the hundreds of tons of rye being harvested were solely for use as seed for the next year. This because the cattle were turned on to new-grown rye before the alfalfa was ready for use.

At the time of our visit the alfalfa was in full growth and heavily infected with grasshoppers and butterflies, so spraying was in progress. The record for one pilot in a single day was 15,000 acres! As we drove it was a remarkable sight to see the rising cloud of butterflies. Counted not in hundreds but in hundreds of thousands, they blew away in the wind as a whitish-yellow cloud. Every stage of development, eggs, caterpillars, pupae and adults all existed together. We were told that this life cycle took about three weeks and was repeated continuously.

Our visit to the pampas ended with flights to a number of Don Juan's other *estancias*, and so back to Buenos Aires and a plane on to Montevideo. Next day *Kista Dan* arrived and after two hectic days of loading an Otter and a Beaver aircraft we sailed for Stanley. There we were met by Dr Stewart Slessor in his ancient Rolls Royce and the Governor's official car. This proved to be a London taxi complete with the official crest and chaffeur-driven, the high roof specially chosen in order to accommodate His Excellency's hat with ostrich plumes when he travelled in uniform. In this I was taken to stay at Government House.

When I had last been in Stanley in 1950 there had been about eighty yards of concrete road and perhaps a dozen cars. Now ten years later this incongruous pair of vehicles could travel on twelve miles of concrete and tar macadam road. The number of licensed vehicles had risen to some 500, many of these being motorbikes. Only a few years later the Falkland Islanders could boast that they had more motor vehicles per head of population than anywhere else in the world.

After five busy days, including a number of receptions, all the new Fids in the ship had been issued with their polar clothing and we sailed for the Antarctic – first stop Deception Island. This volcanic island is like an atoll with a large interior body of water entered by a very narrow deep water channel known as Neptune's Bellows over which tower vertical 400-foot cliffs of volcanic rock. We were struck by the unexpected sight of a derelict whale-catcher hard and fast on a rock in mid-channel. Apparently some time before, on New Year's Eve, this vessel had met a large Argentine ship coming in. When taking avoiding action the catcher had run aground and lost its propeller. The crew began firing distress rockets but this only brought a response of more rockets from the Argentinians who thought that the Norwegians were celebrating the coming year, and sailed happily past them. As all this took place out of sight of the British base, the ship-wrecked crew had to await the arrival of another catcher before they were rescued.

At Deception we spent several days building and then test-flying the two aircraft. The little Beaver was built on board and fitted with floats as we intended to take it south for reconnaissance purposes. This was just as well for after relieving Port Lockroy we encountered increasing difficulty with the sea ice. From the Argentine Islands base we made a number of flights which showed that we would have to sail far to the west before turning south to attempt an entry into Marguerite Bay where we hoped to re-establish the Stonington base.

Three days later we were pushing through heavy pack and my journal records our predicament:

Gradually movement has become more difficult, but the ship keeps going with ice heaving from below as great lumps and plates rise out of the water and fall slowly back into the turbulence of the porridge-like brash. Ahead

John Biscoe and *Kista Dan* at the Argentine Islands

the floes shuffle and rotate as they adjust themselves to the thrusting bows of the ship. If they cannot move they either split into many pieces or stop the ship. Then we go astern and charge again.

After three days we found a patch of water from which the Beaver could be flown. The flight revealed stretches of open water, but between these and the coast lay some fifty miles of unbroken ice. Soon we were calling the plane back, for our pool of water was shrinking and freezing over. When at last it landed the floats sent a shimmering shower of thin ice plates slithering across the newly frozen water.

Once more underway, we made some twenty-eight miles before being held up again by very heavy ice floes. Then came a sixty-five-knot wind which produced sufficient pressure for *Kista* to be tilted eleven degrees to port. Living at that angle for the next eight days was very uncomfortable. Meals had to be eaten holding the plates level, and even single sheets of paper would slide from desk to floor. There was no visible water but the ice was constantly on the move, floes splitting and buckling in every direction. On 2 March the ice activity increased,

... and soon the ship was heaving and twisting, sometimes returning to an even keel, sometimes heeling over as much as sixteen degrees. All around us the ice was buckling and rising in tumbling masses that here and there advanced across the floes like the slow-moving rolling front of a lava stream. From time to time she was squeezed tight and huge plates of ice four feet thick would up-end and drive under her, only to re-emerge with a rush and a great swirling turbulence a few minutes later.

Meanwhile the ship's heading was constantly changing as she was pushed and nudged by the shifting rotating floes ... This evening things have quietened down with the easing of the wind, and the area around us looks like a battlefield, for the floes and brash are stained with great patches of red paint scraped from our hull. The rest appears in various shades of black and grey due to the churning of the water pumped from the bilges during our long stay.

While all this had been going on I had been in touch with the Chilean ice vessel *Pilato Pardo* which had turned back on meeting heavy ice, and the Argentine icebreaker *San Martin* which had lost a propeller blade and buckled thirty of her frames. The Argentine Captain told me he had asked the powerful United States icebreaker *Glacier* to come to his assistance. Since she would then be only thirty miles from our position, I asked her Captain to help us after freeing the *San Martin*. This he kindly did and by 10 March we were once more in open water.

By now all the season's plans were in disarray, and in the end the relief party destined for Marguerite Bay had to be left to winter in an abandoned hut on the Argentine Islands, for we could get no farther south. That was not the end of our misfortunes, for at one time the anchor chains of both *Biscoe* and *Kista* became entangled. This brought the two ships together, and a wing of the Beaver then on the deck of the *Kista* was torn off. Later she was in very heavy seas and the lashings of a large wooden scow on the foredeck broke. The scow went over the side, floated and disappeared in the gloom, never to be seen again.

Apart from all these mishaps we were eventually able to re-supply seven stations in the normal way, and in addition by using the Otter we relieved the Horseshoe Island base in Marguerite Bay. For us in *Kista Dan* the season ended when we arrived back in Stanley on 14 April.

Like this first summer voyage south, I was to make several more visits to the bases before my retirement in 1973. None of them were as adventurous or disrupted as the 1960-61 season, nevertheless each had its highlights.

Kista Dan under pressure

The year 1960 was the Golden Jubilee of the University of Natal, and to celebrate it the University promoted a large educational conference in Durban during July. This was attended by teachers from all over South Africa, and twenty-five eminent educationalists from overseas were also invited as VIP lecturers. For some reason we never understood they also asked Ed Hillary and me to go – presumably as sort of side shows. It was a most happy nine-day visit.

Ed lectured on Everest, I spoke on our Antarctic crossing and also gave a paper on Human Endurance.

Apart from our great interest in the conference itself, we were fortunate in being looked after by British Petroleum (South Africa) who had so generously supported TAE and, it now seemed, were grateful for the publicity they had received in consequence. So it was that I was able to renew the surfboarding I had learnt in West Africa during the war, only now it was on bigger and better boards. One which I found to be really excellent had come from Australia, and a few months later an identical one was presented to me by BP in London.

One evening Ed and I were invited to an exhibition of traditional Zulu dancing, also arranged by the Company, at the end of which we were both given Zulu names, made Honorary Chiefs, and presented with Zulu shields and knobkerries.

Another relaxation was some high-speed water-skiing in Durban Harbour. Among many memorable pleasures I paid a weekend visit to the Drakensburg Mountains with Professor Lester King and Dr Edna Plumstead who was then writing *Fossil Floras of Antarctica* for the expedition *Reports* series. I was also invited to lecture to members of the Indian community – a very pleasant occasion when I detected none of the cultural or racial problems which are spoken of so widely today.

By August I was home again and the time came round for our annual family holiday. As usual we went to the little seaside village of Borth-y-Gest near Portmadoc in north Wales. We had always taken our clinker-built sailing dinghy *Flying Fox*, but the TAE Management Committee had given me £500 for writing the book and I had spent it on acquiring *Pendragon*, a speedboat with which we could now water-ski. So that year there were two boats. Peter took to skiing with apparent ease, for he rose from the water at his first attempt – thereby putting his father's nose out of joint for I had only succeeded at the second essay fifteen years before in Germany.

Borth provided all we needed – sailing, water-skiing, mountains to climb, swimming and fishing. Part of the attraction was the lack of crowds, and in the early years the few boats in the tiny harbour, which we came to call the Bay of the Bobbing Boats. At first *Flying Fox* was the only visiting boat moored in the bay, but in later years it became difficult to find a comfortable anchorage because of the large number of visiting yachts. Fortunately we had made friends with Mr and Mrs Roberts, in whose house we always stayed, and he always managed to find us moorings.

As the years passed we came to know both the people and the surrounding countryside. Climbing Snowdon and lesser peaks, walking the Roman Steps, collecting cowries at low tide on Morfa (Shell Island), all these and other ventures farther afield became annual events. Sometimes there were untoward adventures as when Joyce, Hilary and I decided to walk round the craggy peak of Rhinog Fach and return via the Roman Steps. Joyce was somewhat lame owing to the recent replacement of a hip joint and Hilary had a painful foot from a bone growth which later had to be removed surgically. At first all went well as we followed a footpath and then sheep tracks, until even these petered out. Unknown to us we were now faced with a wide scree of large angular boulders mostly hidden by vegetation. Progress was painfully slow and I began to realize that I would soon be leading the halt and the lame over treacherous ground in the dark. Fortunately we were just able to reach the Roman Steps in time, and after a walk of thirteen miles we regained the car.

Each year there were some such adventures on land or water, but in retrospect for us they were the making of the holiday. Joyce and I had both experienced our own adventures around the world. Now it seemed fitting that the children – and in due course the grand-children – should be initiated into facing unexpected events which are always a part of an active outdoor life. They took to it with relish.

In January 1964 I was again visiting the bases in *Kista Dan*. Our first call was at King Edward Point, South Georgia where another BA's ship, *Shackleton*, was lying, and to her I transferred. We found that the Japanese whalers were working very successfully. They were most helpful, even offering us 100 tons of fuel at only £10 per ton. I learnt that unlike the Norwegians and the British their gunners did not command the whale catchers, nor did they have the freedom to seek whales where they willed. The whalers were despatched by the shore station to areas where the junction of warm and cold waters was reported. Presumably this was where the whales found that the food was most prolific. When our ships sailed – *Kista* for Halley Bay and *Shackleton* for Signy Island – the Japanese waved us goodbye to the blaring of loudspeakers playing 'Auld Lang Syne' in very slow time. We thought it a friendly gesture!

At Signy a new two-storey hut was being built, and I was asked to lay the inscribed foundation stone, really a concrete block. On the occasion suddenly everyone produced cameras and only Richard Stocks, the Base Commander, and I were left to be photographed! As this was clearly an inadequate picture, one man was designated as photographer and, festooned with a myriad cameras, he repeatedly photographed the now reasonable 'crowd' while Richard and I performed our act over and over again.

From Signy we sailed to Hope Bay at the northern end of the Antarctic Peninsula, there to perform the sad task of closing the station which had been a major sledging base for fifteen years. Now all the main scientific work had been done in the area, and it was time to move on. Before leaving I visited the graves of the two men lost in the fire in 1949, and found the crosses still in good condition.

The next call was to Deception where we met the American icebreaker *East Wind* carrying an inspection team to visit all the Argentine, Chilean and British stations under the terms of the Antarctic Treaty. Then on to our Argentine Islands base where we went aground on an uncharted rock while trying to cut a way through heavy ice. Fortunately there was no damage, and after freeing *Shackleton* from the ice with an explosive charge we finally reached the station.

Our grounding was not the last of our troubles. The relief accomplished, on leaving the islands an ominous vibration began to pervade the ship. This was traced to the main shaft thrust-race and slowly we made our way back to Deception. Here the Captain decided that we must visit the Chilean naval dockyard at Punta Arenas for repairs.

The Captain of the Chilean ship *Angamos* advised us to sail via the calm waters of the Beagle Channel instead of through the stormy seas along the coast. This was to have repercussions because territorial boundary disputes between Chile and Argentina made each nation jealous of intrusion.

Making our way slowly north past the South Shetland Islands we were soon approaching Cape Horn. Many of us were surprised not

The new hut at Signy

only to find that it is an island well to the south-east of the apparent tip of South America, but also to experience a flat and oily sea where notorious gales were to be expected. As we passed through the Murray Channel west of Navarino Island the bare rocky coast gradually became clothed with mosses and grass, then low stunted trees cowering in sheltered hollows. Presently the flora grew more luxuriantly until a definite tree-line became apparent at about 2,000 feet. Here and there were small wooden huts, rough and unpainted, presumably belonging to the Fuegian Indians.

Turning westward along the Beagle Channel we passed many glaciers stretching down to the tree-line from the high snow-covered peaks and ridges on either side. A few of these still reached the water but the majority seemed to be in a state of rapid retreat, for here and there the last remnants of glaciers could be seen as patches of 'dead' ice in valleys they once occupied.

During our passage through the Beagle a hot sun shone and a kindly following wind made it possible for us to stand for hours on the upper bridge stripped to the waist as we admired the scenery. Everyone voted it better than Norway, albeit smaller in scale. The narrowness of the channel brought everything so close as to be most impressive.

By 1 February we were secured in Punta Arenas alongside various Chilean naval vessels, including her Antarctic ship *Piloto Pardo*. I enquired about a nearby merchant vessel and was told that she was loading a cargo of Chilean wine. 'Going where?' I asked. 'To France' was the reply – a prime example of coals to Newcastle.

Within a few hours of our arrival a team of Chilean naval engineers began work on *Shackleton*. Through the agency of the British Consul I was able to call upon the Provincial Governor and the Senior Naval Officer of the region, both of them Admirals, together with the naval Chief of Staff. All of them were most welcoming and pleasant. It must therefore have been embarrassing when it became necessary for them, on instructions from Santiago, to summon the British Consul to explain why a British ship had entered Chilean territorial waters without permission. I told the Consul that the Captain of *Angamos* had advised the route, and that with our engine trouble we could not chance the open sea. This was accepted, but perhaps in retaliation I received a demand to carry a Chilean naval officer when leaving Chile to go to the 'Chilean' island of Deception. As this was not in keeping with the spirit of the Antarctic Treaty I said that we would invite an officer to go with us, but it would be some weeks before he would arrive as we planned a programme of marine geophysical work in the Drake Passage first. The demand was then withdrawn and we were allowed to leave via the Magellan Straits without a Chilean on board.

The trip through the Straits was uneventful and indeed uninteresting because the shores are so low-lying. At one time our speed was remarkable because in the narrowest part the strong tidal current can attain seven to nine knots. Before reaching the open sea we could see numerous lighted gas vents from the oil wells on both shores. Then we were on our way south once more to complete the task of relieving the various peninsula bases and Signy.

There our visit coincided with that of *Kista Dan*. So strong was the wind that it was impossible to work between the ships or to the shore, and finally both vessels were compelled to go out to sea where they attempted to find shelter behind an iceberg twelve miles long which had run aground on the island. As we steamed up and down in its lee, the middle of the 'berg began to break up.

First small pieces fell from the cliffs then enormous blocks broke away, tilting and rolling as though some earthquake was upheaving the great 'berg. Soon the fragments, which were themselves small icebergs, separated from the main mass and together with a huge quantity of brash and growlers spread out over one or two square miles of sea. This provided a hazard in the dark and forced us out into the open sea.

When at last the wind abated we returned to complete the relief of the base, and then sailed for the Falklands and home.

As well as his Rolls, which he kept as a hobby, Dick Honnywill also owned an Austin Healey Sprite. On occasion he would lend me this as it was so easy to park in London. One hot sunny day, with the hood down, I drove Sir Raymond Priestley to the Royal Society in it. We progressed down Piccadilly dwarfed by the traffic, with some-what amused glances from the other drivers, and finally stopped at some red lights. A huge lorry came up alongside, and from a great height the driver gazed down in disbelief on our two white heads in the 'Dinky' car. Finally he leant over and commented 'Cor blimey – the sun does bring 'em out, don't it?' The lights went green, and thus reminded of our youthful days we turned refreshed into Burlington House to attend our meeting with so many other white and bald heads, now seeming to form a geriatric community.

Before long Dick replaced his Sprite with a Jaguar XK 150, then one of the fastest cars on the market, and I too acquired the same model. This was the beginning of my love affair with Jaguars. In subsequent years I successively became the owner of each new model of the E-Type – all wonderful cars to drive. When I was 80 my irreplaceable V12 model was stolen and I was compelled to buy a Coupé – the first time in sixty years of motoring that I ever owned a closed car.

Family events continued to occur through the years. Hilary and Howard produced three children, David, Roger and Rosemary, now all grown up and making their own ways through life. After going to St John's, Cambridge, Peter spent two years with the Diamond Corporation in Nigeria, then returned to work with a quarrying company in England. In 1966 he was married to Ann Rowell and they have two children, Caroline and Edward, now also grown up and setting about their own careers.

It has been a great blessing to Joyce and me that our own two produced no problems in their teenage years, and the same can be said of the five grandchildren, all so different yet possessing the

Joyce in the 'E' Type Jaguar

same steadfast stability so valuable in every walk of life. We have indeed been fortunate.

When I had settled down to a steady life in England except for periodical summer Antarctic visits, there were opportunities for other activities. So it was that on his retirement, Gerald Seligman, Founder of the International Glaciological Society, more or less dictated that I should succeed him as President – a post which lasted from 1963 to 1966. I had been a member of the Committee for a number of years, perhaps on the basis that I had seen a lot of snow and ice. Certainly I was not qualified as a technical glaciologist. But in those early days of what is now a prestigious society, acquaintance with the subject was perhaps all that was necessary for its future organization. Whatever the reason, I am extremely proud to have been associated with its Founder and perhaps to have made a small contribution.

In 1967 the British Antarctic Survey left the dying Colonial Office and was transferred to operate under the newly formed Natural Environment Research Council as one of their constituent Bodies. NERC encouraged me to stay on as Director until I was sixty-five, instead of retiring at sixty as is normal in the Civil Service. So it was that I made four more visits to the Antarctic, in 1967, '70, '71 and '73. All these were routine tours of the bases, but each had its unusual episodes.

The main event in 1967 was the building of a new base at Halley

Bay. The old station built in 1956 had been heavily distorted by ice movement, and access was by fifty-foot shafts through eleven years of accumulated snow. The main beams of the huts were nearly all broken by the distortion, and the walls and roofs gaped in numerous places. The internal heat of the buildings melted the outside snow and trickles of water were everywhere. These drips were being caught by plastic sheets hung beneath the ceilings or in gutters along the walls, draining into large buckets which had to be emptied several times each day. This situation alone, apart from the fire risk of living at the bottom of fifty-foot shafts, was an imperative reason for building a new base.

This was done about two miles from the old site and farther back from the seaward margin of the ice shelf. While building was going on a serious emergency occurred when George McLeod suddenly developed acute appendicitis. Unusually but fortunately there were three doctors and a dentist in the ship. With this medical strength the patient was operated on in the depths of the old base. Whether the doctors tossed for who should perform the operation I do not know, but it all took some time because it turned out that George was one of those rare people whose appendix was located on the wrong side.

Three days later they decided to move him to the ship. For this he was strapped into a flexible medical stretcher and hoisted by the local derrick to the surface. Later he told me that dangling in his powerless state from a hook was more terrifying than anything he had experienced during his many years of rock climbing. The medicos' intention had been to strap him on to one of the heavy cargo sledges and tow him the mile or so to the ship by tractor. Realizing that this would be a rough ride over the hard rutted snow route, I persuaded them to man-haul him more gently on a flexible Nansen sledge which gave an easier motion.

Eight days after his operation the ship left for Signy, which we reached in the record time of three days, twenty-three hours and ten minutes. Never had we known the Weddell Sea so free of ice, and perhaps it never had been since Weddell himself sailed into it in 1823. During this time George had been sitting up in bed chatting to visitors, and as witness to his toughness he climbed the hill above Signy base on the fourteenth day after his operation. Less than a month later he was fit enough to be left to winter at Stonington.

Three years later, in 1970, I was again visiting the bases, this time in HMS *Endurance* which that season was occupied in establishing naval hydrographic parties at various points on the west coast of the peninsula.

But it was not until the following year that I again visited Halley Bay, this time in the newly-built BAS ice ship RRS *Bransfield*. Although only four years old the base was already entirely buried, and the ice had distorted the structures in the same way as in the earlier buildings. Our discussions about the reasons for this led to the idea of perhaps erecting base huts inside corrugated steel tubes.

Back in England I was greatly distressed to find that my good friend Dick Honnywill was suffering from terminal cancer. He intimated that he hoped when he was gone that I would keep an eye on Eleanor's welfare in the future. By then she had worked with me for seventeen years and I was only too happy to assent. In 1972 Dick died, and by his own wish he was buried at sea by the Royal Navy.

In the following year, my sixty-sixth, I was due to retire, so I took the opportunity of the 1972-73 southern summer to make my last visit to the BAS bases. It was then that the idea of building the new Halley Bay base inside steel tubes was put into effect. During the re-building we worked in shifts throughout the twenty-four hours until finally there were only fuel drums left to be landed. By extraordinary good fortune I then ordered the cessation of unloading at night. That very evening, when at last there were no men working, a catastrophic collapse of the ice ramp took place. The first lump to calve off nudged the ship from the ice edge, then followed a spectacular break-up of fifty yards of the slope, with huge blocks rising and falling as cracks spread from one side of the creek to the other. Odd timbers, then three cargo sledges, slid into the mêlée of heaving blocks and then disappeared. We were indeed lucky that no one was working, for if they had been they would certainly have been lost. After this the remaining work had to be done with the ship secured to the forty-five-foot ice cliff.

Leaving Halley Bay we sailed for my old TAE base Shackleton, 200 miles to the south. From there we intended to recover the radio beacon for use at Halley Bay. On arrival we found that Shackleton now lay fourteen miles north of the position where we had built it in 1956, showing the annual northward movement of the ice shelf to

Rebuilding Halley Bay

be three-quarters of a mile. There it was astonishing to find the roof
ridge of the hut still showing above the snow in contrast to the rapid
burial of two successive stations at Halley Bay. This was evidence
that the constant southerly winds at Shackleton scoured the surface,
preventing accumulation.

I was surprised to find that coming back gave me a strong feeling
of returning 'home' – quite different from visiting Halley Bay. Yet
the two stations are built on ice shelves with seemingly identical
expanses of endless snow. After many hours of digging we recovered
the radio beacon and bade a final farewell to the station. In 1986,
thirty years after it was built, the ice shelf calved and Shackleton was
borne away in the iceberg, finally to disappear in the Weddell Sea.

Returning to Halley Bay, we awaited the arrival of the two BAS
Twin-Otters which were to make the first flight across 1,000 miles of
the Weddell Sea from Adelaide Island west of the peninsula. An
hour before they were due a low mist enveloped the station and the
landing area, but it suddenly cleared before their arrival and all was
well. Two days later I was flown back to Adelaide, and after visits to
the other bases I sailed for Stanley in *Biscoe*, and so home.

Back in England there were busy months before my retirement in

September. Eleanor retired three months later, and it was arranged that I should use her flat as a *pied-à-terre* in London for writing and dealing with the numerous committees on which I remained. This situation has continued to the present time, and she still hosts many meetings and provides a contact for Antarctic men at home and overseas.

During my years as Director I was an *ex officio* member of the Royal Society's National Committee on Antarctic Research. When I retired the Royal Society asked me to remain on their Committee until a few years later when, no doubt, they discovered my age. I then received their usual very charming letter of thanks for my services, explaining that I had arrived at the normal retirement age from their committees and so 'goodbye'.

It happened that in 1982, when I was seventy-four, I was asked to become President of the Royal Geographical Society. I accepted this with a great deal of pleasure, and by the end of my term it happened that the RGS was looking for someone to represent them on the Royal Society's National Committee on Antarctic Research. They nominated me. So suddenly, amid some ribald comments and much laughter I turned up at the next meeting at the age of seventy-six! Perhaps the surprise was tempered by the fact that in 1974 I had been elected to Fellowship of the Royal Society under their Rule which exceptionally allows those not qualified by science to become Fellows.

In a somewhat similar and curious way in 1972 I had become President of the British Association for the Advancement of Science. I was approached about this, apparently without good reason. But it was not long before I thought I had the answer, for I discovered that the Association was almost moribund and in deep financial trouble. Who would undertake such a task? Perhaps they thought that my recent notoriety over the Trans-Antarctic Expedition might attract badly needed young recruits. On the other hand I had been brought up by my mother to think of the British Association as one of the most prestigious Societies in the country. It was therefore with a considerable sense of pride that I accepted the invitation. Fortunately the Treasurer of the day was Sir Eric Mensforth who, during his five years of office, put the Society on its financial feet again – since when it has never looked back.

5. 'Snowhenge'

6. South Pole, 'Wrack and Ruin' in foreground

7. Sir Vivian Fuchs 1984 painted by June Mendoza RP ROI

Looking back I realize that my retirement made little difference to my way of life. The commitment to BAS had, of course, gone, but somehow there seemed to be as many if not more committees, and in the next few years I was to make a number of overseas visits – to the United States, New Zealand, Antarctica and Kenya. Also it was not long before I became involved with organizing and editing a book entitled *The Forces of Nature* for Thames and Hudson. This was published in 1977.

As soon as that was finished I began, with Eleanor's assistance, to research material for telling the story of the first thirty years of the British Antarctic Survey. This was published by Anthony Nelson under the title *Of Ice and Men* in 1982.

My literary agent, George Greenfield, and I had become close friends. Unhappily in 1975 our twice-weekly games of squash came to an end for he then damaged a foot. We had played together for seventeen years during which time we never knew which of us was going to win – an unusual and very happy situation in the squash world. Sadly I had to look for other opponents, but at my age they were difficult to find. Even so I was able to continue playing until 1981 when I was seventy-three.

In 1977 I was invited to visit Christchurch, New Zealand to be present at the opening of the new Polar Wing of the Canterbury Museum by Prince Philip. This prestigious event was slightly marred by an oversight in the organization. For the occasion a large hall had been cleared of everything but a gigantic Maori war canoe which stood in the middle of the seated audience. In the second row I sat with Lord Shackleton and Sir Peter Scott. As the proceedings were about to begin we became aware of a disturbance in the aisle behind us where about twenty people were gathered. It turned out that they were the Ambassadors and the High Commissioner with their ladies. Leading them to their seats the usher had suddenly realized that no chairs had been reserved and all of the two front rows were already occupied.

After hasty consultations chairs began to appear from behind the scenes and were placed at right-angles to the podium from which Prince Philip was to speak. As these were put into position the various dignatories seated themselves, and it so happened that the Soviet Ambassador was at the end of the line near the door through which they were being carried. Unhappily the attendants, having little room, banged the poor man's knees as each chair arrived. He took it all in very good part and showed much dignified patience, averting what might have turned into a minor international 'incident'.

Two years later the Government asked me to go out to the Falklands to open the new airport in Stanley. This was to replace the temporary airstrip which had been built by the Argentines through some devious arrangement with the Foreign Office. This, and a smaller arrangement for Argentina to provide the islands with petroleum fuel, seem to have been an extension of the last century's efforts to rid Britain of what was then seen as a troublesome problem.

Happily the airport I was to open in 1979 was entirely supported by the British Government, but to perform my function I had to land at the unopened airport in an Argentine plane. The opening was attended by most of the Stanley population. Never have I seen so many Land Rovers in one place at the same time. There were three Guards of Honour – one each from the Falklands Defence Force and the detachment of Marines stationed outside Stanley, and one from the visiting warship HMS *Ashanti*. While inspecting these I thought it appropriate to ask one of the Marines how he was enjoying his posting to the islands. I should have known better – 'I've only been here two days Sir,' was his reply.

The day ended with a fly-past of the two Falkland seaplanes which could not land on the runway, and one small privately owned aircraft which had the honour of making the first official landing. Three years later the runway was used by the Argentine invading force, but happily it survived the attempted bombing by the RAF. Fortunately unaware of what the future held, I sailed away in the *Ashanti*, first visiting settlements in the West Falklands before being carried north to Rio de Janeiro to catch a plane home.

For some time I had been an advisor to Sir Ranulph Fiennes' Trans-Globe Expedition, and by March 1981 his party had crossed the Antarctic continent, and their ship had brought them to Auckland, New Zealand for their first taste of civilization for over a year. With my old friend Admiral Sir Edmund Irving, another expedition associate, I flew out to meet them to discuss the seaborne route to the north and their subsequent crossing of the Arctic Ocean. This visit to the Antipodes also gave me the opportunity to visit the newly built Headquarters of the Australian National Antarctic Research Expedition (ANARE) in Hobart, Tasmania. It was a fine building made largely of glass, which was to be officially opened by Prince Charles in the following week. It seemed strange to isolate the centre so far from its old home in Melbourne where it had been close to university and museum facilities. Perhaps it was intended to bring outside activity to the beautiful but rather parochial Hobart. At least the harbour facilities there were excellent for polar vessels, and in subsequent years ANARE has settled there as a highly efficient organization.

By April I was back in England to pick up the normal busy round of activities before flying to Los Angeles in May to meet the Trans-Globe ship again and launch them on their northern journey. The Mobil Oil Company were generous supporters of the expedition, and they invited a party of six – Jim Peevey from Mobil and his wife, with Admiral and Lady Irving and Joyce and me – to join the party in America. After a visit to the Chairman of Mobil in New York we were taken on a two-day tour to the Grand Canyon, Colorado before going on to Los Angeles.

From Las Vegas we flew in a light plane over the Canyon where hot air rising from a depth of some 6,000 feet created such turbulence that the little aircraft seemed to dance in the sky, making photography almost impossible. Once back at the hotel all our stomachs returned to normal, and we wished there had been time to make the mule trip to the bottom of the Canyon.

The weather was hot and sunny and the views magnificent until we took a trip along the edge of the Canyon to a famous look-out point. There we were suddenly enveloped in a blinding snow storm which made it impossible even to see the tower we had come to climb. When the other visitors discovered who I was, I suppose inevitably, I was blamed for this unseasonal and rare event!

Reluctantly we left the Grand Canyon for Los Angeles, and were greatly surprised by its extent. From our hotel it was thirty miles to the docks where the expedition ship lay near the converted liner *Queen Mary*. She now houses numerous restaurants and entertainment facilities – rather a come-down for the one-time queen of the seas. After two weeks when the final preparations for the Trans-Globe Expedition's voyage north were completed, Joyce and I flew home. It was a memorable flight and the most pleasurable we had ever made. Embarking in the evening, we ate and then slept soundly until called for breakfast before landing at Heathrow. What a contrast to the constant stops when flying west about the world.

Normal life then prevailed until the following September when Hilary's second son, Roger, married Penny Widdick in Oxford. It was a great family occasion, and on 1 February 1988 they gave us our first great-grandchild, Lucy Jane, who is a great joy to us all.

In 1982 I was invited by the Institute of International Studies of the University of Chile to attend a Conference on Antarctic Resources Policy which was held at the Chilean Antarctic station Teniente Marsh. It was the first such meeting ever to be held in the Antarctic itself and it proved a great success. A number of representatives from each of fifteen countries attended, and we were all flown from Punta Arenas to King George Island by the Chilean Air Force. The discussions ranged over the potential Antarctic living and mineral resources, the environment, and conservation. It was a valuable contribution to international conceptions of the Antarctic scene. For me one thing in particular stood out – the expert comment that if prospecting for oil was to begin immediately, it would be at least thirty years before the first barrel could be produced. This is because of the difficulties of prospecting and production in the face of prevailing ice conditions, both on land and at sea. Since no prospect of such production was foreseeable, and in any case its cost could not compete with existing sources, the conservationists were able to relax in the knowledge that the environment would not suffer in the foreseeable future. Perhaps by then Man will have developed alternative means of power and will rely less on the expendable means employed at present.

The trip also involved me in lectures at the University in Santiago and the Chilean Geographical Society, where they kindly made me an honorary member and presented me with the Society's medal. My final engagement was to speak at the English Grange School where George Lowe, my old TAE companion, was then the Headmaster.

In June 1982 I had been elected President of the Royal Geographical Society, and felt that my Chilean visit had been rather a dereliction of duty. Now I was able to enter upon my Presidency with enthusiasm. My duties were greatly eased by the advice and efficient dedication of Dr John Hemming, the Director and Secretary, who gave me every support.

As a side line it was not long before I became aware that my open twelve-cylinder E-Type Jaguar was causing amused comment among the office staff. (This, of course, was before the theft of my beloved V12.) It had not appeared to me as odd, never having had a closed car, not even when I kept hearing entirely inaccurate stories concering the 'spray of gravel' as I departed from the forecourt! But on reflection I had to admit that it might have been thought more seemly for the President to appear in a more sedate vehicle. On the other hand I preferred to believe that to a small degree the E-Type enhanced the increasingly lively image of the Society which was then drawing so many young people as Associates or Fellows!

In July 1983 I was admitted to the Freedom of the City of London, and in August flew to Kenya on a visit to the Geographical Society's Expedition to the Kora River. The camp was beside the river in the arid area of the Kora Reserve and effectively fenced in against marauding lions. The region was one of the last areas of undisturbed bush and was threatened by the encroachment of Kenya's rapidly increasing population. Our intention was to make a complete study of the vegetation and the animals and insects, and indeed the fish population of the river itself. In this way it was proposed to produce a report which would be useful to the Kenya Government when assessing the future management of the area.

The human threat to the Reserve was not only from Kenya. While out there we repeatedly encountered Somali tribesmen who had illegitimately crossed the river with their herds of camels and goats. The Kenya wardens working with us turned them back again and again, but this was largely ineffectual for all they had to do was to move a few miles up or down the river and then cross again.

The expedition Leader was Dr Malcolm Coe, who knew East Africa well, spoke Kiswahili and was an eminent biologist from Oxford. Being in charge of so many young men without African experience he had wisely formulated strict rules to avoid accidents. When I arrived I was unaware that one of these forbade any bathing in the river. So it was that in the Leader's absence up river I joined a party netting fish in the marginal shallows. I was soon wallowing in the cool waters, and with the President's unwitting example before them it was not long before all the others joined me. We all enjoyed the bathing, and the first I ever heard about it being forbidden was much later when the expedition returned home and I took the Chair at Malcolm's official lecture to the Society when he told the story against me!

The wisdom of his rule was demonstrated in the field when a fish net became snagged in a large pool. In an endeavour to free it one young member of the expedition waded in groping along the bottom. Suddenly he sprang back and, with the others, began hauling hard on the net. Soon the dark body of a six-foot crocodile surfaced, closely entangled and powerless to harm anyone; but this was not known to the chap whose groping hands had first encountered the scaly body.

The problem facing us now was how to unwind the net and disentangle the tail and claws. While the others worked on this I found myself standing with one foot on its snout, holding the jaws shut. In the end the net came free with little damage and the crocodile was happy to slide back into the water. This was but one episode during the two enjoyable weeks I spent with the expedition, which proved to be scientifically enormously successful.

Returning to Nairobi where I stayed with the High Commissioner, Sir Leonard Allinson, I made acquaintance with Richard Leakey, son of Louis Leakey with whom I had been at Olduvai fifty-two years before. He had been following in his father's archaeological footsteps and had made numerous important finds. In particular he had discovered the *Homo habilis* skull in the lake deposits at Koobi Fora, north-east of Lake Turkana (formerly Lake Rudolf), where I had been searching for our two lost men fifty years earlier.

Richard was good enough to invite Sir Leonard and me to visit the site and flew us there personally in his own light aircraft. Despite the intervening years of the war and Antarctica it was a great thrill to see again the barren land over which I had travelled so many years ago. Near the end of the flight we spied a group of Ethiopians fishing from a sand spit where they had an encampment. Since they were illegal intruders Richard dived low over their heads, and at the third pass they took to their canoes and paddled away. This reminded me of 1934 when at almost the same spot my King's African Rifles escort drove a similar raiding party out on to the lake.

For some months Peter and Eleanor had been conniving to arrange a secret party in her flat to celebrate our Golden Wedding in September 1983. Their problem was to get Joyce and me down to London without our knowing about it, and to this end Eleanor enlisted the help of the RGS. On my return from Kora, and before I had had any free time at home, John Hemming phoned to ask me to attend a luncheon for some financial wizard who was coming over from the States and might provide some money for an RGS project. As he had a wife with him I was asked to bring Joyce with me. I had hardly caught my breath after the journey home, and remembering that it was our wedding day I was not pleased. I grumbled about the whole thing to Eleanor, saying that such an event was not Joyce's cup of tea and I would not bother her to come too. Eleanor was aghast, and for the only time in our long association she produced a very convincing outburst of disapproval, telling me that Joyce was particularly asked to come and help, that I was being very ungracious, and that instead of telling her how boring it was going to be, if I encouraged her to have her hair done and buy a new dress she would come with pleasure and enjoy the outing.

Somewhat shamefaced at my lack of enthusiasm, and yielding to her stormy outrage, I told Joyce that I would appreciate it if she came and it was arranged that we would motor up together. Eleanor and Peter spent a very anxious weekend in case I was changing my mind again, and early on Monday morning Eleanor phoned to make certain Joyce was coming too as 'the RGS were anxious about their seating plan'!

On arrival at the RGS I left Joyce in the car and hurried up to John Hemming's office, demanding to know what the occasion was all about and how soon could I get away afterwards. John is a very truthful man, and faced with all this he found it impossible to prevaricate any longer, especially as the function we were to attend was now said to be taking place in Eleanor's flat! To my amazement, and his embarrassment, he broke it to me that it was my Golden Wedding Day, and he and Shane Winser, wife of Nigel Winser who was still in Kenya with the Kora expedition, were coming with us to the flat to celebrate. We hastily agreed that Joyce would only be told that we had to go to the flat to pick up some papers I had forgotten, and we all piled into a taxi.

Lookouts had been posted in the road to report our arrival so that the assembly could be quietened down. As we climbed the stairs we found our grandson, Edward, stationed at the top with a camera at the ready to catch our astonished expressions, and were ushered into a completely silent drawing-room full of family and friends where we received a marvellously vociferous welcome.

It transpired that because Eleanor had recently had a hip replacement she had not been able to do half the cooking, as originally envisaged. The full burden had fallen on Ann and Peter, who had made all the domestic preparations in Leicester and carried everything down in their car earlier that morning. It was a wonderful party, and I feel sure that everyone enjoyed their part in the secret organization as much as we did the revelation.

The following year my Presidency of the RGS came to an end and in June I was succeeded by Sir George Bishop. A few days later I found myself back there again giving the first sitting for my portrait to be painted by June Mendoza. I had thought that this might be a somewhat irksome task, and was not looking forward to it. But on the contrary, I found her to be a delightfully interesting person, who was able to carry on lively conversations while actively working. By the end of five sittings, when I believe we had become good friends, I was sorry it was all over, and was able to look with pleasure on the result, marvelling at the skill which could produce it.

In spite of my retirement from the Presidency my connection with expedition matters continued, for I remained President of the Young Explorers' Trust. This has close links with the RGS, especially through the Expedition Advisory Centre which is a joint project of the two Societies and deals in particular with expeditions of younger age.

A year later a number of my activities were brought to a halt when I was suddenly taken ill in Eleanor's flat. The doctor she sent for decreed that I must go straight into hospital but he had great difficulty in finding one with a free bed. Eventually the Westminster agreed to take me but said that temporarily I would have to be placed in the Intensive Care Unit. On arrival I was firmly told that there was no need for me to be there, and I would be moved into an ordinary ward as soon as a bed could be released. That very night I had a severe heart attack while asleep, and awoke not knowing that I had been resuscitated by defibrillation (electric shock treatment). Certainly it was the best place to be in for such an occasion! Six weeks later I was able to travel home to Cambridge.

Since then, after living for fifty years in the same place, we have moved to a smaller house with a much smaller garden, some 400 yards down the road. Although I have had to adopt a gentler way of life, to date I have never looked back.

Three years after my troubles it was Joyce's turn. One day out walking on the Gog Magog Hills with Eileen Wake, our splendid housekeeper who looks after us so well, she suddenly collapsed with a heart attack. Seeking help urgently, Eileen was surprisingly fortunate in finding a man, presumably a Warden, who on hearing of the problem promptly pulled a radio out of his pocket and called for an ambulance. Ten minutes later Joyce was on her way to Addenbrooks Hospital where a temporary pace-maker was fitted that afternoon. Next day she received a permanent one at Papworth Hospital, and the day after that she was able to return home and take up normal life again.

In August 1989 we drove over to Oxford for our grand-daughter Rosemary's wedding to Tim Turan. This was a great occasion, when the reception was held on a boat cruising up the river which was much enjoyed by us all. We were not then to know the tragic circumstances of our next family gathering at Oxford.

The following year, on 27 April 1990, we again went to Oxford, this time for our grandson David's marriage to Susan Hanson on the following day. On arrival Joyce, always keen for a bit of air and a stretch of the legs, suggested a short walk. We set off, but when crossing the road she suddenly gave a little cry – and I caught her as she fell. Passers-by, one of whom turned out to be a doctor, helped me to carry her into the hotel, but she had died instantly, knowing nothing at all about it. We had been married for 57 years, and the shock was considerable.

I was glad to have the support of the family who had also gathered for the wedding next day. The marriage went ahead as planned for neither Joyce, who had looked forward to it so much, nor I would have wished the young couple to have postponed their great day.

On 8 May the cremation took place in Cambridge. So it was that I said goodbye to a life-long friend who had been so staunch an ally over so many years. Her ashes are buried in St Mark's Church cemetary on the Barton Road, where she is commemorated by a plaque and a newly-planted tulip tree.

Sadly Joyce never saw our second great-grand-daughter, Cyan Joyce, who was born to Rosemary and Tim on 21 May. So the generations continue, and the family can look forward to the future with confidence.

Chapter 16

Reflections

Looking back over the years has been both instructive and surprising, but above all I am happy that there has been no cause for me to say 'If only I had …' Some people might think that I was lucky to be born to the parents I had, and that is certainly true; for some the opposite is the case, and they begin life with a handicap. However that may be, I have always believed that usually an individual can and should have the greatest effect on his personal development. Perhaps one of the most important aspects of this is to determine one's interests and to follow that lodestone. In doing what he likes doing a man will be happier, and perform better, than struggling with an incompatible task and half succeeding.

In my case my early interest in nature led to Natural Sciences at Cambridge, and the unexpected opportunity to visit Greenland. So it all began, and my subsequent years in Africa and Antarctica satisfied the urge to see 'what lay over the hill'. The exception was of course the Second World War, which required a new learning in a field foreign to one's nature. To volunteer was natural, but it was with the conscious thought that I was handing myself over for a period of time during which I would have to do my best in a strange world.

I have been asked what has given me the greatest satisfaction – adventure, comradeship or discovery? In the world of exploration they are indivisible. It is the wish to discover that initiates a venture, the comradeship which makes it possible, and adventure is the inevitable accompaniment. The mix has made life worthwhile, the only regret being the long absences from the family.

Fortunately I have been blessed with an understanding wife who herself had travelled the world and, when oppportunity offered, initiated our crossing of Africa and the Sahara itself. Later when the family came she rose to the responsibility when so often alone. To her goes the credit for guiding their early years, which has resulted in the characters of which we are so proud today.

My career has passed through various phases. First the active scene when initiating or participating in expeditions. But these were separated by quite long periods at home when I was writing up the scientific results. Then came the time when exploration became my livelihood, with the twenty-six years of administration entailing the planning, recruiting and provisioning of projects to be carried out by others. This phase also entailed fairly lengthy visits to the field of operations every few years. Thus there was no sudden break from action to sitting at a desk; and this later relieved the scene of retirement, for even then, in the last phase, I found myself travelling the world at fairly frequent intervals until the time of my last visit to northern Kenya at the age of seventy-seven.

In recent years I have found myself more and more involved with helping youthful expeditions in one way or another. Times have changed. In the early 1930s perhaps half a dozen expeditions could be expected to leave the country in any one year. These would be fully adult projects, and perhaps one largely undergraduate expedition from Oxford or Cambridge. Today the number approximates to 400, most of which are university or school expeditions, the latter being unknown in my earlier years.

Today almost all universities have their own exploration societies, and every project is monitored by the university's own organization, by the Young Explorers' Trust, or by the Royal Geographical Society – sometimes by all three. One of the more surprising things about the modern scene is the ability to muster the finance which all these expeditions require. Like the monitoring organizations the scientific bodies able to provide money have also multiplied, but the amounts they can contribute to individual expeditions are small. Their real value lies in the standing that their approval provides when application is made to industry. It is indeed a credit to both large and small industrial companies that they are so supportive. To a degree they may expect some return in the form of advertising, but there is a basic belief in the value of adventurous investigation by young people which later benefits the community.

Another aspect of the changes facing today's budding explorers is the existence of so many nations that have emerged from beneath the Union Jack. Whereas in the past visits to many parts of the world, especially Africa and Asia, could be arranged through the Foreign Office, now the new authorities make their own rules and regulations. Since these tend to be inward-looking, a defensive jealousy of foreign investigations has often arisen, and it is infinitely more difficult to gain entry to such countries and to export specimens for scientific study. It is true that these difficulties can usually be overcome, but the time taken to gain approval and to pass through Customs, both in and out, is frustrating. Sometimes it even precludes an expedition from taking place.

Each generation produces its own behaviour pattern which becomes the norm for those growing up within it. I am sure that my predecessors at the beginning of the century had few if any of the strictures which I experienced in the early thirties. But accompanying these 'advances' society has developed the means of coping with them. The young men or women of today with adventurous ideas have the opportunity to consult numerous organizations which maintain records of past ventures, revealing both their strengths and weaknesses. Equipped with such information, and armed with modern transport and communications, today's expeditions have every chance of success.

It should be said that the agencies through which an expedition has to gain financial support pay particular attention to the gaining of political permission, and especially to safety. Sometimes it may seem that the latter concern is over-emphasized, but in view of the increased number of more youthful groups and mixed parties it is probably wise. In any case the number of expeditions now being promoted annually means that there are inevitably more of those we may perhaps regard as 'accident-prone' venturing into their own unknown.

Through the years I have been asked more and more frequently what there is left to discover? Are expeditions worthwhile any more? It is true that all the world has been seen either from the ground, from the air, or from satellites, but exploration has long since ceased to mean the discovery of new topographical features. Even so it is still possible to make a first ascent, or to be the first person at a particular spot. But the reality of exploration today is scientific study of a region about which little is known. This ranges from making a broad reconnaissance study in some science to attempting the most detailed work. Thus the value lies in the gaining of knowledge and not in the *Guinness Book of Records* type of achievement.

For young people especially there is a need for some adventure, and possibly risk, to accompany their attempt at discovery. Such seeking of hardship is not difficult to achieve, for the natural environment in all out of the way places provides the same problems and the same risks that there have always been. All that is different is that we may have acquired knowledge and equipment with which better to combat these hazards.

In the Antarctic such advances in techniques are especially valuable, for it remains the most inhospitable and least known part of the world. It is remarkable to remember that the first men to spend a winter on the continent were Borchegrevink's expedition in 1898, less than a hundred years ago. Through the years the number of national expeditions and their equipment has increased dramatically. There is now an Antarctic Treaty to which thirty-four nations adhere, communications are via satellites, dog-teams have been replaced by tractors and aircraft, many stations boast laboratories like those at home, and nearly a thousand men winter on the continent every year.

Politically the Treaty has eased the situation, indeed the threat to efficient operations appears to come from the United Nations, the majority of whose members have no knowledge of the continent and what can or cannot be done there. The greater part of this international interest undoubtedly arises from the belief that there must be vast though unknown resources.

It is not surprising that nothing of value has been found since ninety-eight per cent of the continent is deeply covered with ice – the mean thickness being some 6,000 feet. Perhaps the best possibility is oil, and the most likely source is the narrow continental shelf. But this itself presents special problems, not only from the annual formation and drifting of the sea ice, but especially from the ponderous unstoppable movement of gigantic icebergs. These may be many miles in extent, and are capable of scrubbing the ocean bed at a depth of 1,000 feet. In any event even in deep water they would destroy any man-made structure which could not be quickly removed.

To date nobody knows if there is any Antarctic oil, but it has to be accepted that it may be found. Even so the cost of recovery would today make production uncompetitive. This and the possibility of other sources of energy in the future should enable the conservationists to relax.

This is not to say that the future of Antarctica is without its problems. The national claims to sectors of the continent in the early part of the century became contentious in the 1940s. These difficulties were at least temporarily settled by the signing of the Treaty in 1961. The number of signatories then was twelve, all active in the Antarctic itself. Of the present thirty-four, many of the newcomers do not support an active scientific programme, and therefore have little practical knowledge.

So what is to become of the Antarctic? A number of vociferous conservationist organizations would like it to be declared a World Park, immune to any form of development – which would include not only the search for minerals but also the possible impact of a tourist industry. Already many tourists come to the continent by ship or aircraft. These transitory visits are in general harmless. It is the possibility of hotels being built which would undoubtedly contribute largely to the contamination of the region.

Antarcticians everywhere would surely like to see the whole territory preserved in its pristine state. But unhappily it is only too likely that politicians will yield to international commercial pressures. For this reason it is to be hoped that the continent will continue to be managed under the aegis of the Antarctic Treaty, and that it will never be relegated to the babel of the United Nations.

In telling my story I have been aided by my extensive diaries kept during expeditions in the field. At the time it did not seem worthwhile to do this at home too. It was a mistake, as for these periods my memory has had to suffice, and although I can recall my first haircut, at the age of eighty-two much has been forgotten. This I have realized in later years when some chance remark or the telling of an anecdote has triggered a response long forgotten. For me it has been a happy story, and I hope that others will perhaps find some interest, if only in the recognition of how things used to be in years gone by.

Acknowledgements

It is customary to thank those who have played a part in the production of a book. But in this case it is my companions who have travelled with me through the years, in Greenland, Africa and the Antarctic, to whom I am most indebted. There are also innumerable others who have been involved in the events which form the substance of my story to whom I would like to say thank you, for without them the theme would have been slim.

More particularly my grateful thanks must go to Eleanor Honnywill, who throughout the preparation of the book has typed, corrected and advised me; to Tony Nelson, my publisher, for his support and encouragement; and to June Mendoza for allowing her portrait of me to be reproduced. (See colour plate no. 7)

List of Illustrations

List of Maps

Index

Illustration numbers are shown in italic type